PROPHETIC FAITH

IN

ISAIAH

PROPHETIC FAITH IN ISAIAH

SHELDON H. BLANK
Hebrew Union College–Jewish Institute of Religion
CINCINNATI

Wayne State University Press, Detroit, 1967

Originally published by Harper & Row, New York
Paperback edition published by
Wayne State University Press,
Detroit, Michigan 48202

Waynebook 24, paperback reprint November, 1967

Library of Congress catalog card number: 57–9887

To my Dear Companion

who has always helped me understand

CONTENTS

FOREWORD

This is a book about a book of the Bible. It seeks to set forth the thought of the men who wrote the book called Isaiah. It contemplates their faith there revealed. And it does so not as a chapter in the history of ancient religions—though that, too, were a worthy project—but, I hope, as a provocation to religious thinking in our day.

Some things this book is not. It is not an "introduction," it is not a "commentary," it is not a "survey of recent literature upon" and it is not a polemic.

It is an effort to find meaning in parts of the book of Isaiah and to set it forth. Occasionally the interpretations are "new," but new insights must be rare in a literature studied by so many, so long and so earnestly.

From time to time in the body of this work, I acknowledge conscious borrowings. Here, in the Foreword, I acknowledge a debt too great to specify. Two men, Moses Buttenwieser and Julian Morgenstern, exerted a formative influence on me. I have given up trying to define the boundary between their teaching and my understanding. It is still my privilege to consult my colleague, now emeritus, Julian Morgenstern, dean of American Jewish Bible scholars, who guided my early steps in Bible paths. And I belong to the fortunate generation of students who caught from Moses Buttenwieser a spark of enthusiasm and of love for Israel's prophets.

For the thought that hope is a duty, an essential thought in the exposition which follows, I owe a special debt to Leo Baeck, whose death one year ago brought sorrow to many, whose life brought consolation to countless thousands, and who, perhaps of all our generation, best knew the meaning of the words: hope is a duty.

I have done the most of my learning in the give-and-take of the classroom. This is another line which I cannot draw, the line that separates what as teacher I have brought to the classroom from what, with students' help, I have carried away. I thank all students present and past for their part in the making of this book.

Special thanks are due as well to the officers of the World Union for Progressive Judaism for permission to reuse "The Mission of Israel" and to the officers of the Society of Biblical Literature for permission to reuse "The Promethean Element in Biblical Prayer." I was privileged to read the one at the Sixth Conference of the World Union in London in 1949 after which it was printed in the *Report,* and the other as the Presidential Address before the Society at the 1952 meeting in New York after which it was printed in the *Journal* for March, 1953. The two addresses appear, still substantially the same though with some revisions, as chapters VII and XI in this volume. Other studies of mine have contributed to the volume here presented—particularly such as appeared from time to time in the *Hebrew Union College Annual,* and prominent among them my "Studies in Deutero-Isaiah." In germinal form the chapter here entitled "The Isaiah of Legend and the Seventh Chapter" appeared in the *Journal of Near Eastern Studies.*

I am grateful to my colleague and friend Professor Eugene Mihaly for his careful reading of my manuscript and valuable suggestions and to Amy Blank, my dearest critic. I dare say the best paragraphs in the book are those which I wrote when they had done reading my draft. I am indebted to Mrs. Helen Lederer, a gentle lady, for her careful preparation of my manuscript, to Mrs. Fanny Berg for much gracious help with indexes, to Rabbi Bernard Martin for his friendly help with the proofs, to Professor Theophile Meek for his initial encouragement, and profoundly to my father from whom I first learned Bible stories.

The translations from the Hebrew Bible in this book (frequently paraphrastic) are my own unless otherwise designated. References to chapter and verse are usually grouped, one footnote to a paragraph. They follow the chapter division and order of the standard Hebrew text.

September, 1957 S.H.B.

PROPHETIC FAITH

IN

ISAIAH

CHAPTER I

ISAIAH: THE PROPHET AND THE BOOK

The book of Isaiah is a joyous book. But if this is so it is not because the prophet Isaiah was a joyous man. He was not. His book is joyous in spite of him. It is joyous because of the succession of "later Isaiahs" whose contributions all but hide the prophet that was. It was they who supplied the hope and faith which make the book joyous.

Isaiah himself was a prophet of challenge and stern demand. He set high standards, conceived brave ideals, aimed at goals beyond the wider human reach. If you hear him you grow confused because he upsets your notions, if you go with him you run into trouble because you are pushing against the crowd, if you deny him you feel guilty because you know he is right. Ignorance of the prophet Isaiah is the safer way, and the prudent reader will skip the next few pages of this chapter—unless, of course, he has already made Isaiah's acquaintance, under which circumstance there is no more help for him.

Isaiah was a prophet of challenge. That something has often been said did not, as he thought, make it true; nor was the present a firm warrant for the future. It was not that simple, he said; it was not that certain.

The people of Israel had a God; they were as sons to him. He had seen them through their childhood. Indeed he had made them great, made them a foremost nation. God had a people; he cared for it as for a vineyard: breaking the ground, carting the stones away, setting out in cultivated, watered rows healthy cuttings of a noble vine, erecting a proper citadel of a watchman's hut, hewing an expectant vat. Protected and prosperous, seemingly cared for and wanted, Judah, and Jerusalem its fortress, liked to think their God was with them—was theirs. No doubt their public men "pointed with pride," and grew eloquent about "our country" and "this blessed land," and smirked. It was as though indissoluble ties bound their permissive father God to his favored children and thus permanently assured their prosperity.[1] They called these ties a "covenant." Isaiah challenged the assumption that the ties were indissoluble.

Israel served its God. Priest and people agreed that all this bounty was no outright gift. They must make, were prepared to make, a return. There was a sort of religious revival: a flocking to the places of worship, a frequency of occasions for worship regular and special, generous contributions of fat beasts for the altars, an ardent lifting of the hands in prayer.[2] Isaiah saw the activity and the bustle but he challenged the supposition that this was religion.

The people of Israel trusted their God, and with good reason. They remembered his hand outstretched over Egypt, his eruption against the Philistines at Perazim, that he put to rout the kings of Canaan round about Gibeon, that he gave to David the "impregnable" Jebusite fortress, that all his acts were marvelous.[3] And they deduced the future from the past; God's great day was yet to come. All his wonderful works of old would pale before the incandescent glory of that day. Triumph for God and Israel, confusion for their enemies! As for Isaiah, he also read the history, but he read it otherwise.

Trusting God, his people were at ease in Zion. With God (and Egypt) behind them they repaired Jerusalem's walls and thumbed their nose at Assyria. Jerusalem was, and would remain, inviolate. This, perhaps, was the one certainty in their lives—an axiom, that God could never abandon Jerusalem.[4] Isaiah foresaw that he would.

The prophet Isaiah challenged many a comforting inherited delusion. He did not deny the obvious fact that God and Israel were related. He only predicted the early termination of their relationship, said that God was casting his people off—which was no less shocking to them than his denial of an ancient covenant would have been.

God was removing the protecting hedge, withholding his rain and making an end of his vineyard. His sons were rebellious; they had persistently turned away. The lords of the once faithful city had become God's adversaries and would fare as such. Better they had never walked with God. Certainly they would be ill-advised to presume upon this vanishing relationship. Their hold on God was slipping.[5]

Isaiah took no issue either with the thought that Israel must serve God. Men must, indeed, make a return for all God's bounty. Isaiah challenged only the mad supposition that God cared for such irrelevancies as tallow and burning meat or even praise and assemblies.[6] This was upsetting. No doubt, if anyone listened he began to feel confused and helpless—confused because other religious authorities told him otherwise, helpless because how, then, was he to please his God?

As for the meaning of history and the shape of God's "day," as Isaiah read the history he found quite different lessons in it, and he had a dim view of the future. The principle was the same: God is at work in history. Moreover, in times long past, when Israel was "faithful," God had, indeed, most marvelously intervened. This too Isaiah would say. But his agreement went only so far; recent history had another meaning and did not augur well at all. Recent calamitous events might have a sobering effect upon the men of Judah, if only they paused to consider them. Civil strife, social unrest, the wars of their world—if one considered them, they too were God's work and they were his language. They said: turn back. Through history repeatedly God said: turn back; and to no avail. "The people did not return to him that smote them," and God's hand was stretched out still. God would continue thus to speak, Isaiah said, but to the persistently obtuse his work would be "wondrous," "strange," "alien," "terrifying." Indeed, he would have his "day," a day of triumph but not, alas! for Israel: "God alone will be exalted on that day."[7]

Isaiah saw no magic ring around Jerusalem and had no reason to assume that its inhabitants led charmed lives. Among the prophet's many heresies this was probably the worst: that God could abandon Jerusalem. For espousing this heresy, which Micah shared with

Isaiah, the prophet Jeremiah all but lost his life—even a hundred years after Isaiah had said it. But Isaiah said it clearly and strongly and with gruesome symbols. He suggested that Jerusalem was God's *'ari'el,* his sacrificial altar, and that as his sacrificial victim thereon he would consume none but his people. Jerusalem was his furnace, the people his fuel. With change of symbol but with horror unabated, Isaiah pictured God the lion devouring Jerusalem, his helpless prey.[8] All of this is by no means pleasant.

As one reviews the notions cherished by the people of Isaiah's time and then contrasts the prophet's opinions, it becomes obvious that a wide gulf yawned between them. There was such a conceptual difference between them, indeed, as might well preclude conversation. Communication is possible only among persons who share a common language; and it is small wonder that repeatedly Isaiah complained of his failure to touch his people's heart. He said of them: "they did not want to hear"; he might have said: "they could not." In fact he almost did say that they could not, because such is the sense behind an agonized word in his "consecration vision." There, amazingly, God seemed to say to him: "Cover with fat this people's mind, plug their ears, veil their eyes, lest with their eyes they see, hear with their ears, with minds comprehend, and turn back and be healed." This is what the passage seems to say, as though God were loosing at his people's heels an inexorable fate, and they were petrified and wholly helpless. But the true sense behind the word is this: what Isaiah had to say was past belief, incredible; the people would simply be unable to hear it. Taken literally as God's word the verse is bad theology. But, taken as a prophet's anguished comment on his failure, it is good psychology. God gave Isaiah an impossible assignment; such things as he must say to such a people as he must address must be unheard, incomprehensible.[9] In a sermon we hear what we want to hear, in a book we see what we want to see, we understand as we are motivated to understand. We cannot otherwise, and he who would speak to us must say what we are ready to hear, or go unheard.

Isaiah was a prophet of challenge—and, too, of stern demand. Whereas the challenge is a scrunity of platitudes the demand is an affirmation of responsibilities. As the prophet Isaiah knew his God this God made clear demands upon his people and these demands were not the shopworn irrelevancies that then passed for religion.

Yes, Isaiah understood that the relationship between God and people entailed human obligations. When God stocked his vineyard with choice plants, cultivated, and watered, and protected it, "he expected it to yield grapes" after its kind—God, expectant, hewed out a vat for the harvest. Israel had obligations as well as rights; the covenant worked both ways, was a moral relationship. "You shall enjoy the good of the land if you are willing to listen." Isaiah's God rejects the alternative, which is divine favor freely bestowed, gifts of grace, benefactions unearned and everlasting. His God both gives and demands.[10]

What his God demands Isaiah states both broadly and in particular. Broadly stated, God demands that his people know and understand him, that they listen to him, that they keep faith with him. He laments: the ox knows . . . the ass knows . . . "Israel does not know, my people lacks comprehension." He has been disappointed: "they were not willing to listen." He recalls with yearning a "once faithful city." The Holy One of Israel demands that a people which has forsaken and rejected him and persistently turned away yet return, come back, be reconciled. Stated generally this is what Isaiah's God demands, his people's loyalty.[11]

Loyalty is an attitude, the spirit behind the deed. Loyalty means being ready, alert, willing, compliant. God might ask for loyalty in and of itself. But Isaiah's God did not leave the demand undefined. Isaiah supplemented his denial that God wants contributions and encomiums with a disconcertingly specific statement of what, instead, God does require. Isaiah found religion or the lack of it not in the sanctuaries but in the courts and council chambers, streets and market places, and on weekdays as well as sabbaths and occasions. He measured faithfulness in terms of righteousness and justice. The once faithful city was once replete with justice, right lodged there. Justice and righteousness were the vintage which God awaited from the planting of his delight.[12]

But, lest one find refuge in the vastness of abstractions (So, what do you mean by "justice"? "Right" is, after all, a relative matter.)

one observes that Isaiah "got down to cases." He set forth particulars in the form of positive commands: "Give the weary rest." "Correct oppression. Secure the orphan's right. Take up the widow's cause." He phrased his accusations in the form of warning cries: Woe! "Woe to the victors at drinking!" "Woe to them that add house to house!" "Woe to them that acquit the guilty for a bribe!" "Woe to the makers of iniquitous laws . . . to rob the poor of justice." [13]

He faced men and asked impertinent questions. "What is your business here?" he asked of Shebna the royal steward, who was building himself a rock-cut tomb on a lofty place. "What is this you are doing?" he asked of elders and nobles, "that you crush my people and grind the face of the poor." "What you have robbed them of is in your homes," he added pointedly. He was, indeed, too frank, he came too close for comfort; and there were those who thought he should be silenced. It would not have been so bad if he had talked smooth flatteries—but always to be harping on what is right—a preacher should know his place! [14]

Isaiah got nowhere and he knew it; he foresaw the collapse of his people. They were a condemned structure, a high wall, bulging and cracked; they were a crop to be harvested by a grim reaper, an olive tree to be methodically beaten limb by limb, a forest against which axes are raised, a fruit to be devoured. God's executioner had set out from beyond the Euphrates, and with mounting panic Isaiah broadcast black forebodings, shouted his agonized warnings.[15]

It was this Isaiah, gloomy and thoroughly unpleasant, who bequeathed his name to the book. By no stretch of the imagination and not with the best of good will could we call him joyous. Yet, one rabbinic authority, at least, could say that the book of Isaiah is all consolation. According to the *Talmud* consolation and desolation mingle in the books of the prophets; a book like Ezekiel, as the *Talmud* suggests, may begin with desolation and conclude with consolation, or be all desolation like Jeremiah, but the book of Isaiah is from beginning to end consolation.[16] The rabbinic observation is certainly an overstatement but the fact remains that there is a wealth of hope and faith and consolation and joy in the book of Isaiah, though the prophet Isaiah was wholly desolate.

The source of all this joy was not the pr
to the book. This prophet Isaiah, indeed,
first half of the book, in the first thirty-t
by parts of these chapters. With some deg
can be isolated. There is a grim monot
challenge and stern demand, which stamp
nize and label and set aside these writin
sized chapters in length, and what remain
Isaiahs." It was they, not he, who made th
of consolation.

"The later Isaiahs"—it is a term coined for convenience. The hero of the book of Isaiah, the prophet, Isaiah son of Amoz, left a name behind. Not so his less-celebrated successors—they have long been anonymous. For easy reference we have tagged numbers onto them: Greek numbers, "Deutero" and "Trito"—but only so far, though certainly there were more than the first and these two. If we need to speak of all the unnamed in the book of Isaiah together we must invent a term; therefore: the later Isaiahs.

A man would be daring who ventured to say how many such "Isaiahs" there were. And little it is that we know of the prophets whose writings the book contains. As a person the first Isaiah has a recognizable form. He lived in Jerusalem in the eighth pre-Christian century, the time of the great first flowering of literary prophecy. The closing decades of that century were vibrant with the words of Amos and Hosea and Micah—and of this first Isaiah. The evidence for this Isaiah's date is beyond question. By his own statement he accepted his commission "in the year that king Uzziah died," roughly the year 740 B.C., a decade perhaps after Amos appeared at Beth-El.[17] The same Isaiah was later involved in the crisis of the year 701. That was the year that the Assyrian king Sennacherib besieged Jerusalem and Hezekiah in it.[18] Such information we have about the first Isaiah: that he served in Jerusalem from 740 to at least 701 B.C.—but almost no information about the others. We seem to know where the Second Isaiah lived, though even that is not beyond dispute, and approximately when—and that is all. That little is more than we know about the others. As persons they are shadows. It is misleading even to call them Isaiahs—for us they are have only their words. A study of their lives would nt of information. But, properly, it is their faith we their words may reveal it.

faith of the later Isaiahs differs in many respects from the n of the first Isaiah.

The faith of the first Isaiah is freighted with imperatives. It is the religion of the ten commandments, of the "thou shalt not" and, even more, "thou shalt." It is what most of us mean when we speak of "prophetic faith."

The faith of the later Isaiahs is a source of endless confidence—a faith for the valley of the shadow, but equally, for living. It is what most of us mean when we speak of "faith."

The first Isaiah, among the prophets of that eighth pre-Christian century, thought of rejection by the Father. The later Isaiahs spoke of reconciliation with the Father.

The first Isaiah denied that Israel had a covenant hold on God. The later Isaiahs saw the covenant renewed and transformed into a divine commitment.

The first Isaiah knew nothing of a chosen people. A later Isaiah called Israel God's chosen servant.

The first Isaiah looked to a day when God would be exalted though his people perish. Later Isaiahs looked to a day when God and Zion together would triumph.

The first Isaiah conceived of man's defeat, the later Isaiahs of his victory.

The first Isaiah spoke of doom, the later Isaiahs of salvation.

The first Isaiah talked of death, later Isaiahs of life renewed and everlasting.

There is a wide diversity. And yet the first Isaiah is far from forgotten in the procession of later Isaiahs. Now and again reflections appear of his stern visage. His demands are not forgotten. Men still must have compassion, respect one another. Still rights and responsibilities are balanced. His challenge, too, is not forgotten. When there is cause one challenges even a new dogma of despair. A faith and a hope emerge that achieve a synthesis. They are not any more the demand and the expectation of the first Isaiah but their shape betrays his touch beyond all doubt. His book had its fate, but something of him it always retained.

CHAPTER II

THE ISAIAH OF LEGEND AND THE SEVENTH CHAPTER

1. Isaiah in 701 B.C.

The next "Isaiah" after the first was no Isaiah at all, because he was no man but only the shadow of a man. A man's shadow is shaped not by the man alone but also by the surface it falls on. The Isaiah of legend, shaped almost wholly by the popular mind, is a barely recognizable shadow of the historical Isaiah.

The Isaiah of legend makes his appearance at two critical moments in the history of Jerusalem: in the crisis to which the seventh chapter of Isaiah refers and in the crisis of 701 B.C. We are better informed about the latter event.

In 701 B.C., when Sennacherib laid siege to Jerusalem, the historical Isaiah unambiguously predicted his success despite Egypt. Hezekiah the king of Judah had concluded a treaty with Egypt and relied upon that power in the south to deal with the Assyrian foe. But treaty or no, Isaiah foresaw Judah's defeat and the fall of Jerusalem. It was divinely ordained. Isaiah's position in 701 B.C. could hardly be more clearly stated than it is in 31:1–4. This is what in those verses the historical Isaiah says about Hezekiah the king and the other defenders of Zion:

> Alas for those that go down to Egypt for help
> Depending on horses . . .

And look not to the Holy One of Israel
And do not seek God . . .
He will rise against the house of evil doers,
Against the workers of iniquity.
Egypt is human, not divine,
And their horses are flesh and not spirit,
And God will put out his hand
And the helper will stumble and the helped will fall
And they will all go down together.
For so God said to me:
As the lion growls,
The young lion over its prey,
[And] though there be assembled against him
A full band of shepherds,
He fears not their shouting
And is not disturbed by their tumult,
Just so the Lord of Hosts will come down
To lay siege to Zion and her hill.

"Just so," i.e., with undeviating purposefulness, Jerusalem's God (strange behavior for a city's God!) will personally conduct the siege, giving victory to Assyria over Egypt and Zion, defeating the helper together with the helped. In another chapter, too, through the same Isaiah at about the same time, God addressed Zion in similarly unambiguous terms: "And I will camp against you . . . and I will shut you in. . . . And I will raise siege works against you. . . ." Far from protecting, God will attack. God will not help, and Egypt, too, will prove a grievous disappointment.[1]

Probably the last of the preserved words of the historical Isaiah is the touching composition that is now contained in chapter 22. The words already quoted from chapters 29 and 31 relative to the crisis of 701 seem to have been spoken just before or during the siege. The word in 1:4–8, despite its position at the beginning of Isaiah's book, comes from about the same time as these late chapters 29 to 31, i.e., during the siege when all the countryside was scorched and Jerusalem stood as the last untaken fortress. But 22:1b–14 was spoken yet later—in the midst of the unbridled joy that followed on the unexpected withdrawal of the Assyrian foe. Isaiah did not rejoice with the multitude at this high moment. He found no comfort in the relief; still he foresaw only disaster. "This guilt of yours will be atoned by nothing short of death," he still insisted. He did not change his opinion even after the facts had proved it false.[2]

The implications of this situation are great. If Isaiah was of the same mind still in 22:1b–14, which, although it stands in a preceding chapter, is later than 31:1–4—if he was of the same mind still after Sennacherib withdrew, it is wholly improbable that between times he held such a different view as chapters 36 to 39 contain. He was far too fanatical to vacillate in such fashion. Chapters 36 to 39, as we shall see, are not the same Isaiah.

The religion of the historical Isaiah holds out small comfort for a time of danger. His religion is a challenge. He sets out deliberately to shake the confidence of an inflated people. It could happen, he insists. It could happen here. It could happen to you. You are as you are, and what will therefore be is God's doing, and you cannot evade it. God is not safety.

In relation to the event of 701 the historical Isaiah took a well-defined position. He knew with all his God-given insight that Sennacherib would conquer Jerusalem. In this knowledge, as we have seen, he recorded and preserved his estimate of the situation in at least three moments during the Assyrian campaign, just before, during, and immediately after the siege—and the last of these three records proved particularly telling. He knew what he knew even after Sennacherib left and proved him wrong.

So the historical Isaiah was consistent—but he was wrong. As a predicter he had failed, and he was discredited. Yet, though discredited, he was not forgotten; he had sons, he had disciples, what he spoke was on record, his words were not lost.[3]

He was remembered, and as time went on, remembered other than he had been: a later generation credited him at least with the power to forecast more closely the course of events. Hindsight supplied what foresight had not envisaged. The prediction of Jerusalem's miraculous escape, as though God had intervened and delivered his city in the last critical moment—such a prediction was now ascribed to Isaiah. This phenomenon of "prediction after the event" is a common feature of tales about prophets. And certainly what was done was no intentional fraud; it was an act of piety, exalting the prophet and enhancing his memory, and the authors of the fiction surely believed it was fact.

The rehabilitation of the discredited Isaiah takes place primarily in chapters 36 to 39. Here the Isaiah of legend makes one of his two major appearances—his appearance in connection with the crisis of 701. It is not that these chapters 36 to 39 are wholly fiction; it is merely this: that some of the things that Isaiah here does and says are "out of character." The historical Isaiah, as we know him, is quite a different person. And the probability is great that 36 to 39 are as they are and stand where they do precisely in order to "correct" the "wrong" impression of Isaiah which chapters 29 to 31 had given. Their first home, no doubt, was II Kings 18:13 to 20:19 where they still appear, and their author had other purposes than to present the prophet Isaiah as he really was.

The Isaiah of chapters 36 to 39, the Isaiah of legend, "predicted" correctly the withdrawal of the Assyrian forces with Jerusalem unconquered. He spoke of it several times:

So shall you say to your lord [Hezekiah]: Thus God said: Do not be afraid of the words which you have heard, wherewith the men of Assyria's king reviled me; I am about to put a spirit in him and he shall hear a report and return to his land, and I will fell him with the sword in his land.

> This is the word which God said [to Sennacherib] . . .
> I will put my hook on your nose
> And my bit between your lips,
> And I shall take you back on the way you came.
>
> So God said of the king of Assyria:
> He shall not enter this city.
> He shall shoot no arrow here.
> He shall not come near it with a shield.
> He shall cast up no siege works against it.
> By the way that he came, by it he shall go back,
> And into this city he shall not come, God says.
> And I will shield this city to save it,
> For my sake and the sake of David my servant.

Go and say to Hezekiah: Thus said God, the God of your father

David: I heard your prayer; I saw your tear; I add fifteen years to the length of your days. And from the power of the king of Assyria I will deliver you and the city, and I will shield this city.[4]

There is no mistaking the meaning of these passages. In each one the prophet correctly predicts the withdrawal of Sennacherib. But there is much more to them than prediction. There are several other elements present, which along with the element of prediction give a strong impression of the legendary. The stories in chapters 36 to 39 have much in common with the miracle tales of the "early prophets" to be found in the books of Samuel and Kings. Even as, among the early prophets, the "man of God" split the altar at Beth-el and Elijah called fire from heaven, and divided the Jordan, and Elisha defied the force of gravity, even so the Isaiah of chapter 38 set back the sun's shadow on the sundial of Ahaz ten degrees.[5]

Even as David's penitence lifted the death sentence pronounced by Nathan the prophet, even as Ahab's self-mortification lifted from him the death sentence pronounced by Elijah, even as Josiah's humble demeanor secured for him a reprieve through Huldah the prophetess, even so when Hezekiah on his sickbed hearing that he was to die, prayed and wept, God's word through the Isaiah of legend adjourned the evil day for fifteen years. And even as Elisha with nothing but flour extracted the poison from a brew and with only Jordan water cured Naaman of his leprosy, even so this Isaiah healed Hezekiah's seemingly mortal illness with only a poultice of figs.[6]

Like the earlier prophets, too, this Isaiah foresaw events even afar off. God showed Elisha that Hazael would take the throne of his master Ben-hadad king of Syria, and, indeed, Hazael suffocated the king and reigned in his stead. In like manner, this Isaiah predicted the fate of Sennacherib whose sons murdered him at his devotions, one of them to become his successor.[7]

The unerring accuracy of Isaiah's predictions in chapters 36 to 39 confirms the suspicion that the chapters contain legendary matter. It is particularly Isaiah's successful predictions that suggest legend and associate him with the early prophets. The hindsight of legend rather than his own political sagacity or spiritual insight allowed him to predict the wholly improbable withdrawal of Sennacherib when a victory was within the king's grasp—such hindsight as that of the Deuteronomic historian which enabled the man of God to know even the name of Josiah, the reforming king who would after three full centuries defile Jeroboam's altar.[8]

This Isaiah of legend begins to take form. We discover him in the crisis of 701 and note his behavior, his miraculous powers, his ability to predict, his rewarding of Hezekiah's piety, his reassuring manner. But besides his behavior we note with even greater interest his religious position. That God defends Zion is a fundamental dogma in the creed of this Isaiah. In the passages quoted he said so a number of times. "Do not be afraid," "He shall not enter this city," "I will shield this city to save it," "I will deliver you and the city, and I will shield this city." He shared the popular view—or, better, his was the popular view; the people spoke through him, through this Isaiah of legend.

There are other passages in which this Isaiah speaks in connection with the crisis of 701, and one of these is particularly revealing. In v. 5 of chapter 31 the word of the Isaiah of legend follows immediately upon the grim word of the historical Isaiah. The passage from that chapter, quoted above, ends with the terrifying rumble of heavenly wrath:

> . . . The Lord of hosts will come down
> To lay siege to Zion and her hill.

It is an unambiguous prediction of disaster, and it is followed immediately by quite as unambiguous a prediction of deliverance from disaster. Here is clash of controversy. Here in contiguous verses two philosophies collide. Though the one Isaiah is real and the other a figment only, both philosophies are real enough and their contrariety beyond question. Without transition the one makes way for the other. The prediction of disaster yields to the promise of salvation. After the one:

> . . . The Lord of hosts will come down
> To lay siege to Zion and her hill,

the other follows:

As birds hovering
So the Lord of hosts will shield Jerusalem,
Shielding, delivering, sparing, rescuing.

This other, with its repeated assurances, its series of comforting synonyms, is little less than an incantation, a prophylactic spell to soothe all panic. It is faith for a time of peril.

It would be hard to find a better illustration of the clash between the two religions or of the difference between the historical Isaiah and the Isaiah of legend. But there is one other illustration, still related to the crisis of 701. God's word to Jerusalem in 29:3: "I will camp against you" is almost immediately countered by the assurance (in the spirit of the Isaiah of legend):

> As a hungry man dreams he is eating and wakes and hungers, and as a thirsty man dreams he is drinking and wakes and is faint and his thirst is yet unslaked, just so will the multitude of nations fare that lay siege to Zion's mount.[9]

So much for the behavior of the Isaiah of legend at the time of the later crisis.

Now, he also appeared on the scene a third of a century earlier, in 734. In that earlier crisis, when Jerusalem trembled as the forest trees in a storm, before the blustering of Pekah and Rezin he did and said what also in 701 he did and said. The story of Isaiah and King Ahaz, when the kings of Samaria and Damascus attacked Jerusalem, is told in chapter 7 of Isaiah. That is the chapter which, because of the supposed reference to "virgin birth" in v. 14, frequently figures in the news. It is not this, however, which brings us to chapter 7, not the reference to the young woman, and not, either, the messianic prediction supposedly contained in the narrative, but the narrative itself as a further illustration of the faith of the Isaiah of legend. Until that narrative is properly told the disengagement of the Isaiah of legend and the historical Isaiah is not complete. To see each more distinctly, we undertake the somewhat difficult analysis of chapter 7.

The chapter is not a unit. Of the two parts which make up the chapter only the one can be regarded as a legend, the other being a characteristic utterance of the historical Isaiah. The legend is the story with which the chapter begins, the narrative usually called the "Immanuel prophecy." Stated approximately: vv. 1 to 16 contain the legendary Immanuel prophecy and vv. 17 to 25 the word of the historical Isaiah. But an innovation in the analysis of this chapter is here proposed, and it is this: that v. 13 is out of place, not originally a part of the Immanuel prophecy but a vestige of the earlier word of Isaiah, which the Immanuel prophecy now has displaced and which is resumed in vv. 17 to 25. There are other foreign elements in the narrative first part of the chapter, as the translation and notes will suggest, but the change most significant for the interpretation is the proposed removal of v. 13 from the Immanuel prophecy; the removal is significant because without the intrusive v. 13 the Immanuel prophecy has a new flavor entirely.

Although the narrative in chapter 7 is a legend we have no cause to doubt that the international situation was as it is there described. Rezin of Damascus, the king of Syria, and Pekah of Samaria, the king of Israel, joined forces and marched against Judah and her king, Ahaz of Jerusalem. Other sources suggest that Ahaz in distress then appealed to Tiglath Pileser of Assyria and that he responded with an attack upon Damascus. And Judah paid heavily for Assyrian aid. This alliance against Judah, the Syro-Ephraimitic alliance of 734 B.C., was the crisis of the Immanuel prophecy.[10]

2. The Immanuel Prophecy

It is suggested that the Immanuel prophecy, to the extent that it can now be restored, originally had the following form:

(1) And it came to pass in the days of Ahaz son of Jotham, son of Uzziah, king of Judah, that Rezin, king of Syria, and Pekah, son of Remaliah, king of Israel, went up to Jerusalem for war against it but they were not able to conquer it. (2) And it was reported to the house of David, "Syria has entered into an alliance with Ephraim" and his heart and the heart of his people swayed, as forest trees sway before the wind. (3) And God said to Isaiah: "Go now to meet Ahaz, you and your son Shear Yashub unto the end of the conduit of the upper pool, to the way of the Fullers' Field. (4) And you shall say to him, 'Take heed to keep calm; do not fear and let not your heart be faint because of these two smoldering stumps of firebrands, at the

raging of Rezin and Syria, Ephraim and the son of Remaliah. (5) Because Syria [and] Ephraim and the son of Remaliah have devised harm against you saying, (6) "Let us go up against Judah and break it up and conquer it for our side and set up as king in its midst the son of Tabeel," (7) thus says the Lord God: It shall not stand and it shall not come to pass, (8a) for the head of Syria is Damascus and the head of Damascus Rezin, (9a) and the head of Ephraim is Samaria and the head of Samaria the son of Remaliah.'" (10) And again Isaiah spoke to Ahaz saying, (9b) "If you do not believe, (11) ask a sign of the Lord your God; let it be deep as Sheol or high as heaven." (12) But Ahaz said, "I will not ask, and I will not put God to the test." (13) So he said, (14) "Therefore God himself will give you a sign: behold a young woman is with child and shall bear a son and shall name him Immanuel. (16) Indeed, before the boy will know to reject what is harmful and choose what is good the land will be forsaken whose two kings you dread."

If with this translation one goes to the Hebrew text to compare translation and original, or even if one takes it to one of the standard English editions of the Bible, one will notice a number of minor differences and what may seem to be several major discrepancies. These call for explanation.

The major discrepancies are the omissions. We have omitted three whole sentences. We have omitted the second half of v. 8: "In another sixty-five years Ephraim will be destroyed as a nation." There are two reasons for believing that this sentence is an addition: its content and its position. The prediction looks sixty-five years ahead to an event which will then effect Judah's present foe; but the author of the Immanuel prophecy is thinking of relief to come very much sooner—certainly within a few years, according to the concluding verses of his narrative. It is then that Ephraim (and Syria as well) will meet its fate. So much for the content of the half verse. Its position is equally disturbing. It divides a clause right through the middle; v. 9a must follow on 8a with no interruption, as a glance at the passage will show: "the head of Syria is Damascus and the head of Damascus Rezin, and the head of Ephraim is Samaria and the head of Samaria the son of Remaliah." There is no room for a whole sentence where now the comma stands.

The situation is similar as regards v. 15: "He shall eat curds and honey when he knows to reject what is harmful and choose what is good." Both because of its position and by reason of its nature it appears to be an addition. It intervenes between an act and its motivation; between the naming of a child and the reason behind his naming. But also it contains a thought which is foreign to its context: "He shall eat curds and honey" has an eschatological flavor, and there is nothing eschatological about the narrative. The narrative looks only a few years ahead. The added verse is a step away from the original intent of the legend in the direction of a messianic interpretation of the boy Immanuel. The same messianic tendency may have caused the addition of v. 22 to the other composition in the seventh chapter, as we shall yet see.

The third whole verse that appears to be out of place is the thirteenth: "So he said: 'Hear, now, house of David! Is it too little for you to weary men that you weary my God, as well?' " Except for "So he said," which the Immanuel prophecy requires as transition, the verse belongs to the other part of the chapter. Its grim, reproachful mood is quite unsuitable in its present context, but it is the very mood which characterizes the second part of the chapter, the vv. 17 to 25, which follow on the Immanuel prophecy and from which it has been wrongly separated. The removal of the verse from its present position is the real innovation here proposed, and from which has been wrongly separated. The removal of the Immanuel prophecy appears.

A comparison of the translation with the original will also reveal the omission of one clause in v. 9b and the dislocation of another. The proposed translation adopts a suggestion which Carl Steuernagel made a number of years ago.[11] In its traditional form the verse means: "If you do not believe you shall not be established," and this makes good sense and is a thing of value—a thought which we shall return to in the next chapter. But it is suggested as probable that the half verse is a kind of literary accident. The two clauses: "If you do not believe" and "you shall not be established," are almost identical in their Hebrew form, and Steuernagel suggested that the second is only a slightly modified version of the first, which originally is all that there was. Steuernagel thought of the clause "If you do not believe" as a marginal gloss to v. 11. The above translation joins it with v. 11 to mean: "If you do not believe (i.e., if you, Ahaz, are still in doubt) ask a sign of God." This is an offer and not a threat. As the verse has come down to us—"If you do not believe you shall not be established"—it is double-edged. It can mean: if you have faith you shall endure, but phrased as it is in the negative it has threatening overtones—or, rather, it would have if it were original, which this paragraph questions. If also v. 13 were original where it now stands, in the Immanuel prophecy, the prophet would appear indeed to be impatient with Ahaz and the threatening overtones of v. 9b would ring yet louder. It would affect the sense of the entire episode. The offer of a sign would sound like a challenge and the king's refusal like hypocrisy or cowardice. It is different when the suggestions concerning v. 9b and 13 are adopted. Isaiah neither threatens nor shows impatience, and Ahaz is a model of piety.[12]

There are some other, less striking differences between the text and the translation.[13]

The text of the disputed v. 14 is ambiguous at one point only; it is not clear from the Hebrew text who names the child. The form of the verb is the form which would be used if the mother were addressed and told "you shall name him Immanuel." But the king is the one with whom Isaiah has been speaking, and he has been speaking not to, but about the mother. The proposed translation: "and [she] shall name him Immanuel" assumes that the form is a feminine participle, which assumption involves the change of vowels only. This word is then the third feminine participle in a row of participles. Incidentally, the first of the three participles is a feminine stative form, and it simply means: "is with child"—"behold a young woman is with child and shall bear a son. . . ." The writer who used this word certainly did not associate with this pregnancy the idea of virginity.

These notes explain and justify the somewhat divergent translation of that part of chapter 7 which may be called the Immanuel prophecy. If the translation is justified it is before us now for interpretation and evaluation. But its meaning will be clearer if we have before us at the same time the other composition, the second element of chapter 7, the part of the chapter which appears to be the word of the historical Isaiah.

3. The Word of the Historical Isaiah

It is suggested that the word of the historical Isaiah, to the extent that it can now be restored, began with a very brief introductory first-person narrative by Isaiah, probably involving Ahaz and Shear Yashub and possibly still to be found in vv. 3a and 4, after which came vv. 13 and 17 to 25 in the following form:

(3a) And God said to me: "Go now to meet Ahaz, you and your son Shear Yashub, (4) and you shall say to him: (13) 'Hear, now, house of David! Is it too little for you to weary men that you weary my God as well? (17) [Therefore] the Lord will bring on you and your people and your father's house such days as have not passed since Ephraim separated from Judah. (18) And on that day the Lord will whistle for the fly and for the bee (19) and they will all come and settle down in the steep ravines and clefts of rocks, on all thorn-bushes and all water-holes. (20) On that day the Lord will shave with a razor hired beyond the river; it will remove the hair of the head and the body hair and even the beard. (21) And on that day a man will keep alive one calf and two sheep. (23) And on that day briers and thorns will take over any place where there used to be a thousand vines worth a thousand silver pieces. (24) Armed with arrows and a bow will one enter there, for all the land will be briers and thorns. (25) And all the hills which used to be cultivated will be for letting cattle loose and for flocks to trample.' "

In this part of the chapter also, a comparison with the Hebrew text or a standard translation will reveal differences. For one thing, the proposed translation omits a number of presumed glosses. The received text gives the impression that somewhere in the course of the transmission of this material a somewhat pedantic, literal-minded reader provided it with a commentary. To him "fly" and "bee" in v. 18 were merely poetic nonsense, and he identified them, the one with Egypt, and the other with Assyria. His reference to Assyria, though superfluous, was right; but his reference to Egypt was certainly wrong. We have no cause to believe that Isaiah thought of Egypt as a potential conqueror of Judah. Again, taking no chances that the threats in vv. 17 and 20 should be misunderstood, the assumed pedantic reader (again correctly) identified the "days" and "razor" with the king of Assyria. Since the "river" in v. 20 is, without further identification, the Euphrates, the explanation is superfluous. Assyria is, for Isaiah, the staff of God's indignation. The activity of this reader went on beyond chapter 7, and again in 8:7 he added, needlessly, his "king of Assyria and all his glory" to "the mighty flooding waters of the river." The prosaic middle part of 7:25: "You will not come there for fear of briers and thorns," contradicts the foregoing verse and breaks up the thought of the verse that contains it. It may be a note from the awkward hand of the same glossator.

It is somewhat different with v. 22: "Because of the abundant production of milk one will eat curds. For everyone who is left in the land will eat curds and honey." It has the same eschatological flavor as v. 15 already noted above, and the same messianic-minded Isaiah may be responsible for the addition of both v. 15 and v. 22 to this seventh chapter. Whatever the origin of v. 22 it is badly out of context. The desolate waste of its environs affords no welcome for this Eden.

More noticeable in the Hebrew than in a translation is the fluctuation between the singular and the plural where reference is made to "the house of David." In v. 2 "his heart" is the heart of the house of David. The house of David, probably in the person of Ahaz, is addressed in the singular in vv. 4 and 5 and 11; but in the plural in vv. 9, 13 and 14, after which the narrative reverts to the singular in vv. 16 and 17. The disengagement of the two compositions which make up the chapter does not remove this confusion in number. Apparently the biblical idiom allowed some measure of flexibility.

But these matters are somewhat trivial compared to the larger question of the structure of this composition. As for that question, the essential observation is that v. 13, wholly out of context in the Immanuel prophecy, belongs with the words of the historical Isaiah in vv. 17 ff. In tones of indignation and impatience, first, Isaiah calls upon the royal house to appear before the throne of judgment: "Hear now, house of David!" and he then immediately sets forth his accusation: "Is it too little for you to weary men that you weary my God as well?" Upon his indictment, according to his usual manner, follows his sentence:

> [Therefore] the Lord will bring on you and your people and your father's house such days as have not passed since Ephraim separated from Judah.

The structure is characteristic: summons, indictment, and verdict. Its form leaves nothing to be desired, except perhaps the *laken,* "therefore," which must be supplied in thought if not in fact. Again and again the historical Isaiah introduced the divine verdict with the word "therefore." [14]

Verse 13 looks ahead to 17 ff. but it also looks back to a narrative introduction of some sort, however brief. We should at least have been informed as to the identity of the house of David before we are plunged into v. 13. That is why it seems necessary to assume that a part at least of v. 3 originally introduced the summons: "Hear, now, house of David!" in v. 13.

In v. 13 the prophet accuses the royal house: "You weary my God." The fact that he speaks in the first person of "my God" suggests that any narrative that may have gone before was similarly autobiographical. This suggestion becomes a probability when we observe that, in the nearer context of this chapter, Isaiah often speaks in the first person: in chapter 6 throughout, and in chapter 8: "I saw," "and I said," "my mouth," "I heard." [15]

Finally as concerns the introductory narrative, the reference to Isaiah's son, Shear Yashub, must have been a part of it. The lad bears a name of threat and ill omen (as we shall see); and if he did not figure in the original narrative there is no accounting for his presence in chapter 7. The author of the idyllic Immanuel prophecy had no call to introduce this sober tone. Unless the brief narrative which once led up to the word of the historical Isaiah included some reference to the boy he would not now be here.

These several considerations lead to the assumption, then, that narrative matter resembling the quoted words from 7:3a and 4 once introduced vv. 13, 17 ff., namely: "And God said to me: 'Go now and meet Ahaz, you and your son Shear Yashub; and you shall say to him: Hear now, house of David! . . .' "

And so, with some confidence we may suppose that we have isolated the word of the historical Isaiah in chapter 7, and look at it as a composition apart, even as the Immanuel prophecy is a composition in its own right. Having disengaged the two parts of chapter 7 we have them before us and can look at each for what it is. That is the next step.

4. The Two Parts of the Chapter Compared

The chronologically earlier part of chapter 7, the word of the historical Isaiah, is characteristically "first Isaiah." In structure as well as content and mood it bears the stamp of his personality. The prophet summons the king to hear his accusation and to contemplate his dread prognostication. This is his usual manner. What he says, also, is usual; the ingredients of his accusation and prediction are familiar.

His accusation is very brief; it is confined to v. 13. The house of David, he says, "wearies" men and God—a good phrase, which, unfortunately, can mean anything. Standing where it has stood, in the Immanuel prophecy, it took on a meaning which certainly the historical Isaiah did not intend. If it were a part of the Immanuel prophecy the prophet would be (unjustly) rebuking Ahaz for an impious lack of faith, for not "believing." But it is not a part of that prophecy and Isaiah is not condemning Ahaz for his lack of faith. It is continued in vv. 17 ff., but unfortunately these verses do not offer any help in fixing upon the offense of the house of David. Accordingly we are constrained to look to the other writings of the historical Isaiah to discover an appropriate meaning for his accusation.

As we have seen, enough, indeed, is known of the historical Isaiah to justify a statement on his views of God's demands. According to that prophet's knowledge of God, man incurred divine displeasure: by adding house to house, field to field, by calling evil good and good evil, by acquitting the guilty to earn a bribe and condemning the innocent, by devising inequitable laws to wrong the innocent, by grinding the face of the poor. *Per contra,* man pleased his God by obedience to these and like imperatives:

> Wash, be clean.
> Remove from my sight the evil of your deeds.
> Cease doing wrong. Learn to do good.
> Seek justice. Correct oppression.
> Secure the orphan's right.
> Take up the widow's cause.[16]

Perhaps the most striking of Isaiah's definitions of God's demands, and the one most helpful in establishing the offense of the royal house in chapter 7, is one which, because of certain obscurities, is easily overlooked. It is found in Isa. 28:12. Though this verse is not always understood as such, it is really the historical Isaiah's epitome of his teaching. It was the prophet who said to them:

> . . . This is rest:
> *Give the weary rest,* and this is security.

The colon and italics in the quotation are necessary for the understanding. This precept itself is the secret. Follow it and find security. "Give the weary rest" is not simply a divine command; it is a prescription as well, a formula for security. Isaiah has said that not wealth, not power, not armaments, not even sacrifices, but only this is the source of human security: *Give the weary rest.*

We have no reason to suppose that the historical Isaiah thought in other than these familiar terms, when, in chapter 7, he accused the house of David of "wearying" men and God. Instead of pursuing the proper business of kings (he wanted to say), instead of "correcting oppression" and thus "giving the weary rest," the house of David were "wearying men"—and this is tantamount to wearying God.

Thus defying God's will, they were, moreover, incurring his wrath and inviting disaster. So, upon the characteristic accusation in v. 13, there follows the characteristic condemnation. Written in his most bitter mood, the word of the historical Isaiah in vv. 17 ff. is undiluted threat. Invaded by the teeming armies of Assyria, he says, the land will experience depopulation and devastation. Graphically, employing terms that farmers and cattlemen will understand, he portrays the desolation. The descriptions are reminiscent of his "song of the vineyard," especially its ominous close:

> Now I will tell you
> What I will do to my vineyard.
> I will remove its hedge and it shall be depastured.
> I will break down its wall and it shall be trampled.
> And I will make an end of it.
> It shall not be pruned or hoed
> And shall become briers and thorns.
> And I will command the clouds
> That they let fall no rain upon it.

And they anticipate by a few verses the symbol of flood which, too, he employs when threatening invasion and destruction:

> Because this people have refused
> The waters of Shiloah that flow gently
> . . . Therefore behold, God will bring upon them
> The mighty, flooding waters of the river.[17]

Both descriptions, all three, symbolize invasion by Assyria. The historical Isaiah knows that Assyria's advance means Judah's doom, and in chapter 7 he reveals his knowledge to the house of David in the person of Ahaz. His prediction casts a long shadow. Thirty-three years later, in 701, at the close of his prophetic career, the same historical Isaiah will, as we have seen, predict the same fate still for the still unregenerate Jerusalem.

In style and spirit, structure and content, then, the one component of chapter 7 is a representative word of the historical Isaiah.

Quite different is the other component. Now, without the reproachful v. 13, it, too, has a single mood, a single, consistent unambiguous mood, but one which is far from characteristic of the first Isaiah.

There are no shadows in the Immanuel prophecy; it is unclouded promise. When those two hostile kings appeared at the gates of Jerusalem, the heart of Ahaz and the heart of his people swayed indeed "as the forest trees sway before the wind," but thanks to the message of the Isaiah of legend, their terror did not last. This Isaiah arrived on the scene at the critical moment and he came to still the panic in the house of David. Through a literary mischance, that sour note, his son Shear Yashub, came with him; he was there—but he did not spoil the harmony. There was no panic in Isaiah's message: "Keep calm! . . . Two smoldering stumps of firebrands. . . . It shall not stand; it shall not come to pass." That is what this Isaiah came to say; but he wanted to be believed, and so he protested further: "If you do not believe ask a sign." His protestations proved wholly unnecessary; Ahaz believed and piously declined: "I will not ask, I will not put God to the test." And there is no longer any ambiguity in his refusal. The reason, if any, for charging Ahaz with a mock piety was the prophet's apparent impatience with him. But this impatience is confined to v. 13 and that verse is now recognized as out of context. Unprejudiced by that verse one sees Ahaz's reply as an expression of unquestioning faith, piety of the highest order.

All must agree that "testing" God is wrong. Consider, only, the following evidence:

When Gideon received the divine summons to deliver Israel he lacked conviction and made repeated tests with the fleece and the dew. He demanded "signs," but his manner was wholly apologetic, as though he knew it was wrong to do so and an offense against God: "Do not be angry with me; let me speak but once [more]; let me make only this one [more] test with the fleece. . . ." The wilderness generation was, in fact, doomed to die in the wilderness for thus putting God constantly to the test (ten times!) and refusing to obey him, even though they had seen his glory and his "signs" in Egypt and the desert.[18]

One at least of the ten tests had to do with daily bread. Being men of little faith they asked, "Can God spread a table in the wilderness?" And their question is called "sin," "disobedience," and "rebellion." Not to believe in God's providential saving power in spite of all evidence is an offense entailing penalties.[19] The name of the settlement Massah in the desert of Sin memorializes such an act of rebellion. There, too, the people tested God and asked: "Is God among us, or is he not?" [20] The question there resembles the one which Ahaz did not ask—the one to which the name "Immanuel" is a reply. Had Ahaz tested God, had he demanded a sign, the sign should have convinced him that yes, God is among them—but he had no need for a sign.

The author of the Immanuel prophecy agreed: testing God is an offense entailing penalties, whereas trusting him is a virtue. And he attributed such virtue to his hero, king Ahaz. Refusing to ask for a sign the king gave evidence of a faith which merits reward, and, indeed, he was rewarded. The suspicion that the king had doubts was unwarranted. Ahaz showed unquestioning faith. And this the prophet recognized: "Therefore God himself [voluntarily, even without your asking] will give you a sign: behold a young woman is with child and shall bear a son and shall name him Immanuel." It is an appropriate reward for his faith. The reward for his confidence is confidence. He had let God know that he trusted him, and God assured him his trust was well grounded. He may be sure that his God is with him. According to a later chapter the king Hezekiah in comparable distress exhibited comparable piety and the Isaiah of legend rewarded him also with a comforting and reassuring sign.[21]

Speculation as to the identity of the child, Immanuel, or of his mother is idle. For only his auspicious name has any significance. Neither Hosea's children nor Isaiah's sons had any significance in themselves; their only significance lay in their portentous names. And Immanuel is similar. The fact that someone (his mother, or the king) will give a child so pleasant a name: "God is with us"—that, alone, is important.

The name gives expression to the confident expectation of the one who names the boy, the expectation that God, benign, if not indeed indulgent, is on the side of Judah, however critical the times. If his mother names him, the name alone is for the king a comforting reminder of the faith he so recently professed. He will know by the naming that his faith has spread downward and that it is shared now by his once terrified subjects. If Ahaz names him he testifies also, by his choice of a name, that his faith, already proclaimed, now has become his conviction.

How events in the future which were yet to justify the name could be called an *'ot,* a "sign," is no great mystery. The analogous use of the word for "sign" in Exod. 3:12 is the key. That Exod. 3:12

supplies the key has been noted before, but without a full understanding. The usual interpretation of the Exodus passage divides the verse at the wrong place, as though the sign vouchsafed to Moses is to be some future ceremony at that mountain in Midian. Some years ago Julian Morgenstern proposed a better interpretation for the passage in Exodus.[22] According to his proposal, when Moses, impressed by the magnitude of the projected task, hesitantly, reluctantly, asked: "Who am I that I should go to Pharaoh, and bring the sons of Israel out of Egypt?" God's reply to him entirely paralleled that of Isaiah to Ahaz in Isa. 7. To Moses God said: "But I will be with you and this shall be the sign for you that I have sent you." To be sure, God goes on to say that the people will serve him at the mountain; but that is not the sign. The sign is: "I will be with you"—the continuing evidence of God's presence. As a result of this evidence day by day and year after year Moses will know that God has sent him. Just so, in the Immanuel prophecy, the defeat of the two kings will follow. But that is not the sign. As a result of the continuing evidence, day by day and year after year, that God is with them, Ahaz and all his people will rest secure.

So the mood of the Isaiah of legend in chapter 7 is known, and we recognize it. It is already familiar. We associate it with the crisis of 701, though not with the mood of the historical Isaiah on that occasion; rather with the Isaiah whom we met in chapters 36 to 39, the wholly reassuring prophet who stilled the fears of Hezekiah.

The impression is inescapable that the Immanuel prophecy is related to these later chapters. In language, style, and spirit the prophecy and the chapters are very much alike. Ahaz (in the 7th) and Hezekiah (in the 38th chapter) react comparably in their time of distress and are similarly rewarded for their faith. Like chapter 7, chapters 37 and 38 contain two "signs." The sign of the shadow on the sundial in chapter 38 may be the sort of thing the prophet meant when in chapter 7 he challenged Ahaz grandly to demand a sign "deep as Sheol or high as heaven." But there is also the sign in chapter 37 which is to be realized only in the third year, following upon two years of want and hardship, and which, as a "delayed action" sign, closely resembles the sign-promise in chapter 7 that the foes will suffer defeat—by the time Immanuel knows what is good for him.[23] Like chapters 36 to 39 the Immanuel prophecy is biographical, a prophet story and not a first-person narration. Except for chapter 20 there are no other third-person narratives in Isaiah. Moreover, like chapters 36 to 39, the opening verse of the Immanuel prophecy is a quotation from II Kings.[24] This is the direction of the borrowing and not the reverse. For the Immanuel narrative the verse says too much. It says that the two kings went up to Jerusalem for war against it, "but they were not able to conquer it." The quoted words blunt the point of the story. If the two kings were that weak there was no need for Isaiah to come and reassure the house of David. No doubt the words are there only because they were already in the verse in Kings when the author of the Immanuel prophecy adopted it as his opening. Chapter 7, then, depends upon the book of Kings, as do the chapters 36 to 39. Finally, and most significantly, the Immanuel prophecy agrees with the later chapters in espousing the popular religion. In one feature after another the Immanuel prophecy resembles the legendary chapters 36 to 39.

Already in 1895, T. C. Porter correctly perceived that the name Immanuel "expresses not the prophet's faith, but the false faith, the ungrounded confidence of the king and the people." [25] But he did not follow through with his thought. Perhaps the times were at fault. Now, sixty years later, we feel free to go on to the consequence: it is not Isaiah at all, not the historical Isaiah, who is responsible for the Immanuel prophecy; that the historical Isaiah espoused the faith implicit in the name Immanuel is a legend. The Isaiah of legend, and not the historical Isaiah, is responsible for the Immanuel prophecy, and it is not at all surprising that, being the creation of the popular mind, the legendary Isaiah expresses the popular view.

It is possible now to look at these two Isaiahs together, the historical Isaiah and his legendary counterpart. They are very unlike each other.

It was the function of the historical Isaiah to instill in king and people fear, to create unease, to disturb the complacent. It was the function of the Isaiah of legend to relieve the troubled mind, to allay fear, to inspire confidence.

The historical Isaiah depicted the terrifying consequences of royal and national misconduct. The Isaiah of legend suggested the rich rewards of piety.

According to the historical Isaiah the royal house of Judah, with its unjust, oppressive rule, brought upon itself the awful consequences of God's displeasure. According to the Isaiah of legend, Ahaz of Judah pleased God with his "faith"—in the simple, familiar meaning of the word.

To have merit in the eyes of the historical Isaiah, the king and people must have obeyed God's moral demands. The Isaiah of legend saw merit in the piety which required no evidence, the king's willingness to accept the prophet's word and eschew the easy instinct of fear, even when the circumstances were such that "his heart and the heart of his people swayed as forest trees sway before the wind."

5. How the Isaiah of Legend Adopted Isaiah's Two Sons and What He Made of Them

One more observation is in place before we take leave of the Isaiah of legend, and it concerns Shear Yashub and Maher-shalal-hash-baz.

We have noticed in chapter 7 that Isaiah's older son, Shear Yashub, accompanied the prophet when he went to meet Ahaz. It seemed that he first figured in the brief narrative introduction to the word of the historical Isaiah in the chapter, and that the author of the Immanuel prophecy later preserved this detail as a part of his narrative. Both narratives probably contained the words: "Go now to meet Ahaz, you and your son Shear Yashub." Except for the ungarnished remark: that the lad bore a name of ill omen, we have had little to say of him as yet. But the name has acquired a certain importance and should be discussed more fully.

It is easier to understand what happened to Shear Yashub if we observe first what happened to his brother. The names of both of Isaiah's sons were anciently misinterpreted. To both their father gave names which reflected his own despair. But despair was unpopular in his day, and crises were overcome, and in time, by this means or that the bitterness was drawn from the names.

The historical Isaiah approached his wife and she conceived and bore him a son. Prompted by God, Isaiah named this son, uneuphoniously, Maher-shalal-hash-baz, that is to say: "Spoil hastens, plunder speeds." The name expressed a thought which was much on his mind; of the same words he made a large poster and drew to it public attention. And then he included notice of both, the inscribing of the legend and the giving of the name, among the autobiographical data in his book. The notices now appear in the first three verses of chapter 8—immediately following the Immanuel chapter.

There are two conflicting interpretations of the name Maher-shalal-hash-baz in the book of Isaiah; one of these reflects the mood of the historical Isaiah, the other the mood of the Isaiah of legend. Isa. 10:5 f. is certainly a product of the historical Isaiah, and the probability is great that it contains the thought which this son's name reflects. The passage reads:

> Ah, Assyria, rod of my wrath,
> Staff . . . of my indignation!
> Against a godless nation I send it,
> Against a vexing people I give it charge,
> To take spoil and to gather plunder,
> And to make thereof a place of trampling, like
> mud in the streets.

In this passage God speaks of Assyria as his tool, carrying out his purpose, sent by him against Judah, ordered to spoil, plunder, and ravage that offending nation. It is more than possible that the words "to take spoil and to gather plunder" are related to the name Maher-shalal-hash-baz. And if that is so, Isaiah intended to memorialize this thought of his when he so named his younger son. He meant to say: Assuredly Assyria will spoil and plunder the kingdom of Judah—and that right soon. That this is what he meant is suggested also by what precedes and by what follows almost immediately upon the two notices in 8:1–3. What precedes is the grim prediction of Judah's fate at the hands of Assyria, which ends chapter 7. What follows in 8:5–8 is again a prediction of Assyria's destructive invasion of Judah, this time symbolized by a devastating flood.

Clearly the name of Isaiah's second son portended this very disaster, the ravaging of Judah by the anticipated foe. And there would never have been any doubt that this was what Isaiah meant were it not for v. 4 of chapter 8. Isa. 8:4 purports to be Isaiah's reason for choosing the name: "Indeed, before the boy will know to call 'my father' and 'my mother' the wealth of Damascus and the spoil of Samaria will be carried away before the king of Assyria." This is, of course, a quite different interpretation; for Judah it means safety, defeat for her adversaries. It means just what the end of the Immanuel prophecy means ("Indeed, before the boy will know to reject what is harmful and choose what is good the land will be forsaken whose two kings you dread"). It is just what the Isaiah of legend told Ahaz in his hour of crisis. And this, to be sure, is the clue to the origin of 8:4. The misinterpretation in 8:4 of the name which Isaiah gave his second son is only another product of the Isaiah of legend, who confidently believed that God would spare Jerusalem and deal with all foes of Zion. The Isaiah of legend adopted Isaiah's second son and remade him a symbol of divine protection, doing so with the simple expedient of adding 8:4, after the model of 7:16.[26]

The name of Isaiah's other son is subject to similar misinterpretation. There is no reason at all to doubt that the historical Isaiah did name his other, older son Shear Yashub. What he meant the name to signify is less obvious, but that he meant it to presage disaster is almost certain. He already had as a pattern the names which his slightly older contemporary, Hosea, had earlier given his children: Lo-ruhamah (Unloved), Lo-ammi (Not-my-people), and Jezreel (the name also of a place of dire retribution associated with prophetic prediction in II Kings 9). Isaiah had this pattern before him and, as we have seen, soon he himself was to name Maher-shalal-hash-baz with another name of ill omen, a memorial of other grim predictions. This pattern is one of the reasons for supposing that the historical Isaiah meant Shear Yashub to remind all who contemplated him of similarly painful matters.

It is in the now only fragmentary narrative introduction to his prophetic word in chapter 7 that the historical Isaiah mentions this son. That fragment, indeed, is the only reliable witness to this son

Shear Yashub, and it tells unfortunately little: it tells only that the historical Isaiah took this son along with him when he went to rebuke Ahaz, as he does in v. 13, and to threaten him with dire calamity, as he does in vv. 17–25. We can merely note that the inauspicious name of the boy well suited the atmosphere of that occasion.

Probably, like other infants in the Bible, his own brother among them, this lad received his name at birth. And now he is old enough to go with his father to meet the king. There is nothing in Isaiah to tell us what, some years before, the prophet meant when he gave him such a name. Only this much is clear: that he meant nothing good. The evidence is extensive and convincing that the name held out no comfort.[27]

But again the phenomenon already observed: the Isaiah of legend adopts him and makes him respectable. Does this son not, in the legend also, go along with his new father, this time to bring good tidings to the king?[28]

A story is remembered longer and more vividly than a "lesson" and in the minds of many the Isaiah of legend has succeeded in supplanting the historical Isaiah. Consequently, textbooks of Bible history still will say that Isaiah predicted the withdrawal of Sennacherib—which, though an error, is not of much importance. But they will also say that Isaiah could not, indeed, conceive of God's giving up Jerusalem and his temple, and that for this reason, at the last critical moment and near the end of his life, he abandoned the pattern of a lifetime and adopted a "new religion." This is an error, too, and a misreading of the evidence, and it is more serious because it leads to a wholly wrong estimate of the character as well as the faith of the historical Isaiah.

It is surely better to recognize the two Isaiahs each for what he is, and to consider independently the faith of each.

CHAPTER III

THE MEANINGS OF FAITH

1. The Faith that Means Doing

Prophetic religion knows more than one sort of faith. There is, to be sure, the familiar sort, the faith that means believing. But there is the other sort, as well, which has more to do with what a man does than with what a man thinks. In prophetic idiom faith is frequently measured in terms of deeds. An Isaiah or Jeremiah looked at a people's behavior and found faith there or found it lacking.

The faith which those prophets demanded—we can define it first by observing what it was not. It was not for them the false confidence which stemmed from their reliance on the temple cult. Jeremiah was quite clear on this point: "Trust not in vain delusions saying: 'The temple of the Lord, the temple of the Lord, the temple of the Lord are those [structures].' " It was not the complacency akin to arrogance born of an unjustified assumption, the kind of which Micah spoke:

> They lean on God and say:
> "Is not God in our midst?
> No harm will come our way."

It was not either an empty hope, fruit of a wish thought, of the sort which Amos had to deny:

> What will you have of the "day of God"?
> It is darkness and not light.

It was not, either to Jeremiah or to Ezekiel, the soothing doctrine of the false prophets "who cry 'Peace' though peace is wanting." [1] It was not any of these anodynes—which, indeed, Jeremiah called by their proper name: "Lo, you put your trust in unprofitable delusions"; and which Amos and Isaiah knew to be disastrous. Amos threatened:

> Woe to them that are at ease in Zion,
> The trusting ones in the hill of Samaria;

and Isaiah adopted the language of Amos, and challenged the women "at ease in their minds and blissfully trustful." [2]

They all in their day, Jeremiah, Micah, Amos, Ezekiel and the historical Isaiah—all did battle with complacency, opposed what might wrongly pass for faith, a false confidence, popular self-deception, faith misplaced. Faith, for them, was something else.

A word may be known by the company it keeps. One way to an understanding of the Hebrew word for faith, the word *'emunah,* is through acquaintance with its associates. In prophetic writings these verbal associates lend the word resounding overtones of righteousness. Again and again the word is one of a list of virtual synonyms for what is right, just, honest, consistent. It obviously shares with these ideas a common denominator.

Observe the occurrence of the word *'emunah* in the following passages; note in what company it is found and consider whether "faith," with its usual connotation of "believing," is an adequate translation.

In Hosea God says:

> I will betroth you to me forever.
> I will betroth you to me in righteousness and justice;
> I will betroth you to me in loyalty and compassion;
> I will betroth you to me in *'emunah;*
> And you shall know God.

In his Diogenes role Jeremiah sought a man "who does justice, desiring *'emunah,*" and in a later passage this same prophet cited "falsehood" as the negation of *'emunah.* The Isaiah who composed the messianic prediction in chapter 11 said of the awaited king:

With righteousness he shall judge the poor
And decide with equity for the meek of the earth . . .
Righteousness shall be the girdle of his waist,
And *'emunah* the girdle of his loins.

And the Isaiah of the apocalypse had visions of "a righteous nation which observes *'emunim.*" Similarly a passage in Trito-Isaiah explains a calamitous experience as the fate to be expected by a society in which right and *'emunah* are flouted in the courts.[3] In all of these prophetic passages the overtones of "faith" are justice and righteousness, equity, constancy, and truth. "Faith" is assessed in terms of behavior.

A word may be known by its relatives, too. The noun *'emunah* is from the verb *'aman* and is related to the noun *'emet,* which means "truth," and to the adjective "true," *'amen.* And other Hebrew words and forms are near relations also. When, in prophetic literature, persons or things are to be described as trustworthy, dependable, sure, a word is chosen from the *'aman* family. When Isaiah inscribed a tablet with an ominous legend he summoned "faithful" witnesses. To portray the fate of Eliakim, the steward, he contrived a figure of speech and said, God would drive him as a peg in a "firm" place. And as Isaiah could speak of a "firm" place, Jeremiah could speak negatively of waters that are not "dependable." Just so, among the blessings which a virtuous man might expect a later, messianically oriented Isaiah included the promise that his bread would be provided, his water "sure." Not animate yet depending on God's person are the "sure" promises to David to which the Second Isaiah referred.[4] It is with God as with men; his faithfulness means that he is to be trusted, is trustworthy, inspires confidence. It is really because of God, who is constant, that his promises to David are "sure." The same Second Isaiah earlier referred to the Lord who is "faithful"; and some Jewish fugitives in the time of Jeremiah invoked him as a true and "faithful" witness to their oath.[5]

All of the quoted words in these examples: faithful, firm, dependable, sure, are derivatives of "faith"—from the Hebrew stem *'aman,* the stem which yields the noun *'emet* and the adjective *'amen.*

Accordingly, when we come to this same prophetic literature with the question: What is the *'emunah* which God demands? What is the faith by virtue of which a man or a community enjoys God's favor? we are prepared to find, as one answer at least, that behavior and not belief is the determining factor. The faith of a man or the faith of a people will be measured by their faithfulness—justice and righteousness will serve as standards. And so it is.

A clear allusion to such faith appears right at the beginning of the book of Isaiah. It is the historical Isaiah who describes the sorry state of Jerusalem:

> How she has become as a harlot,
> The once faithful city!
> She was filled with justice;
> Righteousness lodged there—
> But now, assassins!

The attribute "faithful" is clearly defined. It is defined by its implied opposites: the "harlot," symbol of disloyalty, and "assassins," symbol of treachery. And it is defined by its implied equivalents: amplitude of justice, the prevalence of righteousness. It is probably not the same Isaiah who speaks a few verses later; nevertheless, he, too, understood faith as the historical Isaiah understood it here. He, too, associated faith with the exercise of righteousness.

> And I will make your judges as they were at first,
> And your counsellors as they were aforetime;
> After that you will [again] be called the city of righteousness,
> The faithful city.

To this later Isaiah who looked forward to a new age when human hopes would be fulfilled, as to the historical Isaiah, a city with faith was one in which justice prevailed.[6]

Two further passages are particularly revealing, one of them also the product of the historical Isaiah, the other in Habakkuk. The earlier, unambiguous word of Isaiah in the utterance concerning the "once faithful city" is a first-rate clue for their interpretation.

The Isaiah passage is Isa. 28:16–17a—the foundation-stone passage, in which, as a matter of fact, the reference to the foundation is less significant than the allusion to "faith." If we leave untranslated the undefined word the passage reads:

> Behold, I am laying in Zion for foundation a stone,
> A testing [?] stone,
> A precious cornerstone of foundation:
> "The *ma'amin* will not be in a panic;"
> And I will make justice the line
> And righteousness the plummet.[7]

The untranslated word is usually translated "the one who believes." But not correctly so. For, in the first place, if the passage contains the words of the historical Isaiah such individualism as the translation implies is anachronistic in his days in his society. In eighth-century Israel the individual had not yet so clearly emerged from the mass as to expect or require God's personal attention. It was the society, the state, the city, the community, which, being wholesome and sound, or sickly and decadent, stood or fell as by God's decree they must, and a person prospered or was swept to his doom along with the rest. If these words, then: "The *ma'amin* will not be in a panic" were spoken by the first Isaiah, the *ma'amin* of which he spoke was no single person but a city, a community, a people. And in the second place, the context calls not for belief but for a certain type of conduct. The *ma'amin* of chapter 28 is the equivalent of the "faithful city" of chapter 1; and the word should not be rendered: "he who believes" but "a people that keeps faith." "A people that keeps faith has no cause for panic"—this is the historical Isaiah's dictum here, and this formula is itself the "foundation," the base upon which to build a religion.

That the formula is itself "the precious cornerstone of foundation" the very next words make clear. For, what follows in the next half verse is not a new thought; it is an expansion of the foregoing. "A people that keeps faith has no cause for panic," God says, "and I will make justice the line and righteousness the plummet." Only consider the function of line and plummet. Masons use them; they use the taut line between two pegs to determine the straight or level horizontal; they use the suspended lead or plummet to determine the true vertical. The line and plummet are instruments of testing, standards. The builder measures his wall against these standards to know if his wall is "right" and "true." And what are the standards against which one measures, not now a wall but a community to know if it be faithful? Justice is the line, righteousness the plummet. A community whose "faith" stands the test when measured in terms of these values, measured against the standards of what is just and right, "will not be in a panic," has no cause for hysteria, is not threatened, and may, under God, endure. The people's faith is weighed in scales of justice; by their deeds they are known. The specifications are quite the same as they were in the opening chapter. There was amplitude of justice, righteousness prevailed in the once faithful city; its faith too was assessed in terms of just and righteous behavior.

It is only a step from these two passages in Isaiah to the one in Habakkuk 2:4. The customary translation of the Habakkuk passage is, at best, ambiguous: "The righteous shall live by his faith." But though the translation is ambiguous the prophet's meaning must, by now, be evident. The sort of "faith" which Habakkuk intends is clearly the sort which manifests itself in just behavior, because, observe! it is not a "believer," who by reason of his "faith" shall live, but, without ambiguity, a "righteous man." By reason of what should such a one live other than by the very righteousness which is his nature? If a man's faith may be known by his righteous conduct—and by now it is clear that it may so be known—there is no reason to look to anything beyond the very nature of a righteous man for his "faith." His faith is not something extrinsic. What else but his righteousness itself is this faith by virtue of which he may be expected to live out his days? This is the meaning of the verse: "By virtue of his righteousness the righteous shall live."

It is attested, then, this one sort of faith—the sort of which a prime ingredient is faithfulness, righteousness, constancy, truth, the sort which, prevailing among men, should make for a just society. It appears as an essential feature of prophetic religion, of the religion of Amos, of the historical Isaiah, Micah, Habakkuk, Jeremiah. Those prophets asked of their people this faith.

Now this faith, this religion, despite the enthusiasm which we frequently muster when we talk of it, has a stern visage. Negatively, it says: there is no unearned security. In its far perspective, on its broad horizons, there is no hiding place for favorites. Affirmatively, it says: See that you implement God's stern demands. The mood of this faith is the imperative. This prophetic religion is not easy; it is not inviting. It is forbidding. It is a religion for the hardy. And, as we might well expect, it had to contend with an alternative formulation, to divide the field with faith of a gentler mold.

2. The Faith that Means Believing

Indeed, it would be wholly misleading even to suggest that the first kind of faith, which is really faithful conduct, is the only "respectable" sort of faith among the prophets. We again recall the faith of Ahaz which the Isaiah of legend commended and rewarded, that other sort of faith—the faith that means believing. Grant that its proponent in chapter 7 of Isaiah was no person but a fictional composite, it still is a prophetic doctrine that to "believe" is pious and that God rewards such piety. And the Isaiah of legend was not alone in commending this other sort of faith. The faith that is a holding still and not a doing, an attitude and not an activity, appears as well in the writings of Jeremiah and Zephaniah, abundantly in the writings of the later Isaiahs, and even, though rarely, in the words of the historical Isaiah, of him who was the determined defender of the faith which means doing.

Also to name this other sort of faith prophets (confusingly) sometimes employed forms of the same *'aman*. More frequently, however, they used the verb *baṭaḥ* for the faith that means "believing," the faith that is confidence. They had, indeed, a number of synonyms at hand to give expression to this popular sort of faith.

This other sort of faith has first of all to be defined by what it is not. Not every believing involves religious faith. Gedaliah refused to "believe" those who warned him of Ishmael's treachery, and he paid with his life for his disbelief. God warned Jeremiah of his brothers' perfidy: "believe them not though they speak fair words to you." Through Habakkuk to his people God announced: "I am doing a work in your days that you would not believe if told." And in one of the servant songs the kings of nations are thought to express their amazement over the servant's restoration, saying: "Who

[ever] believed what we have [just] heard?"[8] "Believing" in these instances has little if anything to do with religion.

Believing may have to do with religion and still not be faith. It may be an un-faith, an illusion. The books of the prophets abound in ironic references to illusions of security. So, for example, among the nations: the pampered princess Babylon who says in her imagined security: "I am unrivalled," will discover her error. Despite Chemosh, Moab will be abashed; the god Chemosh will go into exile along with his people who trust in their wealth. Ammon's god Milcom and all of Ammon's treasures are quite as futile. Indeed all deluded idolators must suffer shame.[9]

And Israel itself could fall prey to the error of misplaced trust. Both the historical Isaiah and the prophet Jeremiah called the reliance upon Egypt a fatal error. We have already noted what Isaiah said:

> Alas for those that go down to Egypt for help,
> Depending on horses,
> And trust in a host of chariots
> And riders in great numbers!

What Jeremiah said is equally blunt:

> The army of Pharaoh which has gone out to help you will return to Egypt, its land. . . . Because of Egypt, too, you will experience disgrace . . . for God has rejected what you rely on.[10]

Even as alliances with Egypt would not avail so, according to Hosea, the historical Isaiah and Jeremiah, armies, military preparations in general, and defense measures within the land were similarly futile. Indeed, reliance on one's own strength is conceit and self-deception. That was the sense of Ezekiel's symbol of feminine vanity: "But you counted on your beauty, and played the harlot because of your fame." Conceit may be compounded with self-righteousness and aggravated by perversity and apostasy. Such faith does not pay.[11]

So, one must be cautious about the faith which is confidence. It may be illusory. All-important is its object. There is no safety in human vanities, in wealth, strange gods, battlements and chariots.

They give only the illusion of security. Prophets counted among errors fatal to men: their reliance upon their own presumed resources not excluding their manufactured idols and false gods.

> They bow low to the work of their hands,
> To that which their fingers have made,

is an accusation which leads on to prediction of disaster.[12] The confidence which is true safety has as its object the true God, and such confidence is a faith which prophets commend.

A passage in the book of Jeremiah contrasts two men, both of whom have trust. The difference between them is that one trusts men while the other puts his trust in God. It is the object of their trust which matters.

> Cursed is the man who trusts in man
> And makes flesh his strength,
> His heart turning from God.
> He shall be like a shrub in the desert
> And he shall not see good when it comes.
> He shall live in the stone wastes
> In a salt land not inhabited.
>
> Blessed is the man who trusts in God
> And God is his trust.
> He shall be like a tree planted by water
> That sends out its roots by a stream,
> That does not fear if heat comes
> And whose foliage remains green,
> That does not worry in a year of drought
> Nor give up bearing fruit.[13]

From the negation this passage in Jeremiah achieves the transition to the affirmation. Faith in God is not futile. It is madness to resist God's will but to trust in him is perfect wisdom.

Religious faith thus narrows down to a believing in Israel's God. This faith finds frequent illustration in the books of the prophets. Explicitly as well as by implication, it has appeared several times on the foregoing pages. Explicitly the piety of Ahaz illustrated the virtue of unquestioning faith. The Isaiah of legend offered to show the king of Jerusalem a sign, if he wished, of cosmic proportions:

deep as Sheol, high as the heavens. But Ahaz in perfect faith declined: Oh, but I do believe! I do not need a sign. "I will not put God to the test." Fully trusting prophet and God, he wanted no proof, and that was his merit. Men who lack the faith that is confidence do put God to the proof; and that, according to biblical sources, is sin and rebellion.[14]

By implication in two other passages already cited the historical Isaiah likewise urged the faith which is confidence in the Holy One of Israel. When he moaned for the deluded statesmen in Jerusalem:

> Alas for those that go down to Egypt for help,
> Depending on horses,
> And trust in a host of chariots
> And riders in great numbers!

he did not, indeed, stop there but went on to name the rejected alternative:

> And look not to the Holy One of Israel
> And do not seek God.

In the other, later word, the sequel to Sennacherib's withdrawal, still disconsolate the same Isaiah mentioned the same wrong choice:

> And on that day you looked
> To the armory of the forest house;
> And the breaches in the city of David
> You considered, for they were many,
> And you gathered water in the lower pool,
> And you counted the buildings in Jerusalem,
> And you tore down buildings to repair the city wall,
> And you built a reservoir between the walls
> For the water of the old pool.
> But—you did not look to him who was doing this,
> And you did not regard him who formed it long since.

It is the last double line, of course, which contains the rejected alternative, the alternative which, to the prophet's mind, it was fatal to reject. In other words, he commended the faith which is "seeking" God, "looking to" God (and not armaments), to the Holy One of Israel who, for their sins, was threatening them with defeat at the hands of Assyria. If he said it explicitly he could hardly say it more clearly. He commended the faith which is confidence in God, the faith that means believing.[15]

It is not in these already cited passages alone but once at least besides that the historical Isaiah commends this faith. The passage reads:

> For thus the Lord God said,
> The Holy One of Israel:
> "By returning and rest you can be saved,
> In quietness and confidence lies your strength."
> But you refused
> And you said: "No!
> Because we will run on horses"—
> Therefore you will run [in flight];
> "And we will ride swiftly" [you said]—
> Therefore swift will your pursuers be.[16]

In view of the reference in this passage to horses and riding, as in others just cited, the occasion was probably Sennacherib's attack and Jerusalem's appeal to Egypt for help. Egypt's aid was in the prophet's opinion only an illusion of safety and he said so, thus suggesting what faith is not. Strength lay not in that direction. Isaiah knew where strength lay and he proclaimed it, but he addressed unwilling ears: "you refused, and you said: 'No!' "

His proclamation contains his explicit demand for faith in terms of believing:

> By returning and rest you can be saved [he said];
> In quietness and confidence lies your strength.

Actually, among the prophetic words which may with assurance be ascribed to the historical Isaiah, this is the only one in which he is quite explicit on this point. At least twice, as we have already observed, he implicitly endorsed the faith which means believing, but only in this last passage explicitly. Yet there can be little doubt that the historical Isaiah wrote the two verses. Both the terms of his reference to Egypt and his lament at the people's refusal are characteristic of the historical Isaiah. Again and again he had the same reason for despair and used the same words to express it: But you refused.[17]

It may seem, then, that the two Isaiahs of chapter 7, the historical Isaiah and the Isaiah of legend, meet at this point in chapter 30—that here the circles of their faith intersect. And this may be right. Also the historical Isaiah could approve the piety of an Ahaz, if by reason of his faith the king would put his trust not in arms and accords but in God. However, one difference is apparent between the faith which this Isaiah vainly asked and the faith which the Isaiah of legend rewarded. By and large they are the same, yet we can observe a small but most significant difference. We note that the proclamation is a formula, a prescription made up of several ingredients; and we further note that one of these ingredients is not quite the same as the other three. That Israel may be "saved," have "strength," Isaiah prescribes: returning, rest, quietness, and confidence. Were it not for the first, the ingredients of his prescription would simply add up to calm inaction, serenity, the fruit of confidence. The ingredients, except for one, are remarkably similar to the faith which the Isaiah of legend required of Ahaz in chapter 7: "Take heed to keep calm; do not fear and let not your heart be faint. . . ." But the final ingredient, the first on the list (is it therefore the most important?), combines less readily with the others. "Returning" is not inaction; it partakes of the nature of that other sort of faith which is more doing than attitude; and possibly this first ingredient tinges all the others with its sober hue.

Perhaps the word "returning" is the stamp of the historical Isaiah's individuality, a necessary ingredient in any formula that he prescribes. Several times, indeed, the historical Isaiah recognized a relationship between a returning or repenting (which is the same thing) and survival. An erring people, which had strayed from the path or abandoned its God, must either turn back or else go on to perdition—this thought he shared with many in the Bible. And so, early and late in his utterances, he referred to repentance. A clause in his consecration vision suggests that an obdurate people condemned to destruction might yet repent and be healed, were it not too fatally insensitive. A somewhat later word of his lamented the failure of his people to recognize the discipline that God had laid on them and to return; for, if they had returned, Isaiah implied, they would have escaped new disasters. And, finally, at the time of Sennacherib's siege, at the end of Isaiah's career, the prophet phrased an appeal: "Return to him from whom the sons of Israel have so resolutely turned away . . . and Assyria will fall. . . ." The command "return" followed by the future "and Assyria will fall" is a normal type of conditional sentence in biblical Hebrew. In this same style Jeremiah phrased a similar divine appeal: "Improve your ways and your doings and I will let you go on living in this place." We could as well translate here: "If only you would improve your ways and your doings"; and in the Isaiah passage: "If only you would return . . ." [18]

The idea of repentance as a prerequisite for survival is familiar in Isaiah and basic, though it is not a distinctive doctrine with him, for he shares it with others. But the prescription as a whole in his chapter 30 seems to bear the imprint of his personality; a man like the historical Isaiah was constrained by his own nature to include, along with "rest, quietness, and confidence," as a prime ingredient some measure of "return." And so, the historical Isaiah and the Isaiah of legend were not in complete agreement on the matter even of the faith which means believing. To the historical Isaiah it meant: believing plus.

The examples of faith which means believing are not exhausted with the few references to the historical Isaiah. If we depended on him alone we would, indeed, be not too well informed about this sort of faith. Jeremiah adds a few examples. Also Jeremiah knew two sorts of faith. Along with Isaiah, as we have seen, he advocated faith of the other sort, faith defined in terms of human behavior, linked with justice and contrasted with falsehood. But also, like Isaiah he knew and commended the faith which is a believing and a trusting in God. Indeed, this faith was an important element in his own personal religion. He could say to God in a moment of personal spiritual crisis in the midst of a "confession": "You are my refuge on an evil day." And in another personal situation he found no better way to reward a friend than to say of him he trusted God. Ebed-melech the Ethiopian eunuch had saved his life, and Jeremiah conveyed to him God's word: " 'I will deliver you and you shall not fall by the sword; you shall escape with your life, because you put your trust in me,' God says." [19]

Zephaniah and the Second Isaiah advocated the faith which is believing. In a bill of particulars accusing Jerusalem, Zephaniah listed: "She did not trust in God"—listed it along with her disobedience and her refusing discipline. Comparably, among the virtues of God's servant the Second Isaiah mentioned the servant's confidence in God and his depending on the Lord. Enthusiastically the Second Isaiah congratulated them that hope in God: "They who hope in God renew their strength." By reason of such strength, he taught, they triumph who hope in God.[20]

Some of the great religious texts of the Bible bear upon this faith that is believing. Some of them are to be found among the words of the later Isaiahs. And one of them is probably the result of a literary accident combined with editorial ingenuity. This is the verse in the Immanuel prophecy which is usually translated: "If you do not believe you shall not be established." Our analysis of chapter 7 suggested that only the words: "If you do not believe" are original there, that the words at first formed the condition of the sentence which continues in another verse, i.e., "If you do not believe ask a sign of the Lord your God," and that the received text is conflate. But someone's ingenuity produced the text as we have it and did so before the time of the Chronicler. By reading the second verb as a passive form he made it mean "you shall [not] be established" and introduced the excellent sense which the verse now has. As others had done, he thus linked faith with survival: "If you do not believe you shall not be established." The present text is older than the Chronicler who put almost the same words in the mouth of Jehoshaphat. Exhorting his troops before battle the king there declaims: "Hear me, Judah and you inhabitants of Jerusalem: Believe in the Lord your God and you will be established. Believe in his prophets and gain the victory." [21] If the history of the verse in Isaiah is here correctly told the verse is a prime example of what have well been called "the unmeant meanings of Scripture." [22] Meant or unmeant the magnificent doctrine, "If you do not believe you shall not be established" has a place in our spiritual heritage—and its "believing" is faith.

Trito-Isaiah reflected the exuberance of the Second Isaiah together with the earlier prophet's understanding of this sort of faith. He, too, linked faith with salvation: "He who puts his faith in me will possess the land and inherit my holy mountain." And, to the Isaiah of the apocalypse, finally, the faith which is a leaning on God was especially dear. He thought of God as the refuge and strength of the lowly poor whose trust he is:

> For you have been a refuge to the poor,
> Refuge to the meek in his time of trouble,
> Shelter from storm, a shade from heat.

This Isaiah is beyond compare in his ability to put his faith in words:

> The spirit of him who trusts you keep in perfect peace,
> If in you he trusts.
> Trust in God forever
> For God is a rock of ages.[23]

Indeed, as we shall yet see, from the Second Isaiah's attitude of expectancy there grew a whole new religion of hope.

CHAPTER IV

ISRAEL'S GOD IS GOD

1. The Second Isaiah

In the days of the Second Isaiah an empire toppled. The prophet saw the crash coming and laughed. He reflected on the prospect and was overwhelmed by a bold surmise. His surmise hardened into certainty and he broke into jubilant song. The sixteen chapters which for convenience we call the Second Isaiah—chapters 40–55—are his rhapsody.

"Sword," according to Rashi, meant different things to different prophets. To Amos and Isaiah, he said, it meant Sennacherib; to Jeremiah and Ezekiel it meant Nebuchadnezzar.[1] Sennacherib was the king of Assyria who failed to take Jerusalem in the days of Isaiah. Nebuchadnezzar was the king of Babylonia who, a century later, plus a few years, in 586 B.C. conquered Jerusalem, destroyed its temple, and carried away its people, among them probably the grandfather of the Second Isaiah.

This last probability is suggested by the fact that the Second Isaiah is maturely grown by the year 538, approximately fifty years later, in Babylonia. It was in that year that Cyrus took Babylon. Cyrus the Persian had swept victoriously westward and in 538 he stood before the gates of Babylon, fading capital of Nabonidus' empire. Babylonia yielded to Persia. The prophet must laugh seeing the swift advance of the conqueror, before whom opposition dispersed as a mist. The feet of Cyrus barely touched the leveled highway. Droll was the impotence of the blustering capital city, seat of empire and house of gods.[2]

When one came to think of it, where, indeed, were those gods of Babylonia? Where was Bel? Where Nebo? Where—they had taken to their heels. But only after a manner of speaking, because, as a matter of fact, they were unable even to run, much less to rescue their worshipers. They themselves had to be carried, ignominiously loaded for flight on the patient backs of the "beasts," their trusting minions—but to no avail.

> Bel is bent over, Nebo bowed down;
> Their idols were entrusted to beasts and cattle,
> Their portable forms were loaded, a burden on weary beasts.
> They bowed down, they bent,
> Altogether they could not deliver their burden;
> The burden itself went into captivity.[3]

It was ludicrous but it gave cause for thought. Who, then, was this astonishing king Cyrus, and whence his invincible power? Why did those gods seem to scurry away at his approach? In the mind of the Second Isaiah there arose a thought so audacious that surely his eyes grew wide and he caught his breath. Could it, then, be Israel's God? Could it be he that summoned Cyrus for his purpose, sped him victorious, and put the "gods" to flight?

Probably, as is the way with "inspiration," this prophet's intuition at once became his conviction. It was for him immediate knowledge, and all the whys and hows were subsequent dressing, and the conclusion was not the end but the beginning of his reasoning. There is reasoning indeed, exalted debate on Olympus, but somehow we know in advance the outcome of the argument. Israel's God is God, and if one wants arguments they are to be had—syllogisms, in fact.

Much of what goes by the name of Second Isaiah is given over to the logic behind the conclusion, and the reasoning is of prime significance. But the intuition, already become conviction, even alone sufficed for jubilation. The future was happening. God, Israel's God, was at work again, and all glorious would the consequences be. The times called for prophets who would comfort God's people, who would announce to them his radiant coming, not now to chastise, but to save them, who would tell them for him: "I favor you; I have not rejected you." Such a prophet was the Second Isaiah. He was a herald brimming with good tidings: Rejoice![4]

The contrast with the early chapters of the book of Isaiah is so marked that readers long have recognized the division. Chapter 40 is the first of a series of connected chapters of surpassing comfort. For convenience we call these chapters "the Second Isaiah." The "Isaiah" part of this designation means only that they are found in the book of Isaiah; we do not know the name of the prophet who wrote them. As we have seen, he appears to have lived in Babylonia at the time of Cyrus. We know no more of him than that. The Second Isaiah was probably responsible for the most of chapters 40 to 55. It is true that chapters 49 to 55 differ in some respects from chapters 40 to 48; it is true that the "servant songs" are in some respects at variance with their context; it is true that the fourth of the servant songs is in some respects unlike the other three; it is also true that chapters 34 and 35 and chapters 56 to 66 are in many respects quite similar to chapters 40 to 55—but nevertheless there is reason enough to consider the sixteen chapters here together. Except for occasional brief passages these sixteen chapters have enough consistency of style and spirit and content to be viewed as a unit apart, and to merit a name; therefore: the Second Isaiah.

The Second Isaiah is the architect among the later Isaiahs—architect and builder in one. There is a religion in his sixteen chapters and he constructed it. He did not create the materials but he designed and constructed the edifice.

A great deal of thinking that is familiar to us as "Judaism" is contained in his pages and emerges as we study them. His creativity is impressive, his influence was tremendous. The present chapter and the three to follow draw upon his spirit. They deal with his argument for the oneness of God, with his conception of Israel the "servant," with his universalism, and with the thought that unites God, Israel, and humanity: the mission of Israel.

This Second Isaiah was the bearer of a broad evangel; he had many bold and encouraging words to speak. But as preparation for his evangel he had first to do valorous battle with all idols. And so, armed with satire, history, and syllogisms, he entered the fray and strove in lofty earnest for his God.

2. Debate in High and Holy Places

His satire is sharp and, like all satire, unfair. He took no pains at all to distinguish between the god and the material representation or symbol of the god. Idol and god to him were all one, and so they were naught but vanity. Idols are made of wood and overlaid with gold; held together with nails they are chained to one place and cannot budge. Immeasurable is the folly of such as make idols. They do not realize that their god is a stick of wood. That same tree that they nurtured serves them both as logs for their fire and as material for their wooden image. At the fire they warm themselves and over it they cook their roast. From the wood thus employed they have at least these benefits, the warmth and the savory food. But they have none of these comforts from the idol which they make of that same tree. For, cry as they may to a wooden god, he cannot help them.

> They lack knowledge who carry about their wooden image
> And pray to a god who cannot save them.

He is a burden more than support. He cannot save even himself.[5]

They toil to the point of exhaustion who make an idol, they with their human frailties. They may, to be sure, enjoy some satisfaction from their labor. The carpenter and the smith, artisans both, derive some pleasure from their creative achievement. They may compliment each other on their craftsmanship:

> They help each other
> And one to the other speaks encouragement.
> The carpenter compliments the smith . . .
> And says of the join: It is good . . .

That much satisfaction men enjoy who create that sort of a god. But, observe the difference between the creator God and the pitiful creations of the craftsmen. At the end of the sixth day, contemplating his work, God was satisfied: He "beheld all that he had made and lo! it was very good." And, indeed, he had reason: "His six days work, a world!" But the idols far from being gods, far from possessing creative powers, these images made of metal and wood, are but impotent creatures of creatures. It is not they, the made gods, but their makers that know the pleasure of creative activity.[6]

The satire against idolatry may not be fair—for certainly Bel and Nebo were not merely identified with their images carried in festal procession—but it is powerful and bitter, and it buttresses the negative phase of the Second Isaiah's argument from prophecy to monotheism.

The negative phase of his argument is the first of his syllogisms. He states it as though Israel's God were challenging all pretenders:

> Present your case, God says.
> Produce your strongest arguments, says the King of Jacob.
> (Let them produce their arguments and tell us
> The things that shall happen.)
> The former things, what are they?
> Tell, that we may take notice.
> Or announce for us the coming events
> That we may know their conclusion.
> Foretell things to come
> That we may know you are gods.
> Yes, do anything—good or bad,
> That we may look amazed or even fear.
> Lo! You are less than nothing
> And what you do is less than naught;
> Misguided is he that prefers you.
> I aroused from the North and he came,
> [Aroused] from the East one who calls on my name,
> And he will tread upon rulers like dirt,
> Even as a potter who tramples the clay.
> Who announced it from the first, that we might know?
> From aforetime that we might say, True!
> Indeed none announced; none proclaimed;
> No one hears a word from you.
>
> . . . .
>
> (When I look there is no one—
> No adviser among these—
> None whom I might ask and be answered.
> Lo! they are all of them nothing
> And their works are naught.
> Vapor and vanity are their molten images.) [7]

"God," the speaker, is "Jacob's King," and they whom he addresses are soon identified: they claim to be gods—but wait! The prophet, speaking for God, invites them to present their case, to produce their strongest arguments. His challenge is provocative. It has an almost jeering tone and is even humorous at one point where, if they are unable to produce the kind of evidence which he demands, God invites the "gods" to do something—anything at all, good or bad, merely to prove that they are animate. One can almost see the miming prophet, himself looking about expectantly, expressing mock anxiety, pausing, listening for a word, alert for a sign, and only after such a pause drawing his conclusion: "Lo! you are less than nothing, and what you do is less than naught."

The proof which Israel's God demands of pretenders is evidence that they had foreknowledge: "Foretell things to come." This is the proof which they cannot produce. The offer is entirely clear. Could they only "foretell things to come" it would be known that they are gods. That is the major premise of this prophet's syllogisms. But it is not they who possess foreknowledge; and the later verses in the passage repeat the thoughts already expressed, the minor premise: "Indeed none announced; none proclaimed; no one hears a word from you," leading to the inevitable conclusion: "Lo! they are all of them nothing and their works are naught."

According to the argument of the Second Isaiah the test of divinity is the ability to reveal the course of future history. The claimant must fulfill two conditions: not only must he possess foreknowledge, but he must also be able to communicate such foreknowledge to his people. But since it is through prophets that a god makes known his intentions, a god to be accredited must have both prescience and prophets—men capable of hearing and articulating his word.

This, then, is the argument developed thus far: no other claimant has produced prophets to substantiate his claims. No prophets of another god have testified to that god's foreknowledge. Lacking such prophets a god deserves no notice; such a one is a fraud.

The argument thus far is only a negation: other "gods" lack evidence of divinity. The negation is repeated in a subsequent passage, in the form of a rhetorical question. The nations are assembled and their gods are challenged:

> **Who among them could foretell this [occurrence]**
> **Or announce to us [in advance] former events?**

"Them" and "us" are not defined but the similarity with the previous passage makes the meaning quite sure: who among their gods reveals the future? The question then gives way to challenge:

> Let them produce their witnesses and be vindicated,
> And hear the testimony and say: It is true.

The challenge is ironical. Since the answer to the rhetorical question must be: none among their gods reveals the future, the sense of the challenge is simply this: they have no worshipers who can testify that they foretold the future; and, therefore, their claims are false, as even they must admit.[8]

And the sense of 48:14 is the same:

> Gather, all, and hear:
> Who of them foretold these [events]?

Again the implied answer is a denial that others possess the power to foretell the course of history.

How may foreknowledge serve as a test of divinity and its absence as a negation thereof? The Second Isaiah appears to argue that no one can infallibly know in advance who is not himself the author of history, the one who alone is capable of putting into effect a preconceived plan, acknowledging no opposition. A man, a creature, may plan a course of action, but such a one can only say: "I propose such a course;" he cannot say: "I shall do so and so." He does not know what obstacles may block his course. Nor for that matter can any god have absolute foreknowledge unless he is the only god—God, whose will no power opposes. Thus, prescience, according to the reasoning of the Second Isaiah, is the attribute of God, the One.

Up to this point he has argued negatively denying such prescience to other gods—denying them thus their divinity. The Second Isaiah has denied to other gods the foreknowledge coupled with prophets which is to him the test of divinity. He has rejected their claims as false. But his argument is complete only when he has shown that there is a god who enjoys such prescience and who may—who indeed must—therefore be recognized as God. To this effect he amplifies his argument in other parts of chapters 40 to 48, supplementing the denial with a positive argument designed to establish the divinity of Israel's God.

For the argument which would establish the divinity of Israel's God the Second Isaiah could draw upon a national experience which had become history. The earlier prophets, of the eighth and seventh centuries, had spoken for God and announced his intent: he would do the incredible, give up Jerusalem, turn his back on his temple, banish his people from their land. He had announced it and now he had done it. Since to the prophets all history was divine history, this two-edged experience—prophecy and fulfillment of prophecy—was to the Second Isaiah a fact at hand to be invoked, a fact known to his contemporaries. And there was another fact, but this one was not yet history. It was a "new thing," which the Second Isaiah was even now announcing in the name of his God—something equally incredible: the imminent deliverance of his people. Even this, seen as a chain of events: the victories of Cyrus the Persian, to be capped by his conquest of Babylon and sealed by his favor to Israel, was not all only promise. The first links in the chain were forged; Cyrus was already on the march. So, to the Second Isaiah, this too was a ready fact. What through him God was announcing as his intent was even then being fulfilled—had in part been fulfilled, as all might see. "Former things" and "things which are new" were facts for his argument.

He develops the positive phase of his argument in a half dozen passages within chapters 40 to 48. In the first God identifies himself:

I am Yahveh, that is my name,

and then continues:

I give to no other the glory due me
Nor my due praise to carved images.
Behold, former things have come to pass;

Things which are new I now foretell.
Before they spring forth I tell you of them.

As in the first quoted passage, so here, the "others" are denied recognition; they deserve no praise. But, what is not stated there is here explicit: Yahveh announces events to come. Such is the meaning of God's further assurance:

It was I who foretold, and it is I who
save and announce,
And no strange god among you.[9]

These two passages merely record the evidence; the others draw the conclusion. In one the rhetorical question:

. . . Have I not announced it in the past
And foretold it, with you as my witnesses?

is followed by another:

Is there a god beside me?

Together the two questions draw the conclusion: the fact that Yahveh "announced" establishes his claim to be God alone.[10]

In the next chapter again the two ideas are coupled:

Who announced this from the first,
Of old foretold it?
Am I not God? Nor is there another—
A god beside me.
[Am I not] God, victorious and saving?
Nor is there any aside from me.[11]

The first question: "Who announced this from the first, of old foretold it?" is not answered in so many words. The hearer is left to supply his own answer; from all that has been said his answer must be: "It was you, of course, who foretold it." Well, then, the argument continues, "am I not God?"

The conjunction of fact and necessary conclusion occurs again only a few verses later.

. . . For I am God, and there is no other God,
There is none like me,
Foretelling the end from the beginning,

From aforetime things not yet performed,
Saying, My counsel stands,
And all that I will I do.[12]

It is in the final phrase of this passage that the Second Isaiah most clearly expresses his meaning. Only one who can say: "My counsel stands, and all that I will I do," only such a one is in a position to foretell "from aforetime things not yet performed." But these are the words of Israel's God. He it is who says: "My counsel stands, and all that I will I do." And he who foretells is the same as he who performs; and he is God.

Once more, though without stating the conclusion to be drawn, God reminds his people of a pregnant fact:

The former things of old I foretold
And from my mouth they issued and I announced them.
Suddenly I wrought and they came to pass.[13]

The fact that Israel's God "foretold," revealed through Israel's prophets in advance of the event, his divine intent, and history, God-made history, then of course fulfilled the revelation, that fact is for the Second Isaiah the proof of his divinity.

Today it is customary to say: The prophets of Israel were not predictors, and there is some truth in the saying. To say absolutely that they did not predict would be false. What is right is this: that it was not their predicting that made them prophets; that prophets who made wrong predictions could yet be called prophets. But although predicting was not the essential function of prophets they did indeed predict—the eighth-century prophets: Amos, Isaiah, and Micah, no less than the prophets of the seventh and beginning sixth century: Jeremiah and Ezekiel. Amos said: "Israel shall surely experience exile"; Micah said: "Zion shall be ploughed like a field"; Isaiah said: "Reliance upon the protection of Egypt will prove a delusion"; Jeremiah said: "The Babylonians will return and storm this city and take it and burn it"; and Ezekiel spoke of similar disasters to come. Of course they predicted—specifically and often.[14]

Their predictions might be fallible, but the truths behind their predictions were unconditioned: absolute and timeless. Fulfillment proved a prophet right, but nonfulfillment did not make him wrong. Isaiah only repeated his grim promise in 701 after the Assyrians had withdrawn and had upset his earlier predictions.[15] Despite the fact that for generations they were not fulfilled, the predictions of this Isaiah and those of Micah yet survived. Apparently others, their disciples, perhaps, or the nation, found enduring values in prophetic words that lent importance even to invalid predictions—though sometimes, to be sure, they tried to "correct" them.[16]

It was probably in the days of Jeremiah and Ezekiel that prophets in their tradition felt compelled particularly to defend their authority. Literary prophecy then was being fiercely challenged. Jeremiah came face to face with prophets who claimed to have a word from God opposed to his. Disputing the claims of those prophets, calling them false, Jeremiah insisted: "The Lord has sent me." [17] As Jeremiah's letter to the exiles suggests and Ezekiel's polemic confirms, Ezekiel in exile knew the same need as Jeremiah knew to defend his prophetic word against a rival. "Let not your prophets beguile you," says the one. "Like foxes [burrowing] among ruins have your prophets been, O Israel," the other warns. In both centers of Jewish life before 586, in Palestine and in Babylonia, the controversy raged, and prophets and people sought criteria by which the true prophet might be known from the false.[18]

The legislation in Deuteronomy 13 and 18 is probably a precipitate of this strife. The gist of the law in chapter 13 is this: that a prophet is to be judged by the content of his message alone, and death is the penalty for bringing a message which tends to apostasy. This basic law was later amplified. If to lend authority to his heretical message such a prophet proposes a miracle, a sign, and the sign occurs (this is the meaning of the addition in vv. 2b and 3a), he is still to be judged by the content of his message alone. God may only be putting his people's loyalty to the test, fulfilling a prophet's predictions, but merely as a bait to snare the unfaithful.[19]

The other law in chapter 18 envisages the possibility that a man may represent himself as a prophet, saying in God's name what as a matter of fact God has not authorized him to say. According to this law such a man, too, has committed a capital offense. The question follows: how expose such a man—how recognize that which, though spoken in God's name, God has not said? And the answer: though spoken in God's name the unauthorized word is the word which "does not follow and does not come to pass." [20]

The addition to the first law and the development of the second contradict each other. In the former passage signs and wonders are ruled out, as unreliable evidence. One must know intuitively or through the exercise of one's rational faculty whether the prophet's message contributes to apostasy, and judge the prophet on that knowledge alone, and not be misled by the occurrence of predicted wonders. The latter passage, on the other hand, accepts as the only valid evidence for the authority of a prophet, the fulfillment of his predictions. These opposing views may be a part of the ferment in the time of Jeremiah and Ezekiel, a reflection of the need to know who among the prophets brought the authentic word.

And the second of the two passages in Deuteronomy, the one in chapter 18, expresses the popular view. The people demanded fulfillment as proof. They taunted Jeremiah: "Where is the word of God? Let it but occur." Scoffing at Ezekiel's prophetic warnings, they said: "The vision which he has concerns days far off; he prophesies for the distant future." Neither prophet wholly rejected the popular demand. Jeremiah accepted for himself the evidence of a realized premonition when his cousin offered him a field. He had the assurance that God fulfills his word; that is the meaning of the almond tree: "I keep watch over my word to perform it." The prophet Jeremiah found satisfaction, such as it was, in the fact that the siege of Jerusalem occurred as he had predicted, and he gloated; before the king, Zedekiah, he said: "Where now are your prophets who said: The king of Babylon will not attack you or this land?" Similarly, to the people's taunt Ezekiel replied: it won't be long now. Through him God said to the people: "In your own days, O rebellious house, I will speak a word and perform it." And of them God said: "When it occurs—lo! it shall occur—then they will know there was a prophet among them." [21]

If Jeremiah and Ezekiel did not reject the popular view the Second Isaiah espoused it. Perhaps the historical situation was responsible. Tentatively after 597, and with assurance after 586, a prophetic heir of the pre-exilic prophets of disaster could call attention to their realized expectations. The nation had experienced the calamity. Even the test of fulfillment proved those prophets credible. The time was ripe for such an affirmation as that which the Second Isaiah conveyed: ". . . My word that goes forth from my mouth does not return empty, not having done what I wanted. . . ." "The word of the Lord stands forever." Now it is known as never before that history fulfills the words of God's prophets. The historical situation was partly responsible, but partly also the purpose of the Second Isaiah.[22]

The Second Isaiah had joyous tidings to replace the evil forebodings of earlier prophets. But good news, too, may be hard to believe, and the assent to hope may be hard to secure. The Second Isaiah, commissioned to comfort, had to awaken belief, inspire confidence. It is natural, therefore, that he should insist upon the credibility of prophets, himself among them. Even as the earlier word had been fulfilled so now this latter word is sure. For the Second Isaiah this is a major concern and a dominant theme. It is against the background of this concern that his persistent reference to realized predictions finds meaning, and it is for this reason that it has an important place within his argument for monotheism.

The Second Isaiah invoked the fact of successful prediction as the minor premise in his second syllogism. It was essential in his reasoning. Reject the premise and you spoil his logic. But with or without his logic you have his conclusion. Israel's God is God.

Now, the prophet has more to say. The argument is only an incident in his larger purpose. Unquestionably he makes the conclusion of his argument here a stage only and a pause on his climb to higher peaks. Historically significant though the conclusion is, for its author it is only a stage.

3. God's Witnesses

When the first Isaiah inscribed a tablet with an ominous legend he called upon dependable witnesses, apparently in order that what he had done might be on record. That is the function of witnesses, to testify when the occasion arises that such and such occurred—that, for example, the prophet Isaiah did indeed say or write down: (Assyria) will quickly plunder, hastily despoil (Jerusalem). That the first Isaiah put his words on record in this fashion suggests that even he was not wholly indifferent as concerns the fate of his predictions, despite his insistence that his words were true notwithstanding contrary appearances.[23]

Isaiah's use of witnesses is pertinent in a discussion of the Second Isaiah's argument because in it, too, witnesses play a role.

The word "witnesses" occurs in one of the passages which comprise the positive phase of the Second Isaiah's argument:

> Have I not announced it in the past
> And foretold it, with you as my witnesses? [24]

The testimony of the witnesses plays a part in the argument. To the people of Israel, so the prophet contends, God revealed events which yet lay in the future. The events occurred and the people experienced them. The people experienced prediction and fulfillment. Without witnesses to the fact that Israel's God had foreknowledge no case could be made for his divinity. But the people of Israel are his witnesses and they have a vital role to play, for through their testimony he is known as God. They are indispensable in the chain of proof.

Witnesses to the divinity of Israel's God are twice contrasted with the discredited or nonexistent witnesses of other gods, God's witnesses held up against witnesses to manufactured idols. Of the idols it is said:

> Their witnesses themselves are sightless,
> And they do not know—so that they will be ashamed.

In a passage where both the negative and the positive phase of the argument occur, the contrast again is drawn: ironically God challenges the other gods:

> Let them produce their witnesses and be vindicated
> And hear the testimony and say: It is true,

and confidently he says:

> You are my witnesses . . .
> And my chosen servant,
> That you may know and believe me,

May perceive that I am that One;
Before me no god was formed
Nor shall there be any after.[25]

The logic of the last-cited passage is at first somewhat confusing: "Let them produce their witnesses . . . and hear the testimony and say: It is true"; and "You are my witnesses . . . that you may know." Are, then, the witnesses themselves to hear the testimony and pronounce it valid? Is it the witnesses who are to gain knowledge, convinced by their own evidence—the witnesses convincing the witnesses? Though unexpected, that appears indeed to be the meaning of the verses, and altering the text only destroys the sense. Unchanged and so interpreted the passage helps also in the solution of a crux within the "servant" passages. For, the servant Israel, too, has the task of restoring Israel—Israel restoring Israel—even as the servant-witnesses are destined to convince the witnesses.[26] An analysis of this apparent confusion leads to a clarification not of the argument only but of the servant concept as well.

An essential premise in the Second Isaiah's argument is, as we have seen, the observation that God revealed in advance events that were to follow. The vehicles of revelation were the prophets and the prophets communicated the revelations to the people. So, in fact, both were recipients of divine revelation, the prophets directly, indirectly the people. As persons the prophets lived their lives and passed from the scene, but the people as a historic continuity in whose midst as a tradition, whether orally transmitted or in written form, the record of that revelation was preserved, this people endured.[27] While thus, in the first place and in a narrower sense the witnesses were the single prophets, in a broader sense they were the people as a whole, the repository of the prophetic revelation.

Ideally conceived the people of Israel were the custodians of the prophetic tradition. But certainly the people were no homogeneous unit. The scoffers of the eighth century had hardly been converted all into enthusiastic prophets' disciples in the sixth. Even as the first Isaiah challenged his hearers:

Hear, indeed, but understand not,
And see, indeed, but perceive not

so to the Second Isaiah God lamented:

> Who so blind as my servant,
> And deaf as my commissioned messenger! [28]

Apparently the people had undergone no essential change. The persecutors of Jeremiah who did not want to hear and the "rebellious house" that opposed itself to Ezekiel begot children and grandchildren in exile and these had still to be convinced.[29] Witnesses had still a double task: the testimony they could bring must not merely convince others—it must at the same time contribute to their own understanding, that they themselves "may know." And this is what the Second Isaiah meant in the verse in chapter 43, which is not confused at all but contains a proper insight:

> You are my witnesses . . .
> And my chosen servant
> That *you* may know and believe me,
> May perceive that I am that One . . .

A people may possess a prophetic tradition, take pride in a rich spiritual heritage—and yet want converting to the ideals which, nominally, it cherishes.

The passage is not unique. There are others in which a witness convicts, or convinces, or instructs, not others but himself. That is the sense of the passage in Joshua: "And Joshua asked the people, Will you serve as witnesses against yourselves that you have to-day chosen the Lord to worship him? and they said, We will." Their testimony, should it be required, would, of course, convict only themselves. That is the sense also of Job's words: ". . . Lo, my witness is in heaven . . . and he will set a man right with God. . . ." Boldly, here, Job represents God himself as witnessing before God on behalf of Job, whom God has afflicted without cause. God with his own testimony must convince God. The same word for witness (*'ed*) is used in the passages in Joshua and Job as is used in the "You are my witnesses" passage in Isaiah. "You are my *'edim,* God says, and my chosen servant [*'ebed*]," thus equating "servant" and "witnesses." These terms being equivalent, the thought in the crucial servant passage, Isa. 49:5, is still this same thought. Though "servant" appears and not "witness," the passage proposes that the servant-witness Israel shall itself instruct the servant Israel.[30]

It is, then, the thought of the Second Isaiah that his people Israel is in a position to serve as God's witnesses, is, in fact, the only people with such experience as, when they tell of it, will prove their god to be God; and he would say, to bring such witness is Israel's role. His thought in 43:10 goes no farther than this: that by its own testimony, by recalling its experience and rehearsing its tradition, the people Israel must convince itself, must know and believe and perceive that its god is the One, before whom no god was, after whom none shall be. But the Second Isaiah does go much farther, and his thought fully developed includes the dissemination of this saving truth throughout the world.

4. "That All May Know"

Here is the broad horizon of God's intent:

> That all may know, where the sun rises
> And where it sets, that there is none beside me;
> I am God and there is none else,
> No God but me.

Not Israel here but the nations are to gain the conviction that Israel's god is God. Clearly again the thought is expressed:

> . . . The earnings of Egypt and the wares of Ethiopia,
> And the Sabeans, men of stature,
> Shall come over to you and be yours,
> They shall follow you, come over in chains,
> To you bow down, to you make entreaty:
> In you alone is God
> And there is none else, no other god.[31]

And yet another passage expresses the thought that Israel's testimony will convince the peoples of the world:

> Lo, I have made you a witness to peoples,
> Prince and commander of peoples.
> Lo, you shall summon a nation you know not,
> A nation that knows you not shall run to you

For the sake of God, your God,
And the Holy One of Israel because
he has glorified you.[32]

Other thoughts here are mixed in with the thought that Israel's testimony shall convince the peoples; "wares" and "chains" and glory somewhat confuse the picture. What is clear beyond question, however, is the expectation that the knowledge of Israel's one and only God shall reach to the ends of the earth. The key words for this thought are contained in the passage here first cited: "That all may know."

It is several times noted that all upon the broad earth in fact do not yet know. The "witnesses" of idols

. . . are sightless,
And they do not know—so that they will be ashamed.

They do not know or understand;
Their eyes are besmeared beyond seeing,
their hearts beyond comprehension.

They lack knowledge who carry about
their wooden image,
And pray to a god who cannot save them.

Cyrus must, indeed, be counted among those who do not (yet) know God.

I summoned you by name,
Naming you though you know me not,

God says to Cyrus, and repeats the thought:

. . . Girding you though you know me not.[33]

Arguing negatively, denying the divinity of other gods, the prophet has suggested as a taunt:

Foretell things to come
That we may know you are gods.

If anyone of them could foretell the future, it is suggested, we would have to recognize that he is God, but their ability to do so is denied. And this denial is the counterpart to the thought "That all may know." If Israel's god succeeds where they must fail then all will know who is God, must recognize that it is he. The negations lead to an affirmation:

> Do you not know, have you not heard?
> The God of the world is Yahveh,
> Creator of the ends of the earth.

That the evidence of his witnesses produces such knowledge has already been noted:

> You are my witnesses . . .
> That you may know and believe me;
> May perceive that I am that One . . .

But the knowledge comes as well from deeds yet to be done, such deeds as the miraculous transformation of the desert, prelude to national restoration. God will do such deeds:

> In order that they may see and know,
> Notice and comprehend at one time
> That the power of God has wrought it,
> The Holy One of Israel has created it.

Evidence and demonstration must lead to knowledge, conviction, belief.[34]

At times, in these chapters, the evidence serves to convince the people of Israel. It is they whom the prophet questions: Why are you despondent? "Do you not know; have you not heard? . . ." It is they who may be convinced by their own testimony. But equally in these chapters it is the nations of the world who are yet to gain the knowledge: Cyrus and the worshipers of idols. Clearest of all is the first cited passage:

> That all may know, where the sun rises
> And where it sets, that there is none beside me;
> I am God and there is none else,
> No God but me.[35]

5. "I am God"

We know, of course, that Israel's God had a proper name, as did the gods of other peoples. Moab had a god named Chemosh,

Ammon had a god named Milcom, the Sidonians worshiped a goddess called Ashtoreth, Babylonian gods bore such names as Bel and Nebo—all of this according to biblical sources.[36] It would be surprising if, in those times, Israel's God had been nameless—but he was not. We know the four consonants of his name: *y-h-v-h,* and we know that they were not pronounced "Jehovah"—that pronunciation mistakes a conventional way of writing the name for the name itself. We have reason to believe that the name was pronounced *yahveh,* so pronounced until men ceased referring to God by his proper name on any but the one most holy occasion in the religious year, employing instead a conventional substitute.

The Second Isaiah did something of far-reaching significance with this name Yahveh. He may have had help from Ezekiel, others may have had a part in it; who was responsible is far less important than the phenomenon itself. He (or they) gave the name Yahveh the additional meaning "God." If Chemosh should say: "I am Chemosh" the declaration would but serve to identify him; we would know that Chemosh, the god of Moab, was speaking. If Milcom said: "I am Milcom" we would know that this god of Ammon was speaking. "Hammurabi . . . am I" says no less; with such words the great king of old Babylonia identifies himself in the prologue to his code of laws. But, unlike these, the God of Israel can say: "I am Yahveh," *'ani yahveh,* and mean "I am God"—and be so understood. It was, primarily, the Second Isaiah who brought it about that *yahveh* could mean "God."

The name Yahveh is not used in the Bible in quite the same way as *'el* and *'elohim* are used. These other terms also mean God, but they are not normally employed as proper names. Unlike proper names they can take the definite article. We never find "the Yahveh" but again and again we find "the *'el*" or "the *'elohim.*" These can be construed with other nouns and with pronouns. We find *kemosh 'elohe mo'ab,* "Chemosh, the god of Moab," and "Milcom, the *'elohim* of Ammon." But *yahveh* is not so construed; it is always "absolute" ("the Lord of hosts" is no true exception). The biblical words *'el* and *'elohim* are generic terms, meaning "god" or "a god."

There are two ways in biblical Hebrew to say "I am God." One is what we might thus expect: *'ani 'el* or *'ani 'elohim,* "I am *'el*" or "I am *'elohim.*" In these expressions *'el* and *'elohim* are instances of what we call "emphatic indetermination." The very absence of the definite article makes them most definite. In English we express this meaning not by using the article "the": "the god," but by omitting the article and using a capital letter instead: "God." The second way in biblical Hebrew to say "I am God" is what we would not expect; it is marvelous. The other way is to say *'ani yahveh,* "I am Yahveh." Wondrously this, too, means "I am God." The Second Isaiah achieved the equation according to which Yahveh is God.

The statement *'ani yahveh* appears quite frequently in chapters 40 to 48 of Isaiah, the chapters in which the great argument takes place. The statement does not always have the same meaning there. Often it means "I am Yahveh," in which meaning it serves as a kind of seal or signature, merely identifying the speaker as Yahveh, Israel's God. But often, too, it has a larger meaning. In the context of the argument from prophecy to monotheism it serves as the monotheistic formula: "I am God"—"I alone am God." The vocable *yahveh* in the formula is no longer the proper noun, the name of Israel's God, no longer a certain god, not "a god" at all but "the god": God.

This is a very important matter. The whole debate leads to this point as its conclusion, and the demonstration that this is indeed intended must be a careful one. In the foregoing sections of this chapter the translation of the formula has been taken for granted; here we must justify it. The statement that *'ani yahveh* in this context often means "I am God" follows upon a number of detailed observations.

In the first place we observe that the alternative translation "I am Yahveh" would sometimes be quite meaningless. In 45:6b or 45:18b, for example, the Hebrew words, rendered word for word, could be translated "I am Yahveh and there is none else." Israel's God could be saying this, but it would be pointless. No one would want to dispute the fact that there is but one Yahveh. What might have been disputed is his uniqueness as God alone. And it is this which here he must be asserting: not "I am Yahveh" but "I am God and there is none else."

The conclusion that this is the meaning of these two identical statements is strengthened by a second observation: that two other declarations in the same context are word for word identical with these, except, significantly, that the generic noun *'el* replaces the proper noun *yahveh* in the formula, thus: "I am *'el* and there is none else." [37] Assuming the phenomenon of emphatic indetermination here, we conclude that in all four passages God means to say: "I am God, and there is none else." *'Ani yahveh* means: "I am God." [38]

A number of further passages point in the same direction. Consider the parallels to the formula *'ani yahveh.* According to the conventions of parallelism synonyms balance synonyms, and one half of the poetic line helps determine the meaning of the other. Thus, if the words "I am *yahveh,* and there is none else" are balanced by the words "No *'elohim* but me" as they are in Isa. 45:5(6), the word *yahveh* will be the equivalent of *'elohim.* Since the conclusion is "no *'elohim* but me" and not "no *yahveh* but me," the first part of the line means not "I am Yahveh" but "I am God"—"I am God, and there is none else, no God but me."

The situation is the same in other passages. In one of them, both of the terms *'elohim* and *'el* are balanced against *yahveh* in such a way that we can only understand *yahveh* to mean God:

> Am I not *yahveh?* Nor is there another,
> An *'elohim* beside me.
> [Am I not] *'el,* victorious and saving?
> Nor is there any aside from me.

First, in this passage as in the foregoing, the generic *'elohim* stands as parallel to *yahveh* and compels us to translate *yahveh* as God. And then, since the parallelism requires a carrying over in thought of the words "Am I not," the question "Am I not *yahveh?*" at the beginning of the challenge is resumed by the question "Am I not *'el?*" And both must be translated: "Am I not God?" We have noticed already that these lines are not the answer to the rhetorical question which precedes. They contain the tremendous conception which the implied answer to that question permits. Put the implied unspoken answer in brackets, and the whole imposing passage reads as follows:

Who announced this from the first,
Of old foretold it?
[You did, O God of Israel; it was you who announced it.]
[Then] am I not God? Nor is there another—
A God beside me.
[Am I not] God, victorious and saving?
Nor is there any aside from me.

The prophet employs the same form in another passage, only substituting a declarative sentence for the rhetorical question:

For, I am God [*'el*] and there is no other,
[Am] God [*'elohim*] and there is none like me.[39]

The longer of these two passages clearly combines elements of the argument from prophecy ("Who announced this . . . ?") with the monotheistic formula ("Am I not God?"). This combination recurs. There is a passage which begins with the words "I, I am God [*yahveh*]"; but probably the repetition of the pronoun is for emphasis and is intended to produce the meaning "I alone"; thus:

I alone am God,
And there is no other savior.
It was I who foretold and I save and announce,
And no strange god among you.
And you are my witnesses, says Yahveh,
And I am God [*'el*].

The thought appears also without the formula.

Thus said Yahveh, Israel's king,
His savior, the Lord of Hosts:
I am first and I am last
And aside from me there is no god [*'elohim*] [40]

But there are more examples of the formula (the evidence is abundant):

Thus says Yahveh, your redeemer,
He who formed you at birth:
I am God [*yahveh*] maker of all;

Stretching out the heavens—I alone;
Spreading forth the earth—who beside me?

The translation of *'ani yahveh* as "I am God" is here confirmed by the phrases which follow: "I alone" and "who beside me?" In part, another verse repeats the thought:

For thus Yahveh has said,
The creator of the heavens—he is God [*ha'elohim*]—
He who formed the earth and made it:
. . . I am God [*yahveh*] and there is no other.

In this passage the monotheistic interpretation of the formula is confirmed by the remark "He is God" where *ha'elohim* replaces *yahveh*.[41]

Now, in these two equivalent passages, a very significant succession of phrases occurs. With the word for God untranslated they read: "Thus *yahveh* has said . . . I am *yahveh*." It is obvious that *yahveh* is here used in both of its two senses. In the first phrase it is the proper noun, the name of Israel's God: Yahveh; in the second it is God, the One; and the succession of phrases means just this:

Thus Yahveh has said . . . : "I am God."

There can be no doubt that the Second Isaiah uses the name Yahveh also as a proper noun. Many times in these chapters the name Yahveh, indeed, appears as such. It is sometimes combined with such a word as "your God":

For I, Yahveh, your God, hold your right hand.

In this combination Yahveh can only mean the particular god of the people, and it does not have monotheistic implications.[42]

Nor does it when Yahveh says:

I am Yahveh, that is my name.
I give to no other the glory due me
Nor my due praise to carved images.

Although here, as elsewhere in these chapters, Yahveh lays exclusive claim to divinity, the words he uses are not the monotheistic formula "I am God," but are comparable to the identification of the speaker by name elsewhere in the Bible: "And God spoke to Moses and said to him: I am Yahveh; I appeared to Abraham, Isaac and Jacob as El Shaddai but by my name Yahveh I was not known to them." [43]

Now the observation that the formula *'ani yahveh* has this double significance in these chapters, and sometimes means "I am Yahveh" and sometimes "I am God," in no wise invalidates the foregoing conclusions. Quite the contrary; it contributes to an understanding of the full and solemn import of the argument. That the Second Isaiah identifies him in whose name he speaks now as Yahveh, Israel's god, and now as God, the One, comports absolutely with that argument. The argument intends to prove just this: that Yahveh is God—that Yahveh and God are the same. The prophet's universalism throughout is combined with the contention that between Israel and the one God a special relationship exists. It is Israel's god, Yahveh, not Chemosh, not Bel, not the god addressed by any other people, who is God—as the Second Isaiah proves to his complete satisfaction with his argument from prophecy to monotheism. Israel's God is God.

CHAPTER V

AND ISRAEL IS HIS PROPHET

1. Retrospect

Israel's God is God, and Israel is his prophet. The Second Isaiah had new dimensions to add to his already magnificent conception. Or perhaps, not to add; no doubt the conception was always all of a piece, and only we, analyzing it at a distance, have to describe it one aspect after another. For, this other aspect of the prophet's thought: its meaning for Israel, may indeed have been there from the start, may have been the very impulse which drove him on to his bold conclusion and may not have been at all some sort of corollary. Had he not come to console and enhearten his people? And was it not his function in history to build them up? Oh, he did not set out calculatingly to devise some form of occupational therapy especially to rehabilitate this miserable remnant of a people in a foreign land. But, if he had done so, he could scarcely have done better. For, what is true of persons is true of peoples, and purpose is a remedy against self-hatred.

Even in the third generation the forcibly displaced Judeans in Babylonia were in "exile." The Second Isaiah could yet say of them: "it is a people plundered and despoiled . . . hidden away in dungeons"; they were "the worm, Jacob . . . the maggot, Israel." He could still resent their captors' behavior: "you made exceeding heavy your yoke upon the aged." To the Second Isaiah they were still "the preserved"; they were to be "restored" and, anguished, he looked forward to the rebuilding of Jerusalem and her ruined places.[1] Yes, the misery of the captive Judeans was still real enough and we can well imagine their state of mind. Not only were their spirits low, they felt small and useless. And probably they had more respect for their captors than for themselves. We find a suggestion at least in the words of the Second Isaiah that they were inclined to adopt the prevailing idolatrous cult.[2] It was probably just this loss of national self-esteem that drove the prophet onward toward his discovery of a place in God's scheme of salvation for his people Israel.

It is from considerations such as these that we come to a study of the prophet's concept of "God's servant." It is a recurrent theme. Throughout the sixteen chapters and especially, there, in four compositions which are commonly though somewhat inaccurately known as the servant "songs," the Second Isaiah refers to God's servant. And it is in this figure that we find what he was seeking: the place in God's scheme of salvation for his people Israel. For, the servant of God is a personification of Israel; and Israel as God's servant is the instrument of his salvation.

Recall the reasoning of the Second Isaiah as the foregoing chapter has described it:

(1) The Second Isaiah invoked an argument from prophecy in defense of his claim that Israel's God is the one and only God. He argued negatively in that he denied divinity to other presumed gods. The test of divinity which he proposed was foreknowledge. And the evidence which he required was the evidence that prophets alone could bring. It was the absence of accredited prophets among the nations which made ridiculous any claims they might present on behalf of their gods. Against his denial of divinity to any other candidates he set his affirmation that Israel's god is God. And his positive proof for this affirmation again was the evidence which prophets supplied. The prophets of Israel's god had brought unquestionable evidence that he possessed the foreknowledge which is the mark of divinity. Israel's prophets were the instruments by which it was known in Israel that this people's god is God.

(2) The role of Israel's prophets was of great significance. But the role of Israel was equally significant. For the Second Isaiah the people of Israel were "witnesses." Being witnesses to a fact—the

fact that their god had foreknowledge of fateful events—the people of Israel were in a position to testify to that unique fact—to obtain the consent of men to the proposition that their god is God. But there is no sharp line dividing the people from the prophets. The people constitute the historic continuity out of which came the prophets who, strictly speaking, alone gave voice to God's intent and evidence of his foreknowledge. But they were also that historic continuity which heard the prophetic word—heard and rejected but, also, recorded and preserved it. They were the soil on which the prophets grew and they were the repository of the prophetic tradition. They were the prophets; they embodied prophecy. And it is in this sense that the Second Isaiah can call the people of Israel God's "witnesses."

(3) There is, however, a limit to the identification. The prophet must distinguish between Israel as an ideal, a prophetic people, and the real contemporary Israel, ordinary men and women, still recalcitrant, still unconvinced by the evidence which they, alone among the peoples, are in a position to adduce. "This you are," the prophet appears to be saying, "but this is your destiny." The distinction between Israel as fact and as ideal removes a difficulty which otherwise one of the "servant songs" presents and opens the way for the proposition that, in these songs as well as their context, Israel is cast in the role of a missionary people and assigned the task of testifying that there is but one God and that the god of Israel is he.

The argument has set the stage for the "servant." Servant and witnesses are one; and the language of 43:10 establishes their identity: "You are my witnesses, God says, and my chosen servant." The "servant" is the personification of the people of Israel: Israel personified as a prophet-witness, as one who has heard the word of God and can testify to his divinity. The figure of the "servant" emerges from the argument for monotheism. It is a natural next step—an obligation—for a people possessed of such a truth to make it known. Thus the people become the "servant" of the God they know.

But if it has been shown that the debate and the "servant" theme are mutually complementary, then it is evident that the debate and the "servant songs" are the product of the same prophetic author.

The demonstration that they belong together obviates any need to regard the "servant songs" as an element foreign to the Second Isaiah. They are neither earlier compositions adopted and incorporated by him, nor later compositions added by another to his writings. They are an integral part of the philosophy of the Second Isaiah.

To say that the servant is the people personified as prophet is to say, in the first place, that the servant is a personification—only a personification, not any real figure, not Zerubbabel, not any contemporary martyr or teacher of the Law, not the prophet Jeremiah, not the Second Isaiah himself, not either the expected messiah—all of these have by someone or other been nominated—not, in other words, any single person but a people personified, a vivid figure of speech. It is to say, in the second place, that the features of this personification are the features of a prophet, that the figure is the figure of a prophet.

This view approaches, but is to be distinguished from that of Wilhelm Gesenius who, more than a century ago, proposed: *"Die Propheten sind hier als ein Ganzes, eine Körperschaft oder moralische Person betrachtet."* He saw in the servant a personification, not of Israel but of the succession of Israel's prophets.[3]

It agrees, rather, with the view expressed more recently by Otto Eissfeldt. Eissfeldt defended the proposition that the servant is the same in the songs as in their context in the sixteen chapters, and that, throughout, the servant is no single person but Israel personified, and personified as prophet. He called attention also to the marked resemblance between the characterization of the servant and the figure of Jeremiah; as Eissfeldt put it, Jeremiah served as "god-father" to the servant.[4]

2. God's Servant

There has been no agreement at all on the question of what the Second Isaiah meant by "God's servant." There is no particular "Christian" view and there is no special "Jewish" view. A survey of Jewish opinion on the identity of the servant from the earliest expressions down to recent time reveals a surprising absence of agreement. A single interpreter among the early exegetes would often explain the servant now one way and now another, as he moved from passage to passage. David Ḳimḥi, who lived in the twelfth and thirteenth centuries, may serve as an example. He identified the servant in the first song with the messiah, the servant in the second and third songs with the prophet Isaiah, the servant in the fourth song with the people Israel, to which last interpretation he gave eschatological overtones.[5]

But in fact the servant is the people Israel, and this is true wherever we look in the sixteen chapters. We are not limited to the four servant songs though these are of primary interest. A number of times besides God refers to "my servant" and the prophet refers to "the servant of God." And these other references are quite as reliable as those in the songs and a good deal more specific. If, for the time being, we leave the songs aside and look only at the other places in the chapters where the servant is mentioned, we are left with little doubt as to the servant's identity. He is the people Israel, chosen by God for his service, commissioned by him as witness to his divinity.

If we consider these several passages here in the order of the chapters we start with 41:8–10 and immediately come upon the equation: Israel—my servant, and the association of servant and choice.

> And you, Israel, my servant,
> Jacob, whom I chose,
> Seed of Abraham, my friend,
> You whom I took from the ends of the earth,
> Summoned from its distant parts,
> Saying to you: "You are my servant,"
> I favor you and I have not rejected you.
> Do not fear for I am with you. . . .[6]

In the second passage, in 42:18 f., at once the other feature also appears: God's servant is described as his "commissioned messenger."

> Hearken you deaf!
> You blind, look and see!
> Who so blind as my servant

And deaf as my commissioned messenger!
Who so blind as Meshullam
And deaf as God's servant! [7]

The next passage has been discussed at length in the foregoing chapter. It combines the concepts: servant, witnesses and choice.

You are my witnesses, God says,
And my chosen servant.[8]

In the following passage, Israel is the servant as he is in the first, and the idea of choice is present.

Now hearken, Jacob my servant
And Israel whom I have chosen.
Thus said God your maker
And he who formed you at birth, who will help you:
"Fear not, my servant Jacob,
Jeshurun whom I have chosen." [9]

The next passage says no more than the foregoing unless, as is probable, it is the original continuation of 44:6–8, now separated from those verses by the satire on idolatry in vv. 9 to 20. If so, the servant, Israel, is urged to remember well those facts which as witnesses the servant people would be called upon to relate.

Remember these things, Jacob
And Israel, for you are my servant.
I formed you; you are a servant to me.
Israel, you will not be forgotten by me.[10]

Another passage adds evidence for the prophetic nature of the servant; the servant speaks a predictive word which God fulfills, and "servant" is a synonym for "his messengers." We observe that though "servant" is singular, "messengers" is plural, which is as we might expect since the servant is not a person but a people. God is

He who fulfills the word of his servant
And accomplishes the counsel of his messengers.[11]

In 45:4 God addresses the conqueror Cyrus, his agent, and speaks to him of his chosen servant Israel—again the combination of servant, Israel and choice.

For the sake of my servant Jacob
And Israel my chosen one
I summoned you by name,
Naming you though you know me not.

Finally, God refers to his servant in the following passage, about which only this much is clear: that the servant has a voice which the god-fearing hear.

Who among you fears God
Hearing the voice of his servant,
Who walked in darkness
Having no light
Trusting in God's name,
Leaning on his Lord? [12]

The passages reviewed make a uniform impression, barring the obscurity in the last of them.

God's servant is Jacob-Israel: 41:8 f.; 44:1 f., 21; 45:4.
God chose his servant: 41:8 f.; 43:10a; 44:1 f.; 45:4.
The servant and God's "witnesses" are the same: 43:10a.
The servant serves as God's "commissioned messenger(s)": 42:19; 44:26.
The servant is expected to see and hear: 42:18 f.
The servant has a voice: 50:10, and speaks a word which God fulfills, gives counsel which God accomplishes: 44:26.

In these passages, in other words, the servant of God is nothing but the personification of Israel as prophet.

These results are clear enough; they have only to be tested against the evidence of the four songs which are yet to be reviewed.

The songs give striking evidence of the Second Isaiah's skill at personification. The Second Isaiah is a master of personification. In the songs he develops his figure of speech until his figment lives and we seem to have a real person before us. He is eminently successful with another figure where no doubt can arise as to its significance.

Get down and sit in the dust,
O virgin daughter Babylon.
Sit on the ground without a throne,
Daughter of Chaldea.

They shall no more call you
Tender and spoiled . . .
Take millstones and grind flour;
Tuck up your skirt,
Bare leg and thigh,
Wade into the ditches.

Now hear this, O pampered one,
Sitting secure,
Who say to yourself:
"I am unrivaled.
I will never be widowed,
Will not know bereavement,"
These very calamities will overtake you
Suddenly on the same day.
Bereavement and widowhood in full measure
Shall befall you . . .

The identity of the pampered princess is beyond question; it is the carefree city of Babylon. But the city has achieved personality, in the prophet's fantasy, and breathes and pouts and grieves and labors. Zion too is a woman; even Jerusalem climbs her high hill and shouts her good news to her neighbors.[13]

And the master of personification is equally convincing when he personifies the people of Israel as God's servant. The vividness of the personification indeed increases as in one of the songs after another God speaks of his servant and the servant speaks of his task.

3. Three Songs

References to the servant in the sixteen chapters suggested the identity of servant and people. A reading of the servant songs leads in the same direction. In them also the servant appears as a personification of the people Israel and the servant's features are those of a prophet. The four songs show some diversity and the fourth is often separated, as a thing apart, from the other three. Although in the end it will appear that all of the songs agree upon the identity and nature of the servant, it is, in fact, better thus to reserve the fourth song for separate treatment and first consider only songs one, two and three: Isa. 42:1–4; 49:1–6; and 50:4–9. Here follows a translation of these songs.

In the first God presents his servant:

42:1 Here is my servant whom I uphold,
My chosen one in whom I delight.
I have put my spirit on him;
He will publish the truth among the nations.
2 He will not cry or shout,
He will not raise his voice outside.
3 He will break no crushed reed,
Quench no dim wick.
In faithfulness he will publish the truth.
4 He himself will neither fade nor be broken
Until he establish truth on earth.
The coastlands wait for his teaching.[14]

In such words God describes the projected activity of his servant. He assigns to him the duties of a prophet. The words are not unlike the words God speaks to Moses, Isaiah, or Jeremiah when he calls them to his service. The "teaching," for which the coastlands wait, is in Hebrew *torah*. The servant is summoned to dispense *torah*.

To prophets *torah* means their own teachings. The first Isaiah applied the term to the living word which he announced, the word of God which he revealed. When his people rejected the *torah* and spurned the word of the Holy One of Israel Isaiah despaired of reaching his generation and determined to seal his *torah* among his disciples. It is clearly his teachings which he hoped thus to perpetuate. He called his people rebellious, false, sons who refused to hear the *torah* of their God, whereupon he recorded his teachings in a book.[15] This living word is what a prophet means who speaks of *torah* and it is this which the servant is to propagate.

Anyone who would dispense *torah* must certainly speak out; and the words of the second verse may not be taken as a denial of speech. "He will not cry or shout . . ." does not mean he will keep silent. The words concern only his behavior in teaching. He will curb his natural enthusiasm, "the sharp sword of his mouth," and preserve a calm demeanor.

The servant's teaching is "truth." This word, occurring three times in this first song, corresponds to the Hebrew word *mishpaṭ,* which also means "justice," "a just order." In this song God says of his servant: "He will publish *mishpaṭ* among the nations" and at the end of the second to his servant he says: "I make you a light to the nations." The light which the servant can bring, this *mishpaṭ* is "truth." [16]

In the second song the servant speaks:

49:1 Hear me, O coastlands!
Hearken, you peoples afar!
God summoned me at birth,
Adopted me when I came from the womb.
2 He made my mouth a sharp sword,
Hid me in the shadow of his hand.
He made me a polished arrow,
Concealed me in his quiver.
3 And he said to me: "You are my servant,
Israel through whom I shall get me glory."
4 But I said: "I have toiled in vain,
For naught and vanity spent my strength";
Surely [though] my cause is with God,
My God has a reward for me.
5c And I am honored in God's sight
And my God has been my strength.
5ab And now God has said—
He who shaped me in the womb as his servant
To restore to him Jacob
And to gather Israel to him—
6 He said: "It is too small a matter for you
to be my servant,
To raise up the tribes of Jacob
And to restore the preserved ones of Israel,
So I make you [as well] a light to the nations,
That my salvation may reach
To the ends of the earth." [17]

Summoned by God, indeed, in the first of the songs, there named God's servant and commissioned to dispense *torah* and *mishpaṭ,* "teaching" and "truth," the servant may well exult as in this second song he does. God had said of him: "The coastlands wait for his teaching," so, here the servant presents himself: "Hear me, O coastlands! . . . God summoned me . . . made my mouth a sharp sword . . . said: I make you a light to the nations, that my salvation may reach to the ends of the earth."

To be sure, the servant here thinks also of himself, not only of "peoples afar." He speaks of the bonds which unite him with God. God has "concealed me in his quiver . . . my cause is with God, my God has a reward for me . . . I am honored in God's sight . . . my God has been my strength." And he speaks of his misery: "I said: I have toiled in vain, for naught and vanity spent my strength." And he speaks of his need "to restore . . . Jacob . . . to gather Israel . . . to raise up the tribes of Jacob . . . to restore the preserved ones of Israel." He thinks of himself, to be sure, and he speaks of these things in his song; yet what is significant is the servant's anticipated readiness to enter upon his prophetic mission.

In the third song the servant speaks again. Still his behavior is that of a prophet—his experience, too, because prophets are abused.

50:4 My Lord God gave me
The tongue of disciples.
To know to relieve the weary
He stirs up a word in the morning.
In the morning he stirs up my ear
To hear as disciples.
5 My Lord God opened my ear,
And I was not stubborn,
Did not turn away.
6 I gave my back to them that smote me,
My cheeks to those that plucked them.
I hid not my face
From insult and spittle.
7 And my Lord God helps me;
So I am not abashed.
I set my jaw as stone
And know I will not be disgraced.
8 At hand is he who vindicates me.
Who dares oppose me? Let us go to court together.
Who has litigation with me? Let him approach.

9 Lo, my Lord God helps me;
Who can prove me in the wrong?
Lo, they shall all wear out like a garment,
The moth shall devour them.[18]

The features of the *'ebed* are clearly drawn in this third song and he emerges as prophet. Prophetlike, he has an ear to hear, he has a tongue to speak, he is a ready disciple. His God instructs him constantly and he both receives the instruction and employs it—"to relieve the weary." Because he is in league with his God adversity does not deter him. Together they shall triumph, he and God, and their adversaries fail.

The first, second, and third servant songs only confirm the conclusions tentatively reached after surveying the eight passages where otherwise the servant appears in the Second Isaiah. At one point the servant and Israel are explicitly equated in these three songs:

. . . You are my servant,
Israel through whom I shall get me glory.[19]

The parallel which we saw to be frequent in the other passages, between being God's servant, Israel, and being chosen, is preserved in the songs, both with the naming of Israel: 49:1 and 3, and without specification: 42:1.

The crux in the second song is no obstacle in the way of the identification of the servant with Israel—as we have already observed. The servant Israel may yet have a mission to Israel. God can shape Israel as his servant "to restore to him Jacob and to gather to him Israel." God can make of his people "a light to the nations" after or along with the small matter of "raising up the tribes of Judah and restoring the preserved ones of Israel." The servant may have a task within as well as without, may be cast as a "light to the nations" and even so still need to overcome its own age-old inertia. This and the fact that the people, no doubt, were only by courtesy of the prophet's figure a unit or corporate personality make it understandable that God's servant Israel would yet "gather Israel to him" and "restore the preserved ones of Israel."

And in these three songs together the servant has the features of a prophet: God's spirit rests on him, God opens his ear, gives him a word. He is as disciples, as were the disciples of the first Isaiah who learned from their master the prophetic word.[20] The servant both hears and can speak, has mouth, tongue, and voice. And he has a message to bring, *torah* to dispense. It is through teaching, by speech, that the servant fulfills his function as servant—therefore the mention of his mouth and voice. It is with the word from his God that he relieves the weary.[21] Though calm persuasion is his manner he will yet "publish the truth"; "the coastlands wait for his teaching." Thus called and gifted, entrusted with a task, according to the three songs (as in the passages previously reviewed) the servant Israel has all of the characteristics of a prophet. It remains to be seen whether in the fourth song the impression is otherwise.

4. The Song of the Servant's Proud Destiny

Of the several compositions dealing with the servant we have yet to look at the fourth song. This is Isa. 52:13 to 53:12, a poem about which many volumes have been written. One approaches the song with reverence, not only because it is the high point reached by the soaring vision of the Second Isaiah but also for all it has meant in the history of the human spirit.

It is because of this song that the servant of God has been called "the suffering servant"—but wrongly so, because that is not at all what the song suggests. Quite the contrary! God and the prophet here portray God's servant as a people destined now to leave behind all grief and misery and to ascend the heights of glory. The chapter quite easily gives the wrong impression. Ambiguity is undoubtedly present and only the most careful study can reveal the true intent of the words. But the difference between what the chapter says and what it has been thought to say is a material difference. Two widely divergent paths may take this chapter as their starting point, the way of defeat and the way of victory. The Second Isaiah meant the song to be a guidepost on the way of victory. An analysis of the song will justify this weighty conclusion.

There is in this fourth song a dramatic alternation of speakers. All, however, speak of the servant. First and last, in 52:13–15 and again in 53:11b–12, God himself describes in glowing words his

servant's coming exaltation. The first description makes
the kings of nations, whose astonishment at the servant's
will be unbounded. And so, in the second part of the song
9, these kings themselves give voice to their astonishme
briefly, near the end, in 53:10–11a, the prophet interprets the events, before God in conclusion renews the promise.

[*God speaks of his servant:*]

52:13 Lo, my servant shall prosper,
Shall rise, be lifted up, be greatly exalted.
14 Even as many were appalled at him,
Because his looks were inhumanly marred
And his appearance unlike a man's,
15 Even so many will be aghast at him;
Kings will be dumbfounded,
Having seen what had never been told them,
Having contemplated what they had never heard.

[*The kings of the nations speak of the servant:*]

53:1 Who [ever] believed what we have [just] heard?
To whom [else] has God's work been thus revealed?
2 This one grew up as a sapling before us,
As one rooted in an arid land,
Having no appearance, no splendor for us to notice,
No shapeliness to enjoy.
3 He was despised and ignored by men,
A man of pains, familiar with sickness,
One to look away from,
Despised—we took no account of him.
4 Yet—he has borne sickness for us;
Our pains he has suffered.
We supposed him stricken,
Smitten by God and afflicted;
5 But he was [in fact] wounded because of
our transgressions,
Crushed because of our iniquities.
He experienced the suffering which might
lead to our welfare;

There was healing for us in his bruises.
6 We all strayed like sheep,
Went each his own way,
And God visited him
With the guilt of us all.
7 He was driven and was meek,
Not opening his mouth—
As a sheep led to the slaughter,
As a ewe is dumb before her shearers—
Not opening his mouth.
8 He was removed from the exercise of
authority and [excluded] from justice,
And who speaks of his generation?
For he was cut off from the land of the living;
Because of our transgressions he was
stricken unto death.
9 They placed his tomb with the wicked,
With the doers of evil his simple grave [?]
Though he had done no deeds of violence
And no deceit was in his mouth.

[*The prophet speaks of the servant:*]

10 God wanted to crush him (? with sickness
To know if his life would give a guilt offering ?).
He shall see descendants, shall live long,
And God's desire shall succeed through him.
11 As a consequence of his life's distress
he shall see light,
He shall be sated with knowledge.

[*God speaks again of his servant:*]

My servant vindicated many,
Bearing their iniquities;
12 Therefore I will give him a portion among the many,
He shall share spoil among the mighty,
Because he emptied his life even to death
And was counted among transgressors
And bore the guilt of many,
Interceding for the transgressors.

Honest interpreters of a text like the fourth song will not conceal the facts (1) that it contains obscurities and (2) that its translation involves conjectures. The translation here offered is no exception; at several points it assumes a text somewhat different from the received text. The first part of the song, which comes at the end of chapter 52, is in considerable confusion and the concluding verses in 53:8–12 are quite obscure in part. Sometimes the fault is easily mended; sometimes we must adopt a less certain conjecture, and once or twice we cannot even guess.

These are the changes in the received text which the above translation assumes:

In 52:14: "at him," *'alav,* in place of "at you," *'aleka;* [22]
"because," *ki,* in place of "so," *ken;*
"marred," with the vowels changed to those of the *hoph'al* participle, *moshḥat;*

in 52:15: "will be aghast," *yirgezu,* in place of the meaningless "shall startle [?] nations," *yazzeh goyim;* [23]

in 53:2: "before us," *lefanenu,* in place of "before him," *lefanav;*

in 53:8: "because of our transgressions," *mippesha'enu,* instead of "because of the transgression of my people," *mippesha' 'ammi;* [24]
"he was stricken unto death," *nugga' lammavet,* in place of "they suffered a blow," *nega' lamo;* [25]

in 53:9: "doers of evil," *'ose ra',* in place of "a rich man," *'ashir;* [26]
"his simple grave," *'aremato,* in place of "in his deaths [?]," *bemotav;* [27]

in 53:11: "he shall see light," *yir'eh 'or,* in place of simply "he shall see," *yir'eh;* [28]
"he shall be sated with knowledge" in place of a phrasing which divides the line before "with knowledge"; [29]
"vindicated," *hiẓdiḳ,* simply, in place of *yaẓdiḳ ẓaddiḳ.*[30]

For a text as obscure as the received text of this fourth song this list of proposed corrections is not too long. But even with these corrections the text is not fully clear. At least two passages still remain most puzzling. Various translations have been proposed for 53:8: "And who speaks of his generation?" none, including this one, very satisfactory. It is best to draw no conclusions based on this half verse. And the part of the verse between the question marks in 53:10 is even more puzzling; the translation is forced and we cannot even guess at its meaning: "with sickness, to know if his life would give a guilt offering." It, too, cannot be used as legitimate evidence in the interpretation of the servant theme.[31]

Probably no chapter in the Hebrew Bible is more generally misunderstood than this famous 53rd. Nascent Christianity saw in the chapter predictions of the "passion" of the Messiah. Jews have often thought it means that Israel is destined, age after bitter age, to suffer, and suffer vicariously, for the sins of men. That the chapter refers to the servant's "passion," his suffering, is beyond question. The only possible question is whether the prophet contemplated that suffering as wholly a thing of the past or as both past experience and future expectation. The answer to that question is not immediately apparent and there is quite enough ambiguity in the tenses of the verbs to justify the uncertainty. All the same, we can answer the question, and the answer is significant and justifies the search.

This is what an inspection of the verbs reveals: that all of the verbs which in this fourth song describe the grim experience of the servant are verbs in the past tense, and, conversely, that all of the verbs in the future tense speak only of success and glory for the servant. If this is right, then the chapter has, indeed, been misunderstood, because, if the suffering is wholly past, it is quite wrong to think of suffering as a program here, and the doctrine is misleading.

What, then, is the situation? The form of a Hebrew verb, as we know, does not always and alone determine its tense. For the clue to the tense of an ambiguous form we must frequently look to the verb that precedes it or follows. Hebrew participles, for example, are flexible as to tense and may be past, present, or future as the context will decide. The combination of an abundance of participles with a generous sprinkling of imperfects, also of uncertain tense, introduces a large element of uncertainty into the fourth song. But, fortunately, the clues to the tense of the ambiguous forms are also abundant and conclusions are possible.

As we have said, the verbs which describe the grim experience of the servant are all in the past tense. In 52:14 the indefinite tense of the Hebrew participle "were marred" is fixed as past by the preceding "were appalled" and, in the same manner, the repeated participle "despised" in 53:3 is fixed in the past tense by the verb "we took no account of him" which follows. In 53:4 "we supposed" leads us to construe as past the participles which follow in vv. 4 and 5: "stricken," "smitten," "afflicted," "wounded," "crushed." "He was driven," in v. 7, justifies the translation of the participle "was meek"; it suggests, also, that the imperfect form which occurs twice in the verse: "not opening his mouth" is to be translated in this fashion, as a subordinate clause which takes its tense from the main verb, namely, "was driven." Similarly in v. 12 the series of verbs in the past tense: "he emptied his life," "was counted among transgressors," "bore the guilt," leaves us in no doubt about the final clause: the imperfect form there must also be construed as a subordinate clause. It does not mean: "he will intercede for transgressors," but, along with its parallel: "and bore the guilt of many, interceding for transgressors." [32] That is it, then; all of the verbs which describe the grief of the servant describe it as over and past.

Not so the verbs that suggest glory and success. Their tense is future. These verbs appear at the beginning, stating the theme of the song, and they appear at the end as the climax of the song. At the beginning: "My servant shall prosper, shall rise, be lifted up, be greatly exalted"; "many will be aghast," "be dumbfounded," "having seen," "having contemplated." The only question here might be about the tense of the two last-quoted verbs, "having seen," "having contemplated." But there need be no question; they stand in circumstantial clauses. These two are perfect forms because the action they describe was antecedent to the state of amazement expressed by the preceding verbs in the future tense. And again, at the end of the composition as at its beginning, the gleaming promise: "He shall see descendants, shall live long," "shall succeed," "shall see light," "shall be sated with knowledge," "I will give him a portion," "he shall share spoil."

And so, throughout the composition, its author portrays the misery as past and looks to a future that is unmixed joy. There are two clauses only that can cast any sort of doubt upon the accuracy of this statement. One is the wholly obscure conditional clause in 53:10 "[To know] if his life would give a guilt offering." Not only may one draw no conclusions from this dubious text, but also, whatever the clause as a whole may mean, the verb, in its context, following the conditional particle "if," cannot mean "will give," and can only mean "would give," which hypothetical activity belongs to the past. The other questionable clause is the end of the also difficult 53:11. This half verse, in fact, is crucial, and the translation: "and their iniquities he shall bear" is possible. But the trouble with such a translation is that any reference to such activity would stand wholly isolated. In the rest of the composition the servant's doleful duty as the bearer of another's guilt is confined strictly to the past.[33] It is incredible that the Second Isaiah should have entrusted to a single clause in this position a thought as important as this thought would be if it means what it might seem to mean—if it were intended programmatically as Israel's destiny, the bearing of the iniquities of others.

This clause could indeed be translated "and their iniquities he shall bear"—but it need not be so construed. We have noted already that the text of the verse is faulty and we have proposed reading *hiẓdiḳ*, "vindicated," in place of the two words *yaẓdiḳ ẓaddiḳ*. If this reading is correct the questionable clause can quite as well be translated as a subordinate clause whose verb will take its tense from the preceding main verb, thus: "My servant vindicated many, bearing their iniquities." This is the same construction as that of the clauses "not opening his mouth" and "interceding for transgressors" in vv. 7 and 12. The word "therefore," which follows immediately in the next verse, supports this interpretation. It is for the past merit that the servant shall be rewarded. And this latter half of v. 11, and 53:1–10a, and the latter part of v. 12 all refer to suffering which shall soon be only a memory.

Accordingly there is in the song no verb with a discordant tense and the significant conclusion stated at the outset is justified. Any suffering involved in the experience of the servant is bygone suffering; his destiny, proclaimed by the Second Isaiah, is all glory. It is just this which is amazing: that such a glorious future is to follow upon such a miserable past.

According to the fourth song and the foregoing analysis Israel, the servant, has a record of suffering now fast drawing to a close. And the prophetic author of the song offers an explanation for the bitter experience of Israel's past. The kings of nations first phrase the explanation:

> Indeed, he has borne sickness for us;
> Our pains he has suffered,

and then more fully:

> But he was [in fact] wounded because of
> our transgressions,
> Crushed because of our iniquities.
> He experienced the suffering which might lead
> to our welfare,
> And there was healing for us in his bruises.
> We all strayed like sheep,
> Went each his own way,
> And God visited him
> With the guilt of us all,

and probably again:

> Because of our transgressions he was
> stricken unto death.[34]

Toward the end of the song in similar words God, too, explains the servant's former grief:

> My servant vindicated many,
> Bearing their iniquities

and

> . . . He . . . bore the guilt of many,
> Interceding for transgressors.

The explanation that the servant suffered for others is preferred in the song against the alternative that he suffered for his own faults: he was buried among the wicked not because he had transgressed but although

. . . he had done no deeds of violence,
And no deceit was in his mouth.[35]

In other words, he was not being punished for misconduct, as, at first, the kings may have thought:

We supposed him stricken,
Smitten by God, and afflicted.

This last remark does not mean: "We wrongly supposed God to be the author of his suffering"; it means that the suffering was not retributive. They were aware that it was God who bruised his servant: "God wanted to crush him," but they recognized that it was not as punishment for deeds of violence and deceit that his God bruised him so.[36]

The experience of the servant exhausts the synonyms of suffering: he bore "sickness," suffered "pains," was "wounded," "crushed," "bruised," "stricken," "stricken unto death," "smitten by God," and "afflicted." God "visited him," wanted to "crush him." In addition to all of this the servant experienced a kind of suffering designated *musar*. The word is found in v. 5 and serves as a parallel to "bruising." [37]

God inflicted the suffering which the servant had experienced but not as punishment for the sins of the servant. Why, then? Why had Israel suffered? Without the usual explanation: the wages of sin, one is at a loss. Why, if not as a penalty? The fourth song contains an answer but the answer only adds to the confusion: "Because of our transgressions," the nations say, "because of our iniquities. We strayed, went each his own way, and God visited him with our guilt." "It was we who should have suffered what he experienced." [38] This is what they say, but knowing this we go on to ask, how so? Why was the affliction thus misdirected? "God wanted to crush him" is still no answer. The now obscure words which follow, something about his life giving a guilt offering, might have been a sort of answer, but they are none as they stand meaningless now. And God cannot simply have wished arbitrarily to destroy his servant, for he would not then be promising renewed life and purpose: "God's desire shall succeed through him." Though "God wanted to crush" his servant, through his servant "God's desire" will yet succeed.[39]

Why, indeed, was the servant afflicted? The author appears to have two explanations, and these go beyond the partial answers. The first involves toil, the second the passive experience of suffering. The first involves the idea of "interceding" for others, "vindicating" others, the second the idea of *musar,* a concept yet to be explored.[40] Both of these ideas are at home in prophetic literature and are particularly evident in Jeremiah. A prophet toils for his people. He spends his soul in intercessory prayer. He intercedes with God in a time of stress and defends his people before their divine judge and accuser. As in a court at law a prophet presents their prayerful plea and would vindicate them. Notably Jeremiah describes his struggles and toil on his people's behalf.

Is good to be rewarded with evil? he asks in one of his confessions,

> Remember how I have stood before you
> To speak good on their behalf,
> To avert your anger from them.

And on another occasion:

> Indeed, Lord . . .
> I have interceded with you
> In the time of calamity and the time of disaster
> On behalf of the enemy.

Jeremiah interceded with God despite the prohibition:

> Pray you not for this people,
> Nor take up any cry or entreaty,
> Nor intercede with me,
> For I will not hear you.[41]

It is the very term for "intercede" which Jeremiah uses in the latter passages that God uses of the servant in the fourth song:

> My servant vindicated many,
> Bearing their iniquities . . .

Bore the guilt of many,
Interceding for the transgressors.[42]

The Second Isaiah agrees with the prophet Jeremiah that "intercession" is a normal and essential prophetic activity.

As against this activity on the part of the servant of God the Second Isaiah speaks also of the servant's passive experience of affliction as similarly purposeful: "He experienced the suffering which might lead to our welfare." [43] It is at this point that the prophet uses the term *musar,* and, in doing so, he again echoes Jeremiah; he adopts a concept which Jeremiah in particular developed. *Musar* is divine discipline, suffering which might lead to someone's improvement, a bitter experience from which the wise might learn. The theme is older than the word; the theme is much older than Jeremiah. Amos listed a series of disasters which were made even worse by the fact that they accomplished nothing. It was his thought that such "acts of God" as famine, drought, ruined crops, epidemics, earthquakes, had a meaning which man, if he would, could read. In Amos' day and land these were God's unsubtle way of calling Israel back from the brink, the charged wire about the pasture, at the edge of the sea cliff. "Yet you did not return to me," God repeatedly laments in the Amos passage. Israel is an "untrained calf." The first Isaiah also had the thought without the word. Loss of territory, decimation of population, civil strife, all went unheeded. The people had not sought out repentant the divine source of their suffering and still, therefore, God's hand was raised against them. They had to "learn the hard way." Both of these eighth-century prophets found meaning in suffering: it was correction, could lead to repentance and on to welfare and peace.[44]

The prophet Jeremiah had a predilection for the idea and employed the term *musar* to suggest it. Several times he stated the thought in the form Amos and Isaiah had given it: "To no avail did I rain blows upon your sons; they did not accept [*musar*] correction." [45] Then Jeremiah contrived a variation. It was probably he, because of his sensitive nature. He himself could suffer in the suffering of others, and he supposed that any sympathizing spectator at a tragedy, experiencing mentally the other's grief, suffering with the sufferer, might similarly learn and benefit—learn as well from the sight as from the experience of suffering. Something there is in the concept of *musar* that resembles katharsis.

In its simplest form, in human society, the idea behind *musar* is the idea that the punishment of offenders serves as a deterrent to other potential offenders. The idea was familiar in Jeremiah's generation from the contemporary deuteronomic laws. A number of times the law calls for the public execution of a serious offender in order that his gruesome fate may be an example and warning to others: "And all Israel shall hear of it and fear; and they shall no more do any such evil in your midst." It is in this sense that Jeremiah compares Israel and Judah, to Judah's shame. The southern kingdom, he suggests, was doubly culpable; having seen God's treatment of Ephraim, Judah could have learned but did not. Judah rejected the object lesson along with the prophetic admonition.[46]

Of the other biblical examples of this aspect of *musar* the one in Exodus is the most graphic. Israel has just crossed the Red Sea. "So God delivered Israel from Egypt on that day. And Israel saw Egypt dead on the shore of the sea. And Israel experienced God's great might employed against Egypt and the people both feared God and believed in God and his servant Moses." [47]

Now, this is the sense in which the Second Isaiah used the word *musar* in the fourth song. Speaking for themselves and their peoples, the kings said: if we understand and take to heart the suffering of the servant Israel we can benefit, avoid what invites calamity, and escape such consequences. This was "suffering which might lead to our welfare." This was the servant's earlier passive experience of affliction to match his activity in "vindicating" and "interceding for transgressors." It was not without meaning for others.

The idea of suffering for others is unquestionably present here in the fourth song; but these are its two forms: the toil of intercessory activity on others' behalf and the pain of affliction endured from which others would learn. The idea is present but it little resembles the "vicarious atonement" which is sometimes thought to be the theme of this song. Granted that the servant was sorely afflicted "emptying his life unto death," granted that he patiently endured the affliction, granted even that an apparent injustice was done and the wrong people punished with the result that the others may say of him: "He has borne sickness for us; our pains he has suffered," "because of our transgressions he was stricken unto death," and that God himself may say: "He bore their iniquities" and "bore the guilt of many," it would still be wrong to derive the meaning that the servant had thus vicariously atoned for the sins of the nations. The process involved no cult mystery. Israel had been a lesson and example for the nations, not an atonement sacrifice. The guilty ones could indeed have learned from his experience, but Israel had not by his suffering wondrously absolved the nations of their guilt.

The fourth song does speak of the servant's suffering. It seeks an answer to the vexing question: why had God afflicted his chosen people? It suggests that their suffering, the "former things": defeat, desolation, captivity, served a broader purpose, made bitterly known God's righteous ways with men, spread broad that knowledge. It is an attempt at an explanation of the people's grief, their grief that now is ending. It is not a program. We have seen this already; the servant's affliction is not presented as a chart and augury for the future. The thought that the servant has suffered has nothing at all to do with the "mission of Israel."

The fourth song admirably supplements the others and strengthens the conclusion that the servant is Israel personified. It is not repeatedly stated and in so many words but it is the inevitable conclusion to be drawn from one broad fact—from the fact that the servant dies and will live again. "He was removed from the exercise of authority; he was cut off from the land of the living . . . stricken unto death. And they placed his tomb with the wicked. . . ." Yes, "he emptied his life unto death." And yet he is destined for life. "He shall see descendants, shall live long, and God's desire shall succeed through him. As a consequence of his life's distress he shall see light. . . ." "Lo, my servant shall prosper, shall rise, be lifted up, be greatly exalted."

When a man dies, a person, he does not live again. Resurrection is not a usual biblical theme. One must descend to the time of Daniel or at least to the time of the Isaiah who wrote the apocalypse

—centuries beyond the time of the Second Isaiah—t
words as theirs:

> Many of those who sleep in . . . the dust shal
> These to eternal life, and these . . . to eternal
>
> Your dead shall live . . . they shall arise.
> Those who dwell in the dust shall awake and sing.[48]

These words do not come from the time of the Second Isaiah—he knew of no personal resurrection. It is just because the servant is not a person but a personification that the Second Isaiah can picture him living again after death. Not as a person but as the personification of a people the servant will merely implement an already familiar hope when he rises from the dust.

The Second Isaiah must be acquainted with Ezekiel's elaborate symbol of the valley strewn with dry bones. There is no misinterpreting that symbol—it is an allegory of national rebirth. As persons the survivors of the national catastrophe after 586, whether among the ruins of Jerusalem or by the "rivers of Babylon," were alive enough to speak of death: "Lo, they say: our bones are dry, our hope is lost, we perish all." In another context similarly they said: "Our transgressions and our sins have overtaken us, in them we waste away; how can we live?" The dry bones in the valley—Ezekiel makes it quite clear—"are all the house of Israel," the people experiencing death in life, the exiles who make up his congregation. And it is to them through him that God speaks: "I will open your graves; I will lift you up out of your graves, my people, and will restore you to the land of Israel. . . . I will put my spirit in you, and you will live." Far from the notion of bodily resurrection Ezekiel was speaking of national rebirth. And it is just this, this idea of national rebirth, which the Second Isaiah adopted. If he did not borrow the expectation directly from Ezekiel he found it among the hopes of his day, cherished by the sons and grandsons of Ezekiel's congregation. A nation may "die" and live again.[49]

Because it was far too soon for a prophet to be speaking of bodily resurrection and because, on the other hand, resurrection as a symbol of national rebirth was already familiar in his day, the conclusion is justified that the Second Isaiah meant just this when he spoke of the one who had died and would live and that his servant can only be the people of Israel personified. Possibly, also, the uncertain words: "He was removed from the exercise of authority" will suggest loss of political independence rather than personal demotion.[50] The servant is the people.

And the people is chosen, here as in the other songs. An air of promise permeates the composition; it is God remaining faithful to an ancient commitment. And, as throughout the chapters of the Second Isaiah, the servant-people has a task according to this last song also, a responsibility as God's witness to further his purpose: "God's desire shall succeed through him." All the preceding pages put content into this hasty phrase. It is freighted with heavy consequences. The song of the "suffering servant" is in fact the song of the servant's proud destiny.

5. After the Manner of Jeremiah

When the Second Isaiah, personifying Israel as prophet, conceived the figure of the servant he thought, no doubt, of his many predecessors in the prophetic succession, men who, as he, had spoken for Israel's God. They were, collectively, the prototype of his servant. But it seems as though Jeremiah in particular hovered before his eyes as he limned in the figure. It was this mental image of Jeremiah that made of his servant-prophet a servant who had known grief, experienced affliction. Or, better stated: the bitter experience of Israel, whom the Second Isaiah here personified as servant-prophet, led him necessarily to Jeremiah for the features of his personification—to that prophet within his tradition who, more than any other, had, like Israel, endured reproach and suffering. Inevitably Jeremiah must sit as model for his portrait of God's servant-prophet.

This is not to say that the servant and Jeremiah are to be identified. The identification has, however, been suggested: in his commentary to Isa. 52:13 Abraham ibn Ezra quotes Saadia to this effect. Saadia, the Gaon of Sura, who died in 942, identified the servant with the prophet Jeremiah, and ibn Ezra expressed his approval: "The Gaon, Rav Saadia, his memory be blessed! interpreted the whole chapter as referring to Jeremiah, and well he interpreted." [51]

But Saadia's younger Karaite contemporary Yafith ibn 'Ali said of Saadia (May it not be said of us!):

> [He] lost his senses in applying it to the prophets generally or, according to some authorities, in supposing that it referred to Jeremiah in particular. His explanation is not indeed of a kind towards which anyone would feel attracted: and we shall show the manner in which it may be refuted: for this man attempted the task of interpreting the book of the prophets upon a plan of evolving their meaning out of his own head, and consequently failed to arrive at any consistent view.[52]

Warned, we observe merely that the view here presented does really differ from Saadia's. The servant is not Jeremiah but Israel—it is the people personified as a servant-prophet, but after the manner of Jeremiah.[53]

The experience of the servant parallels the experience of Jeremiah throughout and in one detail after another. The servant shares so many features with Jeremiah that we are constrained to agree that the Second Isaiah had that prophet in mind when he described God's servant. From the life and writings of Jeremiah, and especially from the confessions and consecration vision of Jeremiah,[54] the Second Isaiah drew detail after detail to give verisimilitude to his symbol.

Two parallels are particularly striking. Twice the Second Isaiah appears to be quoting the very words of Jeremiah. Once the words have to do with the prophet's dedication:

[Jeremiah:] The word of the Lord came to me, saying: Before I shaped you in the womb I knew you, I dedicated you before birth, appointed you a prophet to the nations.

[The servant:] God summoned me at birth, adopted me when I came from the womb.[55]

The second parallel concerns the prophet's submissive behavior:

[Jeremiah:] I had been as a tamed sheep led to the slaughter, not aware that they were plotting against me.

[The servant:] He was driven and was meek not opening his mouth—
as a sheep led to the slaughter, as a ewe is dumb
before her shearers—not opening his mouth.

These two contacts are very close as if the Second Isaiah, in fact, had borrowed Jeremiah's phrases.[56]

Dedication is a theme which the servant and Jeremiah emphatically shared. Both knew that God had adopted them.[57] Their dedication was the dedication of their mouth and speech,[58] and both regarded the divine word as a potent, irresistible force.[59] Both referred to their reception of the divine word and their willingness to accept the heavy responsibility of declaring it.[60] Both Jeremiah and the servant called the living word which they brought "teaching," *torah.*[61] In the enthusiastic fancy of the Second Isaiah the servant, Israel, was the people in whom Jeremiah's prediction of a "new covenant" had found its fulfillment; it is through him that God calls Israel the "people in whose heart is my teaching." [62]

The servant shared with Jeremiah all of the tribulations of a true prophet. Both were beaten,[63] both endured sickness and pain,[64] disgrace and insult.[65] In one respect, significantly, the affliction of the servant surpasses the affliction of Jeremiah. The biblical record reveals that Jeremiah was repeatedly threatened with death and only narrowly escaped, and that is all; but the servant was done to death.[66] The fact that the Second Isaiah, unfolding his personification, permitted the servant to die a martyr's death does not suggest that he knew something about Jeremiah, the model for the servant, which has been lost to tradition; it does not suggest that Jeremiah was executed. On the contrary, the Second Isaiah forsook his model at this point. It was inevitable that he do so: the servant was to be restored to life; Jeremiah was not. The people, whom in reality he meant when he spoke of the servant, did die and were to live again. A personification is both a fiction, a figment, a figure of speech, and a reality, a fact. And a writer employing the device of personification may slip intentionally or unintentionally from fiction into fact. So the Second Isaiah did at this point. The servant who died was no longer the shadow of Jeremiah, as up to that point he had been. But even in their attitude toward the threat of death the two are comparable. Jeremiah said before the judges: "As for me, I am in your hands. Do to me what seems to you good and proper." And the servant "emptied his life even unto death." [67]

Even the thought that the servant suffered not as a consequence of his own misconduct but for the sake of others is reminiscent of Jeremiah. Jeremiah protested his innocence. In his confessions he laid his plea before his Judge and asked that justice be done him, the injured party.[68] It is in the expectation that he will be vindicated that Jeremiah asks a hearing, and the servant comprehends in one bold statement the whole complex of Jeremianic confessions, when confidently he says:

> At hand is he who vindicates me.
> Who dares oppose me? Let us go to court together.
> Who has litigation with me? Let him approach.[69]

Both the servant and Jeremiah had such surpassing confidence that it helped them through crises of discouragement.[70]

One feature that they shared remains to be mentioned: both looked beyond Israel to the nations. It is perhaps germinal in Jeremiah,[71] but it swells to a major theme in the Second Isaiah and his sense of mission is characteristic of the servant, as we have seen.

It is true then: the servant and Jeremiah have a great many features in common; and we are forced to conclude that, creating the servant figure, the Second Isaiah remembered Jeremiah the prophet. He had intimate knowledge of him and he drew largely on that knowledge in the characterization of his servant-prophet Israel. How the Second Isaiah came to know so much about Jeremiah is a question in itself,[72] but the evidence suggests that he knew not only the life experience of his predecessor but his writings as well and, not the least among them his intimate papers, his prayer confessions. That Jeremiah served as model for the servant is established.

Many of the features of the servant, to be sure, are features which Jeremiah shares with all of the literary prophets, and possibly it is because we know too little of the lives of the others that we find the similarity with Jeremiah so striking. Lacking other information, we find that the Second Isaiah personified Israel as a prophet notably comparable to Jeremiah, probably choosing Jeremiah from among the prophets, because he knew him to have been a man of grief. To personify a people wasting in exile his servant-prophet must include such details of mental and physical anguish as are associated with the person of Jeremiah. Among the prophets known to tradition he was the one to exemplify a servant who had suffered.

6. "My Servants, the Prophets"

But the servant also has much in common with all prophets. For one thing, the servant knows himself possessed of the word of God which he must speak. It is not Jeremiah and the servant alone—all of the biblical prophets describe themselves as men over whose mouth and tongue God disposes, whose speech is his. Through the mouth of prophets God announced his will and purpose, revealed (in advance) his intentions, became articulate.

Amos less obviously suggests the mouth: "If the Lord God speaks who can but prophesy?" but the consecration visions of Isaiah and Ezekiel match Jeremiah's in their specific allusions to the prophet's mouth and God's word. Even as God touched the mouth of Jeremiah and said: "I have put my words in your mouth," even so one of the seraphs first took a coal with tongs from the altar in Isaiah's vision and touched with it the impure lips of Isaiah, after which that one could offer himself for God's service as prophet. So, too, Ezekiel, at the climax of his consecration vision, ate the scroll which the hand of God proffered, the scroll inscribed on both sides with "lamentation and moaning and woe," and heard God say: "Now go to the house of Israel and speak my words to them." [73]

The same conception of a prophet underlies the objection which Moses raised in Midian when God would send him forth as his prophet: "I am not a man of words . . ." but "heavy of mouth and heavy of tongue," and God's ensuing rebuke: "Who gave man a mouth or who makes one dumb? . . . Go, and I will be with your mouth and instruct you what to say." What is probably another source in the same chapter in Exodus substitutes Aaron for Moses as prophet because, God says: "he can certainly speak"; "and you will speak to him and put words in his mouth and I will be with your mouth and his and instruct you what to do. And he shall speak for you to the people and he shall be mouth to you and you shall be God to him." This "being mouth to" Moses is what is later called being "prophet": "And Aaron your brother will be your prophet [*nabi'*]. You will speak [to him] all that I command you, and Aaron your brother will speak to Pharaoh. . . ." But Moses remains the favored example of a "prophet." To him God spoke "mouth to mouth." A future prophet to be accredited must be like Moses to whom God said: "I will raise up for them from the midst of their brothers a prophet like you and put my words in his mouth and he shall speak to them all that I command him." The prophet Balaam patiently explained to Balak: "Now that I have come to you, can I [for myself] say anything at all? That word only which God puts in my mouth can I speak." Micaiah made the identical claim: "As God lives, only what God says to me can I say," and when rival prophets led by Zedekiah brought an opposing message, he insisted: "God has put a spirit of falsehood in the mouth of all these prophets." It is perhaps natural, also, that, since the words of one man's mouth were contested by the mouth of another, the blow aimed at Micaiah should land on his jaw, designed as it was to shut his mouth. And it is natural, too, that the rivals of Jeremiah should say: "Come, let us smite him on the tongue and hear no more of his words." [74]

And so it may be said in general and not with reference to Jeremiah alone that one essential characteristic if not the essential characteristic of a biblical prophet was that God employed the prophet's mouth; with his speech the prophet served God, was articulate for God, communicated God's word. That the servant is so characterized was noted above: "God gave me the tongue of disciples"; "God made my mouth a sharp sword"; "he stirs up a word in the morning"; "the coastlands wait for his teaching." [75] That the servant is characterized as a man of speech is clear. But it should be noted also that throughout, the Second Isaiah lays great store by speech and the word of God. So important to him is this word that it is wholly expected when he makes of the servant of God, the symbol of Israel, a man of speech.

The chapters of the Second Isaiah begin and end with an evaluation of God's word: it endures eternally, is unerringly fulfilled.

Grass withers, flowers fade,
But the word of God endures forever.

As rain falls
And snow from heaven,
And does not return
Without watering the earth
And making it fruitful and verdant,
Giving seed to the sower and food to the eater,
So is my word which goes from my mouth;
It does not return unfulfilled
Without doing what I wanted
And accomplishing that for which I sent it.

A matter is certain once "the mouth of God has spoken." God's word has such effective power that by it heaven and earth were made:

My hand founded the earth,
My right hand spread forth the heavens;
I summon them—
They appear.[76]

The role that prophecy plays in the Second Isaiah's argument for monotheism itself illustrates the importance he attaches to speech. It was the failure of other gods to foretell that proved them vain—and the fact that Israel's god did so foretell that proved him God. And Israel, having knowledge of God, is constrained to bear witness, to give voice to that knowledge.

For his present purpose, too, the Second Isaiah is concerned that the validity of the prophetic word be recognized: to produce the conviction of Israel's joyous future. Through him God is foretelling anew. God is bringing (Cyrus) the fulfiller of his counsel:

I spoke and I am accomplishing it;
I formed it and am doing it.

And not only Israel's joyous future; the Second Isaiah needs to produce the conviction that his prophetic promise for mankind is equally sure. Based on God's word it is sure without question:

A word has gone forth from my mouth as a sure purpose

And will not fail,
Every knee shall do me reverence,
Every tongue confess me.

God is one who speaks his sure purpose, and not in secret. The word giving voice to his saving purpose is *torah:*

Torah proceeds from me,
I arouse my truth as a light for men.

This *torah,* "teaching," appears not only in the servant song: "the coastlands wait for his teaching," but in the passage just cited, and again:

God wished for his sure purpose
To make the teaching great and glorious.[77]

Everywhere, then, in the sixteen chapters God's word, the prophetic word, and the word of God's people (they are hardly to be distinguished) have surpassing significance, and it is not by mere chance that the Second Isaiah characterizes the servant of God as he does, as a prophet whose role and function it is to speak for God.

But is a prophet a servant? In relation to God a prophet may be called a messenger, *mal'ak,* or an agent, *meshullaḥ,*[78] or he may be called a servant, *'ebed.*

There are fourteen passages in the Bible where prophets are called servants in so many words. It is quite possible that all of these passages are later than the Second Isaiah. If they are, then they did not influence him in the choice of his figure when he named his personification of Israel "the servant of God," but on the contrary, the Second Isaiah influenced the authors of these passages who recognized the prophet in his servant. And this is probably the order of events. But whether or not these passages were written under the influence of the servant songs they do permit one certain conclusion: that it was quite proper and reasonable to refer to prophets as God's servants.

More of these passages occur in the book of Jeremiah than in any other book. In the book of Jeremiah they are a recurrent formula: "I sent to them all of my servants the prophets, persistently, but they did not hearken. . . ." Almost as frequently the expression occurs in II Kings and with only a little more variety. The passages containing the term in II Kings refer for the most part to the *torah,* the warnings, and the predictions now fulfilled which God communicated to the people "by the hand of his servants the prophets." Different only is the threat: "I will smite the house of your master Ahab and take vengeance on Jezebel for the blood of my servants the prophets. . . ." Almost a stereotype again is the one reference in Ezekiel, in which God asks of Gog if he be the invader announced by God's servants the prophets of Israel in bygone days.[79]

Two passages remain, one in Zechariah and one in Amos. These two passages seem quite clearly to have been written under the influence of the Second Isaiah with his thought that God reveals his purpose through the prophets, his servants. If, as may well be, the stereotyped references to God's servants his prophets are all post-Exilic, it is quite possible that the passage in Zechariah is the parent of them all, the link between the Second Isaiah and the formula. "Your fathers, where are they?" God demands of Zechariah's generation returned from exile. "And the prophets, do they live forever? But my words and decrees which I commanded my servants the prophets, did they not befall your fathers, so that repentant they said: As the God of hosts designed to do to us according to our ways and deeds he has done." A younger contemporary of the Second Isaiah, Zechariah appears to have been impressed as the Second Isaiah was impressed, by the evidence of fulfilled predictions, from which evidence he, too, drew conclusions for his times. Both of them insisted upon the validity of the prophetic word, and like the Second Isaiah, Zechariah equated prophet with servant of God.[80]

The passage in Amos (which is almost universally regarded as secondary in its context) is even more strikingly dependent on the Second Isaiah. It is one of the premises for the argument from prophecy—one which, surprisingly, the Second Isaiah does not himself express in so many words but leaves to be inferred. "The Lord God does nothing," it says, "without first revealing his counsel to his servants the prophets." The principle has no significance in its context, where Amos' purpose is to show and demonstrate by analogy that a prophet is constrained to speak. The added verse contains a different thought: that through prophets in advance,

God reveals the course of history. Because the verse in Amos, secondary in its context, both contains this thought essential in the argument of the Second Isaiah and employs his designation of prophets as God's servants, it appears indeed to have been added under his influence.[81]

And this whole series of varied as well as stereotyped biblical passages which link servant and prophet suggests that, beginning at least with Zechariah, biblical authors understood the servant of God as prophet.

Two other passages contain the equation. In one it is Moses who is called "my servant." Moses of whom it was said: "There has not yet arisen in Israel another prophet like Moses whom God knew face to face"—it is this prophet to whom God refers as "my servant Moses." The narrative defends Moses as a supremely gifted prophet, gifted as to speech, the essence of prophecy, a prophet with whom God speaks mouth to mouth. Moses is attacked, according to the narrative, and needs this defense. He is defended against the implications of the question: "Did God speak with Moses alone? Did he not also speak with us?" The question is a demand for spiritual autonomy. The narrative containing it is one of a number of passages reflecting this demand. The Korah story is among them. There, the two hundred fifty laymen express their indignation against Moses and Aaron in the words: "All the congregation, all are holy, with God in their midst, and why do you lord it over the community of God?" A very good case can be made for the hypothesis that the demand for religious democracy evident in these and in related narratives, was a feature of the early post-Exilic period. If such a conclusion is right and the narrative defending Moses is to be dated in the period following the Second Isaiah, then the designation of Moses the prophet as God's servant may be but another reflection of the Second Isaiah's equation: servant—prophet.[82]

The one remaining passage may or may not antedate—may or may not be the source of his equation. In Isa. 20, God says: "As my servant Isaiah went naked and barefoot three years . . . so the King of Assyria shall drive off the captives of Egypt. . . ." Chapter 20 is a biographical narrative about Isaiah in the third person. The other such narratives in Isaiah, in 7:1 to 16 and in chapters 36 to 39, are legendary additions to his book and, being biographical, chapter 20 may also be secondary, and if so, not necessarily older than the Second Isaiah. Nevertheless, it could be original with the first Isaiah and could have been known to the author of the servant songs.[83]

If now we ask: May we call a prophet God's servant? the answer is obvious: again and again in biblical literature prophets are called "God's servants." And why should they not be? They served him as one serves a master, speaking as they were commanded. Like Amos ("If the Lord speaks . . .") and Jeremiah ("Like a raging fire . . .") they knew themselves helpless. "You have enthralled me, God, and I am enthralled. You have overpowered me and prevailed"—so Jeremiah, himself the model for the servant, voiced his own estimate of his relationship to God.[84]

So, then, it is proper to see in the servant the figure of prophet. When the Second Isaiah personified his people Israel as the servant of God he was thinking of prophets. He was thinking of Jeremiah, among the prophets, because Jeremiah and Israel had in common a history of suffering, the experience of affliction. But he was thinking also of all prophets, men who put their mouths and tongues and speech at God's disposal, who spoke for him, giving warning and instruction, and who testified for him as witnesses. And he was thinking of prophets as men who do God's bidding, his messengers, his agents, the servants of God entrusted with a mission.

7. "Would That All the Lord's People Were Prophets!"

Israel, personified as a prophet after the manner of Jeremiah, Israel as the servant of God, has a responsibility, a task, a mission—that is the capstone in the structure which the Second Isaiah erected.

Again and again the Second Isaiah alludes to this mission. He does so in the servant songs: My servant, God says,

> . . . Will publish truth among the nations . . .
> . . . Establish truth on earth.
> The coastlands wait for his teaching.

Through the Second Isaiah to Israel God says:

You are my servant,
Israel through whom I shall get me glory.

. . . I make you a light to the nations
That my salvation may reach
To the ends of the earth.

The servant says of himself:

My Lord God gave me
The tongue of disciples
To know to relieve the weary.

And of the servant who suffered, the Second Isaiah said, in the last of the songs:

What God wants shall succeed through him.
. . . He shall see light;
He shall be sated with knowledge.[85]

Outside of the songs as well, in their context in the sixteen chapters, their prophetic author refers to the task of God's servant Israel. He refers to the "servant" as his "commissioned messenger" and as his "witnesses." And this equation: servant—commissioned messenger—witnesses, turns the discussion back from poetry to prose, from figurative language: the personification, to logic: the syllogistic argument by which from the fact of prophecy the Second Isaiah derived the final fact that Israel's God is God. Israel the servant, begetter of prophets, heard the prophets' testimony, preserved the prophets' word, is a prophetic witness, possessed of a saving truth.

Thus intimately is the servant's mission related to the great argument. It is a consequence of the argument. It implements the argument. The conclusion that Israel's God is God is, to begin with, merely an intellectualization. If it is to be meaningful in human society, men must do something with it, and herein lies the need for a servant of God with a mission to mankind. One might put it this way: the mission of the servant Israel is to convert a theology into a religion.

It is easy to be misled by the personification. Israel, personified, has the character of a prophet, resembles Jeremiah. But Israel is not Jeremiah, is not any single prophet or person. Israel remains a people, an aggregate of persons. The nature of the personification serves merely to suggest how the Second Isaiah pictured the people. The national character of Israel as he saw it was prophetic. The Bible contains another such characterization of Israel and a comparison is instructive. According to the author of Exod. 19:5 f. God said to Israel at Sinai: "If you will really obey me and observe my covenant you shall be my special possession among the nations—for all the earth is mine—and you shall be to me as a kingdom of priests and a holy nation." Israel, a "kingdom of priests" among the nations—that is one conception. It is a notion shared by one of the later "Isaiahs," the author of Isa. 61:5 f.:

> Strangers shall stand and pasture your flocks,
> Foreigners shall be your farmers and vinedressers;
> But you shall be called: the priests of God,
> Shall be known as the ministers of our God.

The idea seems to be this, that one nation is set apart for a special service within the community of nations. Just as within Israel the tribe of Levi and the family of Aaron were reserved for the priestly function and served the whole of the nation as priests, so Israel, the family of Aaron among the families of the earth, is set apart as a kingdom of priests to minister to God for them all. This is one conception. But there is another. For the Second Isaiah, a prophet, the relationship between Israel and the rest of mankind is in general the same as for the writer with priestly leanings who wrote Exod. 19:5 f. He agrees: Israel has a role to play, a specialized function among peoples. Different, however, is his conception of Israel's role. No kingdom of priests, Israel is to him a people of prophets among the peoples of the earth. In times past a handful of prophets in any one generation served God's revelatory purpose for Israel, a single people. But for the society of men no such few—rather a whole people must serve. And for such service no people is better suited than Israel, prepared as it is by its long experience with prophets—true prophets—and equipped as it is with knowledge of the one true God.

The thought opens a wide panorama. The Second Isaiah was

the prophet of expanding horizons; there is no restraint to his language; his God is incomparably great. In relation to God

> Nations are like droplets spilling from a pail,
> May be reckoned as the motes that settle on the pans
> of a balance;
> He can take up islands as though they were
> particles of dust.

He is "the one enthroned on the earth's horizon, and the earth-dwellers are like grasshoppers." "To whom will you compare me?" he demands. "Who has a conception of the extent of God's spirit?" He made the stars also:

> Lift up your eyes and see.
> Who created these?
> It is he who brings forth the host of them by number,
> Calling them all by name.
> By reason of his abundant strength, he being
> replete with power,
> Not one is missing.

Right at the outset the Second Isaiah makes clear the incomparable greatness of God; the quotations are all from chapter 40.[86]

But the thought is not limited to the one chapter. Israel's God is the creator—one is not to lose sight of the fact. He is

> . . . the creator of the heavens who stretched them out,
> Who laid down the earth and brought forth its yield,
> Who gives breath to the people upon it
> And life to all who walk thereon.

God's command alone sufficed to bring to being earth and heavens:

> I summon them; they appear.

Evil and darkness are no rivals of his; he made them also:

> Shaper of light, creator of darkness,
> Maker of peace, creator of evil,
> I, God, am all of these.[87]

Even as God is unbounded in space, so he knows no limits of time:

I was first, and will be with the last.

Before me no God was formed
And after me there will be none.

I am first and I also am last.[88]

And if "it" means the earth in 48:16 the implication of this verse is the same:

From the time when it came into being I was there.

Infinite and eternal, the God of the Second Isaiah, the creator, is the master of human history as well. Though Cyrus does not know him Israel's God has summoned Cyrus for his own ends. God's activity is not aimless. Through lesser goals, apparently, God's activity moves to a desired end. Cyrus, "fulfilling God's desire," will rebuild Jerusalem and the temple. God's servant, Israel, will live again, have descendants, a long life, "and God's desire shall succeed through him." God is, indeed, one who can say: "My counsel stands, and what I will I do." God's desire is as broad as his creation: "Not as an empty waste . . . to be inhabited he formed it." There is not one word but several which denote God's purpose, but it is the breadth of vision of the Second Isaiah which is here to be noted. His concern is with the "ends of the earth"; he demands the reverence of every knee, the confession of every tongue. The God of the Second Isaiah is the Lord of all creation, the master of human history, who does as he wills and has a people to prosper his desire.[89]

For the far horizons of the Second Isaiah's vision no single prophet suffices. His prophet is a people, their stage the world, their day the centuries.

The Second Isaiah vested his people Israel with a mission to the peoples of the earth. According to the proud ideal of him who conceived the servant, the people Israel as a historic continuity has the responsibility of dispensing knowledge of God to them that walk in darkness, of being a light to the nations. In his vision, Israel was a light that would not fade, a reed that would not be broken, until it had established truth upon the earth, thus prospering God's desire.

His people, to be sure, was an aggregate of persons, and, idealist though he was, the Second Isaiah had enough contact with reality to recognize the double aspect of his people's task: to be a light to the nations, but also to restore Jacob to God, to bring to him Israel. There is a word in the mouth of Moses which well expresses the hope of this prophet. It concludes the narrative of Eldad and Medad in Num. 11, one of that cluster of narratives developing the theme of religious democracy.[90] So that Moses should not bear alone the burden of religious leadership God prepared to share his spirit with seventy others of the elders of Israel and summoned them for that purpose to the Tent of Meeting pitched outside of the wilderness camp. Eldad and Medad, stubborn, remained behind in the camp; yet when the spirit descended upon the others at the tent it fell upon them in the camp as well, and all together the seventy "prophesied." Disturbed by their dissidence Joshua would discipline the two, but Moses rebuked his narrower zeal: "Are you jealous for me? Would that all the Lord's people were prophets, that the Lord would put his spirit on them!" (Num. 11:29). So, the Second Isaiah; he wants no monopoly on prophecy. His wider vision knows how great the task. He assigns to his whole people the heavy privilege: prophets all, a prophetic people. But with a pang of regret he seems, in the midst of his rhapsody, to pause and to say with Moses: "Would that they were! Would that all the Lord's people were prophets, that the Lord would put his spirit on them!"

The whole grand view that broke upon the gaze of the Second Isaiah encompassed humanity but it by no means excluded Israel. No sooner had the thought dawned upon the prophet that Israel's God is God—than he saw with startling clarity the implications for Israel of its burden of saving knowledge, Israel's place in God's unfolding purpose. Exultantly aware of his people's opportunity he conceived the figure of God's servant. In passage after passage of his ecstatic vision the Second Isaiah called upon the servant of God, this people of destiny, to assume its high role. Everywhere in the chapters, in the songs and in their matrix, in the first three songs and in the fourth as well, in that misnamed song of the suffering servant which is far from an invitation to martyrdom, as well as in the other three, the prophet portrayed Israel as the servant of God.

In a general sense he created this servant in his own image or not alone in his image but in the image of all prophets who spoke of God and for God—prophetic witnesses to his divinity. In a narrower sense, remembering his people's record of suffering (now ending), he chose the man of grief among his predecessors, chose Jeremiah as subject and drew a vivid likeness. Though as yet imperfect, the people of Israel, so like Jeremiah in many respects, is the servant of God, its goal to make known God's name in all the earth. This high privilege the Second Isaiah conferred upon Israel, people of prophets. If Israel's God is God Israel is his prophet.

CHAPTER VI

"FOR THE SAKE OF HIS NAME"

1. Isaiah 52:5

Now, if God is to become known in all the earth, if every mouth is to confess him and every knee to do him reverence, if his house is indeed to be known as a house of prayer for all the peoples, then how he is regarded is of prime importance. The world's salvation is delayed when his name is profaned; when it is hallowed redemption may approach. When, therefore, men and God do what in their different roles they do, it is a matter of concern whether their doing is or is not "for the sake of his name." Human behavior and divine behavior have a meaning in the larger scheme of things. How a man conducts his affairs may determine his success or failure but it may also further or retard God's hopes for human society. And how God treats his people Israel may, if one may think in those terms also, diminish or enhance his reputation among men.

In Isaiah 52:5 God complains: "my name is despised." For the thought the word "profaned" is more commonly used: God's name is said to be profaned. The negative is matched in other contexts by its contrary: "the sanctification of his name." And this sanctification is the equivalent of action undertaken "for the sake of his name." The ideas of the profanation and the sanctification of God's name and the idea of such activity, human or divine, as may be undertaken for the sake of God's name are the approach to a notable aspect of the religion of the later Isaiahs and, indeed, to a whole important phase of biblical thought.

It is, accordingly, profitable to look more closely at this one poetic line in chapter 52 which touches on the theme of profanation. Unfortunately, the text of the verse is not in good order. Probably it once said with emphasis and repetition what now it says less strongly in its closing words alone. The unsatisfactory character of the present text is obvious. It reads:

Their masters wail, God says,
And constantly, daily my name is despised.

The opening words: "their masters wail," introduce a thought without relevance. As soon as the "masters" are identified, how wrong the verb is becomes apparent. The masters can only be those princes and satraps that hold the Judeans in miserable captivity, and the last thing that they would be doing here is wailing. The attitude of the lords of Babylon is proudly exultant, and chapter 47 contains the Second Isaiah's vivid estimate of that arrogance and its consequences. The context here clearly requires a different predicate.

The improbability of "their masters wail" is generally recognized and the commentaries seek substitutes. Suggesting various emendations, commentaries obtain such varied meanings as: "My temple is cast down," "Because of violence my sons wail constantly," "Behold, those who wait for me are become a by-word" or, more moderately: "Their rulers mock" or "boast." These and other attempts to improve the text only demonstrate its unsatisfactory character.

The structure of the line is no more satisfactory than its sense. There is little balance between the two cola. "God says" stands isolated and is an unexpected repetition of the same two words in the preceding line. "Constantly" and "daily," which are synonyms, would normally balance each other in the two different halves of the poetic line. As it is, they stand together and throw the line off balance. And, finally, "my name is despised" is no proper parallel for "their masters wail."

But, with justifiable conjectures, it is possible to restore sense and form and obtain the following good meaning:

Their masters defame me constantly,
Daily is my name despised.[1]

This, now, is a perfect line, with synonymous parallelism and an artistic chiasm, "constantly" now balanced by "daily" at the center of the line.

All of the expressions in the line thus restored are idiomatic and occur elsewhere. In just this fashion, the synonyms "constantly" and "daily" are balanced in Ps. 72:15:

> That they pray for him constantly,
> Daily bless him. . . .[2]

The expression "their masters defame me" is also proper. One may not object that in it, God, the speaker, is construed as the direct object of an offensive verb *ḥll*. It is true that usually not God but "the name of God" is contemplated as subject to profanation. Usually, indeed, but not exclusively! God appears again as the direct object of this verb in the received text of Ezek. 13:19: "And you [women with your magic arts] have profaned me among my people for handfuls of barley. . . ." Also, in Ezek. 22:26 God does not say: "And my name. . . ." he says: "And I am profaned among them." [3] It may be that the Second Isaiah himself spoke, in another context, of the profanation of God for, in Isa. 48:11 the verb "be profaned" lacks a subject. We must either assume and supply "my name" as subject there: "How should my name be profaned," or read the verb as a first person form: "For my own sake, for my own sake will I do it; for, how should I be profaned?" The Dead Sea Isaiah Scroll published by Burrows has this latter form, which fact may be significant—or not, since the reading there may be a mere chance "correction." Finally, according to a rabbinic tradition, "him" in Mal. 1:12 is an intentional substitution (a *tiḳḳun sopherim*) for an original "me," i.e., "and you profane me when you say: the table of the Lord is polluted." [4] Accordingly, although the forces that shaped the text avoided or sought to eliminate expressions in which God was the direct object of profanation, commonly introducing circumlocutions, at least two such expressions remained undisturbed, and one other survived in rabbinic tradition. This being so, no exception on these grounds can be taken to the reading here proposed for Isa. 52:5: "their masters defame me." [5]

Nonetheless, since the cushioned idiom, "to profane the name of God," occurs nearly twenty times as against these four only in which God is the object of the verb, the idiom "to profane the name of God" is indeed to be recognized as the more usual. If it is the less common idiom which the author of Isaiah 52:5 here employed, he probably did so merely out of a sense for literary style—because the word "my name" occurs in the immediately following parallel clause.

So much for the critical note. The new reading: "Their masters defame me constantly" is a perfect parallel to the final colon: "Daily my name is despised"; and this line follows perfectly on the first half verse, the whole verse now reading:

> Now therefore what have I here, God says,
> Seeing that my people are taken away for nothing?
> Their masters defame me constantly,
> Daily my name is despised.

The history of this text is of interest. In the Septuagint the end of the verse is expanded. Instead of just "daily my name is despised" the Greek translation contains the longer statement "because of you daily my name is despised among the nations." Although the Greek translation differs from the received text it would not be appropriate to make any changes in the Hebrew text based upon the Greek. The translator was only interpreting—correctly interpreting. This is what the author meant: *because of you* my name is despised *among the nations*. The translator could have gone farther. He could have said: "because of your condition, because you languish in exile." In view of the beginning of the verse he could have done so without scruple. But he appears to have been satisfied with his "because of you"—the phrase seeming clear enough in its context.

But one cannot be too careful; his interpretive gloss: "because of you," was ambiguous after all, and a later writer took advantage of the ambiguity. In his letter to the Romans, Paul cited the end of this verse from Isaiah and gave it an unintended meaning—a meaning made possible by the ambiguous phrase "because of you" in the Septuagint. Had he been quoting the Hebrew text he could hardly have used the verse as he did, but the Greek facilitated his misuse of the text. Paul used it to mean: if you scorn the law my name will be despised among the nations.

> You who say that one must not commit adultery, do you commit adultery [Paul asked]? You who abhor idols, do you rob temples? You who boast in the law, do you dishonor God by breaking the law? For, as it is written, "The name of God is blasphemed among the Gentiles because of you." [6]

The quotation from Isa. 52:5: "The name of God is blasphemed among the Gentiles because of you," now recognizable only by way of the Septuagint, is certainly no literal translation of the Hebrew text (". . . my name is despised"), but it is just as certainly the lineal descendant of that fragment of a verse from Isa. 52.

Divorced from its context, the statement that God's name suffers profanation "because of" his people can mean either of two things, (a) that God is defamed by the shameful *conduct* of his people, or (b) that God is disgraced because of the disgraceful *condition* of his people. Without a doubt, as the context proves, the author of Isa. 52:5 intended the latter meaning, and Paul's reference to his words in the former sense introduced an unmeant meaning.

One talmudic authority understood the Isaiah verse as its author meant it. He said: "There are four things which the Holy One, blessed be he, regrets he ever created, and these are they: the exile, the Chaldeans, the Ishmaelites, and the evil impulse." In support of the claim that God regrets the first of these creations of his, the exile [*galut*], this teacher quoted God's own impatient query in the verse from Isaiah: "Now therefore, what have I here, God says, seeing that my people are taken away for nothing?" [7] This rabbinic author applied the verse correctly. God does not, in Isa. 52:5, reprimand the people for their misconduct; rather he regrets their misery for which he holds himself responsible.

Paul's thought is not, however, foreign to the Hebrew Bible. Both meanings are found associated with the idea of profanation.

Paul's meaning, that God's name may be profaned by the *misconduct* of his people, indeed occurs a number of times in the Bible. With this meaning the formula "to profane the name of God" occurs ten times, once each in Amos, Jeremiah, Ezekiel, and

Malachi, and six times in the Holiness legislation.[8] In these ten passages it is specifically the "name of God" which is subject to profanation. Other passages where not the name of God but sundry also sacred objects are contemplated as exposed to profanation occur predominantly in fifth- and sixth-century sources, Ezekiel, the Holiness legislation, the Second Isaiah, Malachi, and in a few even later passages.

The awkward syntax of the purpose or final clause containing the formula in Amos ("And a man and his father go to the maiden in order to [?] profane my holy name") suggests that the clause is an addition, and the doubt as to its originality in Amos grows when we fail to find the formula in any other writings earlier than the sixth century. An inspection of the remaining passages which contain the formula in this meaning suggests that the one in Jeremiah is the earliest.

In all the prophetic literature there is no more impressive example of religion in terms of social conscience than the narrative in Jer. 34:8–22. The episode there described occurred during the final days of Jerusalem. Jeremiah experienced a moment of triumph during the siege of the city. Whatever their true motives may have been, the lords of Jerusalem did for once the right thing, as Jeremiah knew the right. They obeyed a long-neglected law and freed their slaves (in order to have fewer mouths to feed? hoping that the slaves, now freemen, would the more willingly defend their city? because the respectability of the aristocracy required them to be law-abiding? because God could, after all, be offended and this gesture might set matters right?—in a crisis one tries anything, even the religion of Jeremiah). They freed their slaves and the crisis passed; threatened from Egypt the Babylonians lifted the siege. It was then that the lords of Jerusalem "profaned the name of God"—they revoked the newly granted freedom of their slaves. "You turned about and profaned my name and took back each of you his male and female slaves whom you had set free . . . and constrained them to be your slaves again." Outraged, Jeremiah assured the treacherous slaveholders that now they had sealed their fate, indeed. Were the whole army of Babylon dying of wounds in the camp they would yet rise and set fire to Jerusalem.[9]

This powerful narrative of the ministry of Jeremiah may have the incidental distinction that it introduces into biblical idiom the expression "to profane the name of God" and does so in the sense here clearly indicated. In the preserved literature the flagrant breach of faith by the slaveowners of Jerusalem is the first offense to be designated *ḥillul hashem,* "the profanation of his name." It was a breach of the moral code, an offense against justice, a betrayal of faith, that first attracted to itself the invidious epithet, *ḥillul hashem,* "the profanation of his name."

More commonly, indeed, in biblical times, the offensive conduct so designated was not an offense against justice but an act of apostasy or of ritual defilement. Lev. 20:3 may serve as illustration: ". . . I will cut him off from among his people because he has given of his seed to Moloch, defiling my sanctuary and profaning my holy name." Most of the actions which bring the people's conduct into this category are sufficiently similar to permit the one example to serve as a definition. And, whether ethical or ritual, concerning human society or God, the conduct, or rather the misconduct, of God's people could be and was frequently called a profanation of his name. Paul was unfortunate only in his choice of a text; there is sanction enough in the Old Testament for his use of the thought.

2. The Second Isaiah's Debt to Ezekiel

The formula with its other meaning, expressing the idea that God's name may be profaned, not now by the conduct but by the *condition* of his people, that God might be in disgrace because of Israel's fate—Ezekiel appears to have been the first to use the formula with this meaning. As a matter of fact, Ezekiel and the Second Isaiah are the only prophets to use the formula in this sense. It is of minor significance, as we have seen, that the Second Isaiah refers to the profanation of God, where Ezekiel speaks of the profanation of his name. In this meaning (God or God's name profaned by the condition of his people), outside of the book of Ezekiel, the expression "to profane God's name" occurs in these two places in the Second Isaiah only.[10]

In Ezekiel it appears nine times, in chapters 20, 36, and 39, and

Ezekiel must be considered responsible for this usage. He originated it and the Second Isaiah adopted it. The classic and possibly first preserved expression of the thought appears in chapter 36: the people of the house of Israel polluted the land with their conduct and God in his anger scattered them among the nations. When they came there (now God is speaking)

> they profaned my holy name, it being said of them: "These are the people of God and they have gone from his land." So I am concerned for my holy name which the house of Israel profaned among the nations. . . . Not for your sake will I do it but for the sake of my holy name which you have profaned among the nations . . . and I will sanctify my great name . . . and all the nations shall know that I am God . . . and I will take you from the nations and gather you . . . and bring you to your land . . .[11]

What the people had done is here only remotely responsible for the profanation; the immediate cause is their condition. It is a familiar thought. In the defeat of a people the nations see the defeat of that people's God. In the expression "to profane the name of God" the word "name" is, to be sure, a circumlocution, a buffer between the holy God and the offensive verb "to profane"; but it is something more as well. The word adds a connotation; it connotes reputation, fame, prestige, recognition. To profane the name of God is to defame him, to damage his reputation, to lessen his prestige, to retard the process by which he achieves recognition, to put off the day on which it shall be known "where the sun rises and where it sets" that he is God. Ezekiel suggests that by the scattering of his people God has done his fame no good.

And the author of Isa. 52 makes this thought his own. As the foregoing chapters have suggested the Second Isaiah would have it known abroad that Israel's god is God. He here agrees with Ezekiel that Israel's pitiful condition is an obstacle to that end. He hears God admit, in the words of the passage here considered, that the exile is a truly unprofitable, if not, indeed, disadvantageous business:

> Now therefore what have I here, God says,
> Seeing that my people are taken away for nothing?

> Their masters defame me constantly,
> Daily my name is despised.

And he hears God's resolve:

> For my own sake, for my own sake, I will do it,
> For how should I be profaned?
> I will not relinquish to another the glory due me.[12]

The *locus classicus* for this theme, quoted above from Ezekiel, contains not only the idea of the profanation of God's name but the idea of its rehabilitation as well. This latter is *ḳiddush hashem,* "the sanctification of God's name," God's activity on his own behalf, "for the sake of his name." The one theme, of course, is the obverse of the other, and the two are normally paired. The theme here newly broached, the idea of God's activity on his own behalf, "for the sake of his name," is the more fertile, a dynamic concept.

From the negative then to the affirmation: man may act, God may act "for the sake of his name."

"I am concerned for my holy name. . . . Not for your sake will I do it but for the sake of my holy name. . . . And I will sanctify my great name." God's holy name has been profaned and God is determined to rehabilitate it, to restore its holiness. That is the meaning of "sanctify," a transitive form of the root *ḳadosh,* "to be holy." With dubious exceptions it is God who, according to Ezekiel, restores the holiness of his name. He himself gets himself holiness, obtains for himself honor (*kabod*). He does so by means of his activity on his people's behalf. Ezek. 20, like Ezek. 36, contains the theme in its whole complexity. In that chapter Ezekiel traces the long history of unregenerate Israel, whom age after age God has treated with more consideration than the people deserved and always solely: for the sake of his reputation, which might have been damaged if, once having promised his people good, God failed to accomplish it. His failure could be misconstrued. His reputation among the peoples depends—this is the thought—upon the fulfillment or nonfulfillment of his promises, no matter what the circumstances. The nations demand performance and have no understanding for the finer distinctions—the extenuating circumstances. So:

> I considered pouring out my anger upon them, spending my wrath against them in the land of Egypt. But I acted for the sake of my name, that it should not be profaned in the sight of the people among whom they were, before whom I made myself known to them, promising to bring them out of the land of Egypt. So I brought them out of the land of Egypt.

The process repeated itself, God always fulfilling his promises, but only out of concern for his reputation among the peoples: for the sake of his name.[13] In chapter 20 as in chapter 36, God announces his intention to regather his exiled people, thus to restore the holiness of his name.[14] So like this material in Ezek. 20 and 36 is the passage in Isa. 48 that the Second Isaiah must here depend upon Ezekiel. The relation is even more striking if, instead of looking at Isa. 48:11 alone, we couple v. 11 with v. 9 of the same chapter:

> For the sake of my name I will be patient;
> For the sake of the praise which I should receive I will restrain my anger against you
> And not consume you . . .
> For my own sake, for my own sake, I will do it
> For how should I be profaned?
> I will not relinquish to another the glory due me.

Undeniably the Second Isaiah has here adopted the thought of Ezekiel.

His dependence upon Ezekiel probably goes farther even than this. To some extent Ezekiel may have anticipated his insight that Yahveh is God. In Ezekiel the Second Isaiah may have found some elements even of this major theme, the debate with the gods. A comparison of the Second Isaiah's argument for monotheism with certain common expressions in Ezekiel justifies the conclusion that his debt to his predecessor is fairly great.

The first such expression in Ezekiel is the formula: "It is I, Yahveh, who have spoken." With only minor variations the formula occurs eleven times in the book of Ezekiel.[15] Four times more it is expanded significantly to read: "I, Yahveh, have spoken and will perform it," or: "I, Yahveh, have spoken a word and will perform it."[16]

A passage in Ezek. 12 furnishes the key to the understanding of this formula.[17] A proverb is current in Ezekiel's day concerning the land of Israel. People say: "Time passes and every vision fails." Ezekiel has to contend with the taunts of his contemporaries whose skepticism is the fruit of their experience with the evil forebodings of such prophets as Jeremiah and himself. It is their experience, the people opine, that prophetic predictions of evil remain unfulfilled year after year, that "every vision fails." It is obvious to them that the expectations of a prophet of doom have no reality, except perhaps in the remotest future. Their proverb challenges Ezekiel to produce compelling evidence that Yahveh has in truth inspired this prophet's threatening words. They imply that any event whatsoever which could be regarded as the fulfillment of any "vision," if not forever delayed, would convince them.[18] Ezekiel tacitly accepts the validity of the reproach, but, like Jeremiah, he answers the challenge with a bare assertion.[19] He announces God's answer: I will silence the skeptical house of rebellion. Visions will not now as heretofore fail of fulfillment because: "I, Yahveh, will speak whatsoever I will speak, not speaking alone but fulfilling; it shall be no more delayed; for in your days . . . will I speak a word and will perform it." [20] In the following paragraph, Ezekiel is defending the authenticity of his own prophetic call—as indeed the polemic against the unauthorized prophets in the next chapter testifies. But here in this paragraph he is defending the concept: prophecy; and he defends it by attributing to Yahveh the assertion: "I will speak a word and will perform it."

That paragraph and the formula "It is I, Yahveh, who have spoken" are clearly related, and what the formula does is this: it sets a seal upon the words to which it is appended. They are invariably threats or promises, and it stamps them as the words of Yahveh. But what could be the purpose of thus designating certain utterances? Only this: words so authorized must find their fulfillment if Yahveh is to be believed. And if they find fulfillment Yahveh must then be believed. It is as though Yahveh here were saying as a challenge: "I stake my reputation on it! These threats, these promises, shall come to pass. It is I, Yahveh, who have uttered them. Believe them! Remember, too, that I announced them in advance, and know by the outcome that my word is sure!" Before the Second Isaiah, Ezekiel here lays store by predictions fulfilled, attaches significance to realized prophecy. This apears to be the meaning of the formula: "It is I, Yahveh, who have spoken."

A second formula has a related meaning. It is not very common, occurs only twice, but it has the sound of a formula: "And they shall know that a prophet was among them." [21] A "prophet" in this formula is: one who declares God's intentions with men. This is an important connotation of the title "prophet" in the time of Ezekiel. It appears in the first occurrence of the formula: "You shall say to them, 'Thus says the Lord God'; and whether they listen or whether they refuse, being stubborn, they will know that a prophet was among them." When the formula occurs a second time its sense is very much sharper: the prophet declares what he declares and he is indisputably right. If, through Ezekiel, God says: "When this comes to pass—and lo, it comes—then they shall know that a prophet was among them" he means: the occurrence of the event which the prophet declared in advance proves that he who declared it was in fact as in name a prophet. In more general terms it means: through his prophets Israel's God can and does, in fact, reveal his intent. It means two things: that the word of the prophet deserves respect, and that God's word thus revealed is a factor to be reckoned with. Woe to such as brush it lightly aside! [22]

Is Ezekiel whistling in the dark? Is he saying: Just you wait? When the Second Isaiah formulated his argument from prophecy he could point and he did point to fulfilled predictions, and they were the foundation of fact on which his proof was based. Ezekiel does not invoke any such evidence. He merely says: "It shall be no more delayed . . . in your days I will speak a word and will perform it." "It is I, Yahveh, who have spoken." "When this comes to pass . . . they shall know that a prophet was among them." Ezekiel is almost in the position of those prophets of whom he deprecatingly speaks, the prophets "who say 'God says' though God did not send them and hope he will authenticate the word." He does not have the evidence at hand. Until 586 all he has is conviction, the conviction that he is different from those others of whom God says: "They say: 'God says' when I have not spoken." [23]

If Ezekiel had the evidence it would prove not only that "a prophet was among them" but something else as well: that he, the God of Israel, who spoke through the prophet was God. This is the implication of that other ubiquitous formula in the book of Ezekiel, "And they will know that I am God."

This third formula, with only slight variations—it is not always "they," but sometimes "he" or "you," singular or plural—occurs about seventy times in the book. It exhibits some little variety but the verb is always a future form: "You will know . . . ," "they will know . . ." The formula occurs in chapters 1 to 39 only but in all of the strata of those chapters. The fact that it does not occur in chapters 40 to 48 adds to the impression that those chapters are an appendix added after chapters 1 to 39 had attained their present form. But the fact that it does occur everywhere else—even in the apocalyptic chapters 38 and 39, for example—gives rise to the impression that it belongs to a late stage in the editing of chapters 1 to 39. If this impression be correct, then it is hardly the prophet Ezekiel himself who is responsible for the formula: And they shall know that I am God. But the reasoning behind this formula is very like the reasoning which the Second Isaiah sets forth in his great argument. And if a late editor of Ezekiel's book liberally sprinkled his edition of that book with the formula in question, he probably did so under the influence of the Second Isaiah. Nevertheless, the alternative remains that Ezekiel himself first expressed the thought and phrased it as a formula, which formula then later editors of his own book repeated.[24] Whether or not he himself expressed it, it is wholly probable that Ezekiel was moving toward such a formulation. It is probable in view of his thinking as it appears in the expression: "They shall know that a prophet was among them" and in view particularly of the concept: "for the sake of his name." For, the motivation in this concept is the same as in the formula: "They shall know that I am God." The formula means: they shall know that I (Yahveh, the speaker, the God of Israel) am God (the one God, unrivaled).

Who shall know this? An inspection of the seventy passages or so in which this formula occurs, reveals: that in a little more than half of the instances of the formula it is the people of Israel themselves, and that in the remaining instances it is the foreign nations who shall know. And what will convince them? In more than two-thirds of the instances it is some national disaster which they themselves experience. That is to say: When disaster befalls Israel, Israel will know, when disaster befalls Ammon, Moab, Edom, Egypt, or Magog, that nation, whichever it be, will know that Yahveh is God. In the remaining passages it is the miraculous restoration of scattered Israel to peoplehood after the national disaster which will produce in them, and, to a lesser extent, in others, that conviction. A few examples will add concreteness to these observations: (a) Israel will learn through the experience of disaster who is God—"I will not look with pity on you nor show compassion, for I will visit your ways upon you and your abominations will be in the midst of you, and you [Israel] will know that I am God." Alternatively (b), Israel will learn through the experience of salvation—"And they will know that I am God when I break the bars of their yoke and deliver them from the power of those that have them in servitude." (c) Another nation will learn through the experience of disaster that Yahveh is God—"I will perform acts of judgment against Moab, and they will know that I am God." Alternatively (d) another nation will learn through observing the good that God will do for Israel—"And I will sanctify my great name which is profaned among the nations, which you profaned among them; and the nations will know that I am God, says the Lord Yahveh, when I am sanctified through you in their presence." [25]

What reasoning lies behind the assumption that the occurrence of this or that national disaster or the restoration of the people of Israel after a national disaster will produce the conviction that Israel's god is God? Apparently the same sort of reasoning as that which led the Second Isaiah to the same conclusion: reasoning from the premise that a god who fulfills his word is God. The foregoing paragraphs suggest that this is so, the interpretation of the formula: "It is I, Yahveh, who have spoken" and its relation both to God's insistence: "I will speak a word and will perform it" and to the assurance: "They shall know that a prophet was among them." It appears to be Yahveh's implementation of his threat or promise previously announced by his prophet which is to produce the conviction that his prophet was prophet and that he is God. This is remarkably like the reasoning of the Second Isaiah.

Two other contacts are apparent. Both prophets were frustrated by the skepticism of their own people in their generation, and felt the need of bringing such evidence as must convince the people. So, the Second Isaiah asks his people to witness to facts which will convince them themselves and assigns to the servant Israel the task of bringing Israel back. And in the same manner, Ezekiel anticipates such events, the fulfillment of such threats, the accomplishment of such promises, in Israel as must convince Israel.[26]

On the other hand, and this is the second contact, both prophets look beyond Israel to "the nations." The argument of the Second Isaiah, coupled with the testimony that Israel is to bring, must, so he believed, force upon the nations the conviction that Israel's god is God; and bringing that testimony is a major task for the servant —to be "a light to the nations." [27] So, for Ezekiel, the fulfillment of Yahveh's threats and promises will convince the nations also: "and they will know that I am God." And it is "for the sake of his name" that he acts.

The formula, then, both in its logic and in its motivation, has intimate contacts with the thinking of the Second Isaiah. But the formula is linked also with several other thoughts of Ezekiel and it is not necessary to look elsewhere for its origin beyond the inspiration of Ezekiel himself. It appears to be a significant original contribution of the prophet Ezekiel, which a later prophet knew well how to exploit.

The Second Isaiah, then, who inherited so much from the prophet Jeremiah, borrowed also from Jeremiah's younger contemporary Ezekiel. He seems to have adopted Ezekiel's propositions that Yahveh speaks and fulfills, that he speaks through prophets and authenticates the prophets in the fulfillment, that in the fulfillment lies also the proof that he is God, that the proof must be accepted by Israel and by the nations as well, and finally, that in history again and again Yahveh acts precisely for this purpose, "for the sake of his name."

What the Second Isaiah took over from Ezekiel he used to great advantage. As already we have seen he went on beyond Ezekiel. History helped him. Between Ezekiel's time and his own, history had fulfilled the words of God's prophets. Jerusalem had fallen and instead of Ezekiel's "lo, it comes," through the Second Isaiah God could say: "they came to pass":

> The former things of old I foretold,
> And from my mouth they issued and I announced them.
> Suddenly I wrought and they came to pass.[28]

So the Second Isaiah could draw his conclusion. And he did so emphatically and as a central theme in his message. Though the formula "And they shall know . . ." appears seventy times in the book of Ezekiel it is still somehow peripheral there. When the Second Isaiah picks it up he looks at it from all sides and ends by converting it into a program. It is no tired formula in the Second Isaiah. It is a thought being worked over, stated now this way and now that. It finds clearest expression in the words:

> That all may know, where the sun rises
> And where it sets, that there is none beside me;
> I am God and there is none else,
> No God but me.[29]

The universalism of the Second Isaiah shapes his message.

Eager to consolidate and propagate the knowledge that God is God the two prophets looked about for hearers and this one's range of vision was not as broad as that one's. Whereas Ezekiel looked first at Israel and only now and then allowed his gaze to wander to the nations, the eyes of the Second Isaiah roamed constantly among the nations and only now and then returned to rest on Jacob. The Second Isaiah built a spacious mansion on the foundations which Ezekiel had laid.

3. "Where the Sun Rises and Where It Sets"

These considerations do not exhaust the theme: "for the sake of his name." It is to be found also beyond the pages of Ezekiel, who seems first to have given it expression, and beyond the Second Isaiah who expanded it notably. It is found for example in such Pentateuchal narratives as Num. 14:11 to 20 and Exod. 9:14 to 16. In the one in Numbers, Moses prevents God from destroying the rebellious people in the wilderness by appealing to God's self-interest: "Now if you kill this people as one man," Moses says, "the nations who heard your fame will say: 'It was because God was unable to bring this people to the land which he promised them that he slaughtered them in the desert.' " In the other narrative God explains to Pharaoh why he did not with one bold stroke merely withdraw his people from Egyptian bondage. Had he done that he would have had no opportunity to display his power, performing miracles in the midst of Egypt. "This is why I let you stand," God says to Pharaoh, "to show you my strength, to publish my fame [lit., name] in the whole earth." "This time I will stretch out my hand with all my visitations upon you . . . so that you will know that there is none like me on earth." About this show of strength the priestly narrative of the events leading to the exodus has interesting and relevant things to say. This narrative is introduced in Exod. 7:3–5 and concludes in 11:9 f. The introduction calls the heralded events signs and miracles and foresees that they will not convince Pharaoh, and the conclusion admits that this was so. To make it quite sure that Pharaoh would not too soon give in, God, in fact, repeatedly hardened his heart. Only the stretching out of God's hand on the night of the first Passover could persuade Pharaoh.[80] Until this event Pharaoh was quite unimpressed; Pharaoh held cheap the feats of magic which Moses and Aaron performed. Different, however, was the effect of the miracles on persons less obstinate than the divine Pharaoh, *viz.*, his court magicians. Matching their skill with Aaron's they first do well enough. They make snakes out of wands (though Aaron's is biggest and swallows the others), turn water into blood, and bring up frogs out of puddles. These tricks are easy to duplicate. The court magicians experience their first defeat when they cannot turn dust into lice. "This is the finger of God," they inform Pharaoh confidentially, but he pooh-poohs it. They are really impressed when far from making the soot of the furnace produce sore boils on others they themselves are so grievously afflicted that they cannot stand up before Moses. Aaron and Moses not only defeat, they also make utter fools of them.[81]

The interesting thing about this story is the way it parallels Isa. 47. One has only to substitute Egypt for Babylonia and magicians for astrologers to find the narrative from Exodus in the chapter from the Second Isaiah. The Babylonian exile is a repetition of the Egyptian enslavement. As the taskmasters there imposed rigorous labor so here: "Upon the aged you have laid your heavy yoke." And the exodus from Egypt and the miracles performed for Israel in the wilderness form the pattern for the return, centuries later, from exile:

> Leave Babylon, flee Chaldea.
> Celebrate it with a joyous shout, publish it,
> Make it known to the end of the earth;
> Say "God has redeemed his servant Jacob.
> And they did not thirst though he led them
> through waste places.
> He made water gush from a rock for them.
> He split a rock and the waters flowed."
>
> Not in haste shall you leave,
> You shall not go fleeing;
> For God shall be going before you,
> The God of Israel shall be your rear-guard.

Elsewhere, also, the two are equated, confused: Egypt and Babylon, exile and bondage, return and freedom. In part, no doubt, this explains the pervasive interest in the exodus everywhere in the Bible and the institution of rehearsing its story, which has never been lost in Jewish tradition and practice.[32]

And so it is not strange to find in the priestly narrative in Exodus, in the defeat of the sorcerers of Egypt, an echo of the Second Isaiah's anticipatory derision of the court astrologers in Babylonia. Of them, addressing Babylon, the Second Isaiah wrote:

> Let them deliver you who chart the heavens,
> Who gaze at the stars,
> Who tell month by month
> What things shall befall you.
> Lo, they will be as stubble,
> Fire will burn them;

They will not save themselves
From the flame.

He probably has these same futile witnesses of Babylonian gods in mind when he draws the contrast. God

Frustrates the signs of praters,
Makes fools of diviners,
Turns back sages,
Making nonsense of their knowledge;
But he establishes the word of his servant,
Fulfills the counsel of his messengers.

It is hard to avoid the impression that the priestly author of the narrative in Exodus had tongue in cheek and expected his hearers to know what he meant when he afflicted the Egyptian sorcerers with the pox.[33]

There is a further contact. The miracles in Egypt were intended as credentials. They would demonstrate to the people of Egypt that prophets were among them. They would even prove the superiority of the God of Moses and Aaron over the gods of the sorcerers. Before the magicians are prostrated with sores they indeed admit: "It is the finger of God." The miracles are not plagues but signs. For the priestly author they are the demonstration which convinces Egypt that the God of Moses is God.

In other words, God undertakes to deliver Israel from Egypt for the sake of his name, and we are led back to the verse with which we began. In that verse God said:

Now therefore what have I here
Seeing that my people are taken away for nothing?
Their masters defame me constantly,
Daily my name is despised.

It now appears no accident that this verse is introduced, as it is, in the verse preceding it, by a reference to the sojourn in Egypt. As that sojourn was a reproach to God, because it was the reverse of his promise to the patriarchs, so now the exile is a disgrace to him, and he bestirs himself to clear his name.[34]

It is all for his greater glory—this should be understood. Defeating the sorcerers and drowning Pharaoh, making fools of astrologers and smashing the brazen doors and iron bolts of Babylon's gates, bringing his people from the house of Egyptian bondage, driving them before him as sheep on a new-built highway across the wilderness of the peoples from exile, doing all these things God is only acting for the sake of his name that they may know "that I am God"—"that all may know, where the sun rises and where it sets" [35]—in Babylonia as well as in Egypt.

The admission wrung from the sorcerers of Egypt is only one of several; for, a number of biblical narratives make the point that Israel's God is God, as all must recognize. Following upon the exodus Moses met his Midianite father-in-law and told him "all that Yahveh did to Pharaoh and Egypt on Israel's behalf, and the trouble they had on the way and how Yahveh helped them . . . and Jethro rejoiced . . . and said: Blessed be Yahveh who delivered you from Egypt and Pharaoh. . . . Now I know that Yahveh is greater than all the gods. . . ." Elijah put the matter clearly at the test on Carmel: "The god who responds with fire, he is God." And when Baal failed and Yahveh succeeded: "All the people saw and fell on their faces and proclaimed: 'Yahveh, he is God! Yahveh, he is God.'" Elijah's disciple, Elisha, cured the leprous Aramean general, and this Naaman, too, came and stood before Elisha and declared: "I am convinced that there is no God on earth except in Israel." [36]

Whether by the performance of miracles or by the execution of justice and the doing of acts of salvation, Israel's God supplied the evidence which obtained from his own people and from others the acknowledgment that he is God. Whether he acted to clear his name of reproach or to impress with his saving power he acted in order that all might know that he is God. Whether the prophetic authors burdened their God, as Ezekiel did, with the need to act himself on his own behalf and for the sake of his name, casting off all suspicion of weakness or inconstancy, or whether, as did the Second Isaiah, they assigned to their people the double burden, to avoid all such conduct as would discredit their God, and to witness as prophets, possessed of a momentous truth, to his divinity, they had a common property: they were men with a mission.

Jealous for God they cared how men regarded him. They dared to hope that his name would be known "where the sun rises and where it sets." They saw the joint efforts of God and his people bent to that single end. What Israel did and what Israel experienced, its ways and its history, both were relevant. Through unseemly actions God's people might profane his name, through fitting conduct hallow it. But that was not all; God, too, acted for the sake of his name and Israel's fate was evidence of his acts. Being the people of God Israel occupied a peculiarly sensitive position among the families of the earth and what happened to this people always had significance. Through Israel's history God was known. Suffering or benefiting, Israel revealed God's nature and his will, his purpose and his glory. Thus passively, without effort, after affliction enjoying his bounty and tasting victory, as well as actively, steadily pursuing justice, bringing light to the nations, the people of destiny went about its god-given mission.

CHAPTER VII

THE MISSION OF ISRAEL: BIBLICAL ORIGINS

1. One God

Behind the idea of a Jewish mission lies the idea of one world God. This idea probably had its beginnings in Judaism in the thinking of Amos but it did not achieve its fullest expression until the time of the Second Isaiah more than two centuries later.

Starting with Amos the pre-exilic prophets prepared the way for the eventual definitive formulation:

They did so by their refusal to accept the popular loose interpretation of the covenant, which made of Israel a favored nation.

They did so by teaching that God might make use of other nations as means for the execution of his purposes.

They did so by their rejection of distinctive ritual acts.

They did so by their emphasis upon ethical conduct, which knows no racial boundaries.

And they did so by proclaiming the principle that God could be worshiped outside of his land, beyond the borders of Israel.

In these ways they laid the foundation upon which the Second Isaiah was to build. They widened the base; they drew lines of influence from Israel's God to the nations of the earth. But it remained for the Second Isaiah to storm the heavens and empty them of the vanities of the nations.

He did so with a two-edged syllogism—this we have seen. He set forth his major premise. He alone is God, he said, who can declare in advance what is to be; for, only an unrivaled power, a power opposed by no greater force, one whose articulated will fears no antagonist, can thus announce the future. He drew from history his minor premise, from experienced facts, and he phrased it both negatively and positively. Negatively, he observed: the presumed gods of peoples other than Israel had failed to declare what was to be. Therefore, he concluded the one and only God is not among the gods of other peoples. He accompanied his negation with elaborate and devastating satire directed against the pretentious gods of metal and wood and their dim-witted interpreters. The positive form of his minor premise led him to a positive, far-reaching conclusion. Unlike the vanities of the nations, he said, Israel's god through Israel's prophets had announced what was to be—and not announced alone but accomplished it. He, therefore, is God, the one and only.

The Second Isaiah lived after the conquest of Jerusalem by the Babylonians, after they destroyed Jerusalem's proud temple and deported the Judeans. That these events were inevitable had been the oft-reiterated burden of God's word articulated by the first Isaiah, by Micah, Jeremiah, Ezekiel. The Second Isaiah lived long after Assyria destroyed Samaria and deported the Ephraimites, which events, also, Amos and Isaiah had unmistakably declared to be God's will, well in advance of their occurrence. Through chosen mouths a god had spoken words scarcely credible: he had announced the doom of his own people—and the incredible had occurred. Therefore this God's word is sure. If now his prophet comes with a new word—a consoling message of restoration and future glory—this word, too, will not return to him empty. It was a major concern of the Second Isaiah thus to gain credence for his comforting promises. But more than this it was his purpose to produce the conviction that Israel's God is he, besides whom there is no other.

His proof, it is to be observed, was based upon the fact of prophecy, the historical phenomenon of Israel's prophets. It was not the prophets of any other people but the prophets of Israel alone whose speech supplied the proof that Israel's god is God. It is this fact that led the Second Isaiah to a corollary directly related to the idea of a Jewish mission. In Israel these prophets arose; of Israel they spoke; to Israel they addressed themselves; it was the people of Israel who heard and preserved their words. Who, then, but Israel would bear testimony that the God in whose name these prophets spoke is indeed God? This is the core of the mission idea: "You are my witnesses, says Yahveh, and I am God."

Neither according to the Second Isaiah nor according to Ezekiel before him was God content merely to be; he desired also to be known. Nor for them was the One God a mathematical concept, a logical abstraction. Biblical man thought and spoke of him in human terms—as of a personality with positive attributes and strong emotions, and with virtues and weaknesses, comparable to the attributes and emotions, virtues and weaknesses of men. "My thoughts are not your thoughts, neither are your ways my ways" is immediately explained in what follows: "For as the heavens are higher than the earth so are my ways higher than your ways and my thoughts than your thoughts." For biblical man "other than" meant "higher than." [1]

And among the manlike feelings which they attributed to God was the feeling of jealousy. At first God was jealous of the gods of other nations and wanted them to have no part of the worship of his people. The earlier prophets condemned those in Israel who served other gods. Israel's god was, so to speak, in competition with Baal and with Ashtoreth and the others—and he wanted what was his, he was jealous for his prerogatives. He demanded *da'at,* "knowledge of him"; and knowledge of him meant not only awareness of his true nature and demands but also, and more significantly, acknowledgment or acceptance by his people of his authority. So it was from the beginning of the prophetic movement—from Elijah onward, if not, indeed, from the time of Moses.

But later, for Ezekiel and for the Second Isaiah, this was not enough. For these prophets "knowledge of God" had come to mean acknowledgment that he alone is God and there is none else, not the acceptance by Israel of him alone among the gods, but the recognition that he is one, unique and unrivaled, besides whom there is simply no other. And, accordingly, these prophets thought of God as jealous not only for Israel but for all mankind—concerned that all men should acknowledge his authority. Somewhat grudgingly at first, Ezekiel promises the exiles national restoration not because Israel is deserving (Israel deserves no more than the present calamity) but rather because God is jealous for his reputation among the nations. These have misconstrued his actions; in them the suspicion has arisen that the captivity proves the impotence of Israel's patron god, his inability to prevent their humiliation. But "Why should they say among the nations: 'Where is their God?' " The nations are, of course, greatly in error; his treatment of Israel was a demonstration not of weakness but of strength.[2] Nevertheless, so they think, and God's reputation has suffered; his prestige is at an ebb. And therefore, for the sake of his name, purely for the sake of his name, now he will restore Israel; and then they, the nations, will know—by their own standards they will know—that he is God. Basic to this argument is the implicit characterization of God as one who is jealous for all men's homage.

The Second Isaiah reaches the same conclusion but the route he takes is more attractive. It is his view also that God desires the homage of all men. The goal is the same: universal acceptance of a universal God; but the motivation is different. Whereas in Ezekiel it was "so that not"—so that God's name should not be profaned among the nations, in the Second Isaiah it is "in order that"—in order that his salvation may reach to the ends of the earth. Any idea present in Ezekiel of personal injury (if we may use this term of God) is replaced in the Second Isaiah by a different urge: it is because God has something to offer the nations, something for their welfare, that he covets their recognition.

What men think of God is largely conditioned by what they think of themselves. If the God of Ezekiel felt the need to justify himself in the eyes of the nations this may mean that Ezekiel and his generation were afflicted (as well they might have been under the circumstances) with a measure of self-hatred, and cared what others thought, and felt apologetic. And what miraculous thing has happened during the intervening decades, that, less than forty years later, a Second Isaiah can conceive of a God thus reconciled with himself? Whatever the cause, the fact remains that this prophet's God was self-confident and unabashed; he was not one to hide his light under a bushel. So must a God be who would send forth his people to acclaim him among the nations—and so must a people be to set out on such a mission: they must have faith in their God born of faith in themselves.

There can be no doubt that this people in the decades following the appearance of the Second Isaiah (and Cyrus) thought of God as the world God and of Judaism as the world religion of the future. According to Zechariah a time would come when ten men of the variously tongued nations would take hold of one Jew's robe and say: "Let us go with you, for we have heard that God is with you." In an anonymous passage now found in Jeremiah, possibly from Zechariah's time, a similar thought appears: "Nations shall come to you from the ends of the earth, and they shall say 'Our fathers inherited only wind, unprofitable vanity.' " The Second Isaiah represented God as affirming in the form of an oath:

> Every knee shall do me reverence,
> Every tongue confess me.

A disciple, one of the later Isaiahs, took up the thought and announced God's purpose in unmistakable terms:

> My house shall be called a house of prayer for all peoples.

The author of Solomon's prayer at the dedication of his "house" is equally sanguine:

> The stranger also, the non-Israelite who comes from a far land because of your fame—for they will hear of your great name and power and outstretched arm and come to pray towards this house—hear in heaven where you dwell and do all that the stranger asks of you, so that all the peoples of the earth may know you and fear you as does your people Israel. . . .

The anonymous author of Ezek. 47 conceived the happy symbol of the spring flowing from the threshold of the temple, and as a swelling stream, bringing healing everywhere and life. Another anonymous author used the same figure and went on to say:

> And God shall be king over all the earth. On that day God shall be one and his name one.[3]

Enviable was the unreserved enthusiasm of these generations, conscious as they were of the truth of their tradition, with confidence in their own spiritual insight, believing themselves alone in possession of the knowledge of God, and fearlessly commending that knowledge to all who sought salvation. They were proud of their heritage and generous to share it. Their God has expressed the will to be known "where the sun rises and where it sets" and has made his offer: "Turn to me all you ends of the earth and be saved." Through his servant this shall be.[4]

2. Israel's Passive Role in the Process of Salvation

The spokesmen of these generations thought of Israel as playing a double role in the process of universal salvation: a passive as well as an active role. The passive role is relevant to the mission; the active role is the mission itself.

According to Ezekiel, not Israel but Israel's God would act in a manner calculated to produce the conviction that he is God. The frequent phrase: "and they shall know that I am God," with its twofold reference, "they" being Israel itself at times, at other times the nations of the world, implies activity on the part of God alone, jealous for his name. For this activity Israel assumes no responsibility. To convince the nations that he is God, Israel's God will do two things: he will intervene in history, miraculously visiting disaster and ruin upon those very nations, whereby they will learn that he indeed is God; or, he will miraculously restore the fortunes of his own conquered, decimated, impoverished people, observing which the amazed nations will attain to understanding. In neither aspect of God's activity does Israel here have any but a passive role.

As to the first, it is to be observed that the harbingers of salvation were not always generous to the candidates for salvation. Ezekiel was not generous when he conceived of divine visitations upon the peoples as the rod which would bring them to knowledge. Malachi was not generous when he coupled the universalistic sentiment: "God is great beyond the borders of Israel" with God's promise to destroy Edom, the foe and despoiler of Israel, which chastisement would serve as evidence of God's dominion. God, indeed, says through his prophet Malachi, as through the Second Isaiah: "From the rising of the sun to its setting great is my name among the nations" and "I am a great king; my name is feared among the nations," but it cannot be denied that in this context the title "king" has the connotation "despot." [5]

Speaking as he did of Edom's expectations, Malachi was echoing a thought occasional in the Second Isaiah but not closely related to his major themes. The Second Isaiah suggested that God was purchasing the release of his people from Babylonian captivity with the nations and kings falling before his anointed Cyrus and was thus earning for himself general acclaim.[6] Though examples of this notion are not uncommon, the thought has no great significance in connection with Israel's mission—the thought that the nations will learn who is God only when the rod of God's avenging anger descends upon them.

Not much more significant is its counterpart, the other aspect of God's activity. According to this thought Israel would play a very pleasant though still wholly passive role in the unfolding of the divine plan, the role of a recipient only of divine favor. In many passages it is suggested that God will so reward, bless, and benefit Israel that all the nations, seeing the privileges which Israel enjoys, must perforce be attracted to the God from whom such blessings flow. But in this event the missionaries have no responsibility other than to sit back and accept the material fruits of the abundant salvation of God. Then, when others see their enviable lot, they will clamor for admission to the fellowship of those whose God confers such superior benefits. This thought also is frequent in the final chapters in Isaiah and in other writings later than either Ezekiel or the Second Isaiah, and probably dependent upon them: a people strange of appearance from a distant land will bring tribute to Zion, the place of God's name; "all nations will call you fortunate for you will be a land of desire"; "and Jerusalem shall be an object of praise and glory for all the nations of the earth who hear of all the good that I do [for her inhabitants] and are amazed and startled at all the good and well-being that I produce for her." [7]

The pattern includes the picture of the new Jerusalem resplendent with gold and silver, precious stones and structures of the finest workmanship: "gold for bronze, silver for iron, bronze for wood, iron for stone." "And all your border precious stones, and all your builders taught of the Lord." This is Jerusalem whose "gates are open continually, not closed by day or night, to admit the wealth of nations." Caravans of merchants stopping off at Zion, impressed by the splendor of the new city, will go on to distant ports, evangelists of the God who adorned it: "they will publish the good tidings of the praiseworthy works of God," "and they shall rehearse my glory among the nations."

> Their seed shall be known among the nations,
> Their offspring among the peoples,
> And all who see them shall recognize
> That they are the seed whom God has blessed.

> It shall be that just as you could be used by the nations in the phrasing of a curse, O house of Judah and house of Israel, so I am going to save you and you can be used in the phrasing of a blessing; fear not, take courage.

In all of this Israel merely receives. The strangers passing through in merchant caravans even take over what little missionary activity is involved in the process.[8]

Variations of this theme are numerous: Zechariah expects distant peoples to aid in the rebuilding of the sanctuary, an expectation which the author of Isa. 60 shares. According to this Isaiah: the nations will offer their services—not the commoners among them only but royalty as well—to rebuild the walls of Zion. They will also tend the flocks and farms and vineyards and make a leisure class of the people of Israel, who, if they have any duties at all, are called upon only to serve as priests:

> You yourselves shall be called "the priests of God,"
> Shall be known as "the ministers of our God."

Serving as priests will probably be no arduous task, because from among the "nations and tongues" "levites" will be chosen to assist the "kingdom of priests," this according to a possible understanding of an ambiguous verse in the last chapter of Isaiah. Nevertheless the augmented priesthood—the whole people!—would not be idle, for hope ran high. An exuberant prophet of that day announced as God's word:

> On every successive new moon
> And on every successive sabbath
> All flesh shall come to prostrate themselves
> Before me, God said.

And again there is a parallel in Zechariah:

> And it shall be that all who are left over of all the nations that come against Jerusalem shall go up every year to prostrate themselves to the king, God of Hosts, and to celebrate the festival of tabernacles.[9]

Imagination ran riot and, as a contrast to its actual low estate, the people dreamed itself an extravagant compensatory dream—justified only by a firm faith in the salvation promised them by the one world God, the eternal creator of all and author of human history.

The willingness to leave everything in the hands of God—at least everything connected with the coming of his kingdom—is a position that religious men have espoused in all centuries, even in ours. But events of recent decades comport badly with the hopes described in the foregoing paragraphs. Recent Jewish history has not been such as to arouse envy in the hearts of men and entice them to seek fellowship with Israel and shelter with Israel's God. On the contrary the dispersal of Central European Jewry in the thirties and the genocide of the forties invests that hope with irony.

Is it proper, then, to consider this recent, and all such suffering of Israel known to history as falling within the category of missionary activity? The thought is indeed familiar. The figure of the "suffering servant" so-called, in Isa. 53, has been taken to suggest suffering as a mission. Suffering is a passive enduring and thus no active mission; nevertheless it could be considered relevant in a discussion of the mission theme.

A people that has intimately known suffering may be allowed the consolation of discovering a meaning behind it. In order to justify the ways of God with man Israel has said: it is our mission to suffer. Our suffering atones with God for the sins of mankind. We must accept it as an episode in the inscrutable process which leads to man's ultimate redemption. Or else, speaking without mystery, sociologically, we have said: the mere fact of Israel's endurance, the people's continued existence despite diabolical efforts to pluck this thorn from the side of nations, is a service, has therapeutic value for society. Formulated either way the explanation includes suffering for Israel in a divine plan for the salvation of men.

The thought that in God's plan this people's grief may serve some purpose, inscrutable or manifest, is not *per se* to be rejected. But this must be observed: the Second Isaiah laid down no program of suffering for Israel. Our analysis of chapter 53 led to the quite different result, that the prophet does not there condemn the servant-people to a career of suffering, to pain as a destiny; he speaks of past, not future affliction. He foresees for the people a joyous future of such proportions, indeed, as to strike with amazement all who learn of it. The gulf is not too wide that separates the thought here: "Lo, my servant shall prosper, shall rise, be lifted up, be greatly exalted" and the idea of the new Jerusalem studded with precious stones which closely follows.[10] God's message concerning his servant in this chapter is not a laying on of burdens; it is, as throughout the writings of the Second Isaiah, a message of consolation. Israel will arise from the valley of the shadow. "He shall see descendants, shall live long, and God's desire shall succeed through him." [11]

The idea behind the passive phase of the mission is this: that Israel may learn and men may learn lessons from Israel's history. They may observe and know that there is a God, that he works on earth, that nations do his bidding, that his ways are just, that a corrupt society must collapse, that God reveals his will, that as well his promises as his threats are sure, that salvation is his to give. He who is wise will read such lessons from the pages of Israel's history. To him the record of that people's bitter experience is an incentive to repentance, a motivation to obedience, an alarm to arouse a dormant conscience, a spur to deflect a man from evil. As regards suffering this was the thought of the Second Isaiah. He thought only of the record of suffering, as we have seen, and did not advocate a philosophy of surrender. Martyrdom is no mission. As for the sure promise, it is an invitation.

It is only by a courtesy that this passive phase of the mission can be called mission at all. Inactivity and mission are contraries. To receive at God's hand, be it reward or penalty, to be the inert product of history is a poor substitute for a mission. But more than one among the prophets conceived an active role for the people in God's process of salvation.

3. Israel's Active Role: The Mission Proper

One conception of Israel's active role is slightly bizarre: It is also of minor significance and is to be noted for systematic reasons only. It corresponds to the paradoxical notion already observed that God's destruction of Israel's foes could somehow irrationally serve a universalistic purpose. It is the counterpart to the observation that "Israel's mission is peace." Though "the dead cannot praise God" it appears that some of the biblical authors thought knowledge of his name might be spread by Jewish arms and advocated a militant program of proselytism by conquest. The thought occurs a number of times in the Bible, particularly in passages dating from the period of Zerubbabel and onward, and even the Second Isaiah permitted himself the paradox.[12] There is no evidence that this thought went beyond the theoretical in Bible times, but it is an interesting theory, though not, indeed, to be commended for our times.

The Second Isaiah had the clearest of all prophetic views of Israel's active mission, and this view corresponds more nearly with what we mean today when we speak of the mission of Israel. We have already examined it in some detail and refer to it here in order to place it in a larger context. Following his lead the Jews of his day—or any among them who listened—thought of themselves as keepers of the light and teachers of the truth. The prophet had referred to them as men who had God's *torah* in their hearts, a people to whom God had said: "I have put my words in your mouth." Having his revelation in their heart and his words in their mouth, they must, of course, speak for him, even as a prophet could not choose but speak what his God had disclosed to him. It is God's will that knowledge of him be universal:

Teaching proceeds from me;

I arouse my truth as a light for men.

And, according to the Second Isaiah, he had chosen his people as the instruments of his revelation. The prophet assigned Israel the prophetic role of speaking for God and of God.[13]

According to one who followed the Second Isaiah and caught his spirit there is a covenant between God and Israel under the terms of which the people is obligated. And the people's obligation is to speak. "This," God says through his prophet, "is the wording of my covenant with them: 'My spirit which is upon you and my words which I have put in your mouth shall not depart from you, nor from your children, nor from your children's children, now or ever more.'" [14] This is, of course, the point to which the reasoning of the Second Isaiah had led him. Israel, he had claimed, was peculiarly suited for the role of a people of prophets, since, through its history, and in that history most especially through the teachings of its own prophets, it had been privileged to learn that saving truth. Had not Israel's prophets, in fact, supplied the evidence which of necessity led to the conclusion that God is God? And had those same prophets not spoken to Israel? Who, then, but Israel could best witness to the imposing truth?

The Second Isaiah dramatized the prophetic role of Israel in the figure of the servant of God, as we have seen. He equated the "choice of Israel" with the prophet's call to service. Prophetlike, the servant Israel was called or chosen, commissioned or sent, and authorized to speak. His mouth and tongue, like a prophet's, are at God's service. He may rebel but he cannot refrain from speech. He carries out the divine purpose. He has met with opposition, as did all prophets; he has even suffered shame, as did especially the prophet Jeremiah; but he persists.

Behind the figure of the servant stands the idea of the mission of Israel, and here it is a prophetic mission. Formerly a chosen few served to transmit God's word to the one people Israel, but now, to make God known to all the peoples of the earth, nothing less than his whole people Israel will do—not here a "kingdom of priests" but a people of prophets. Israel is to be a "light to the nations," an instrument of universal salvation.

Whereas Ezekiel had thought of God as acting so that his name should no more be profaned among the nations, the Second Isaiah thought in terms of God's positive purpose: that his salvation might reach to the ends of the earth. The Second Isaiah was without apology; the true missionary spirit was his: he was enthusiastically evangelistic. He was convinced that Israel's God had something of value to offer—an abundant reward for such as acknowledge him. And this reward he called "salvation." With self-confident words the God of the Second Isaiah invites the nations: "Turn to me and be saved, all you ends of the earth!" [15] In chapters 40 to 66 of Isaiah the word "salvation" occurs with great frequency and is a key word—one of two key words; "sure purpose" is the other—for the understanding of the mission idea in Bible times.

The English word: salvation is a translation of any of the three Hebrew nouns: *yeshaʿ*, *yeshuʿah,* and *teshuʿah,* all derived from the verb *yashaʿ* meaning: "to help, save, or deliver." Often, according to its context, the verb means no more than "to deliver persons or nations or armies from peril," from an enemy or from any threat to their safety. It does not always have theological implications; one man may save another from danger, one army may save another from defeat. But, for the Second Isaiah and his followers, God is the source of salvation and in addition to its negative connotations: deliverance from, it has achieved a positive sense: a bestowing, a giving to. It includes all that a man may wish—all that one may expect from a benevolent God, whose generous will is unopposed.

The Second Isaiah developed the argument which proved to his satisfaction that God's will is unopposed, that he is unrivaled power. To the argument from the facts of prophecy fulfilled he added another. It was Israel's God, he declared, not the Babylonian Marduk surely, nor even the Persian Ahura Mazda, but Israel's God who brought Cyrus victorious to Babylon to overthrow that proud seat of empire—and why?—so that Cyrus should release God's people and rebuild his temple. God's will is triumphant, triumphant again as it was in earlier days when he employed Assyria and used Babylonia as rods of his wrath, fulfilling the word of doom articulated by his agents, the earlier prophets. Now, in the upsurge of spirit following recent events, the grim past is forgotten.

Israel's God is not only without rival but he is also generous. And any man who acknowledges him may share in the rewards which he has to give—and can give, being unique and all-powerful. With him is salvation.

This argument is fundamental in the thought of the Second Isaiah. Depend not upon man, the creature, you creatures of the earth, he seems to be saying; depend rather upon the creator of all. Put not your faith in idols, the creation of men who themselves are creatures, nor even in the figments which these idols purport to represent, when God the supreme reality is at hand, when he invites you to partake.

> Wherefore spend money for what is not bread?
> Your gain for that which does not satisfy? [16]

The Second Isaiah would enlarge the fellowship of those whose God shapes history. It is better to enjoy the company of such a God than to dwell in the tents of those vanities that parade as gods. Great is the salvation in store for such as know him.

His salvation is, first of all, security, security from the sword, from pestilence, and from famine; but it is also blessing, the blessing of the womb, of the field, of the barn; and it is life and length of days. It is these earthly and homely blessings; for the age had not yet come when men thought in terms of heavenly reward.

God's salvation is these things and it is something more—something on a larger scale, commensurate with the expansive spirit and broader horizons of the Second Isaiah and with his characterization of God as the one world God—universal in time as well as in space. Salvation is the goal God has set for mankind, the realization of the divine purpose. Creation is purposive. Out of chaos God created this world;

> Not to be an empty waste did he create it.
> To be inhabited he formed it.[17]

Once because of human depravity he had been constrained to destroy with a cosmic flood all flesh and start anew with the family of Noah. Again, for men's arrogance, he had found it necessary to divide mankind into a Babel of tongues and scatter them over the earth. But this was not the goal of his desires for humanity. Eventually the family of man must again be united. Their reunion is the goal; it is salvation—a *berit 'am,* a covenant uniting men. And the new covenant is to be a firm commitment (*ḥesed*), an eternal covenant of peace.

In a flood of anger I hid
My face a moment from you.
But with unending constancy I love you,
Said God your redeemer.
For this is to me a Noah's flood.
As I promised that the flood of Noah
Would never again deluge the earth
So I have promised not to be angry with you
Or rebuke you.
The mountains may yield
And the hills totter,
But my commitment to you never,
Not my covenant of peace.
So God has said, who loves you.

Although this promise is addressed to Israel it is relevant to the theme of universal salvation both by reason of the allusion to God's promise nevermore to destroy mankind and because of its new definition of a "covenant": an enduring commitment. Such seems to be the connotation of the phrase *berit 'am:* God's purpose to unite mankind in an enduring peace.[18]

Nouns derived from the Hebrew verb *yasha'* express the idea of salvation. This idea has been considered. But the authors of Isa. 40 to 66 also use nouns derived from the verb *ẓadaḳ* to express a closely related idea. They use the nouns *ẓedeḳ* and *ẓedaḳah* in a justifiable but somewhat individual sense which can perhaps be best expressed by the words: "[God's] sure purpose," and this is a second key word for an understanding of the mission.

The expression "sure purpose" is a proposed translation of the Hebrew noun *ẓedeḳ.* It is a somewhat novel rendering and needs a bit of explaining. Perhaps it is more an interpretation than a translation, but it does give the meaning as well as the overtones of the Hebrew word here, which is what a good translation should do. The two English words together: the adjective "sure" with the noun "purpose," give the sense here of the Hebrew noun *ẓedeḳ*.

Ẓedeḳ and its feminine cognate *ẓedaḳah* are, of course, the words which usually mean "righteousness." *Ẓedaḳah* is usually paired with *mishpaṭ,* "justice." And the words *ẓedeḳ* and *ẓedaḳah* are used a number of times by the later Isaiahs with this familiar and usual meaning, for example:

> Who swear . . . not in truth and not in
> the right [*biẓedaḳah*].
>
> Preserve justice and do right [*ẓedaḳah*].
>
> As a people which has done right [*ẓedaḳah*]
> And not abandoned the just order of its God.

In these and other passages in Isaiah the noun is used in the familiar sense of "righteousness" and "right." [19] But especially the Second Isaiah, and others probably under his influence, gave it another sense in which both "sure" and "purpose" figure.

The connotation "sure," i.e., "assured, unerring," is unmistakably present in many of the occurrences of the word in chapters 40 to 66 of Isaiah. This connotation is a natural one in view of the usual habitat of the verb *ẓadaḳ*. The verb is at home in the law courts and it is associated with the winning of a case at law. The court distinguishes the winner from the loser in a case at law with forms of the verbs *ẓadaḳ* and *rashaʿ*. The language occurs, for example, in Deut. 25:1, which reads: "If there is a case between men and it comes to court and the court decides the case and declares one the winner and declares one the loser. . . ." In this verse the expression: "And declares one the winner" corresponds to the Hebrew words *vehiẓdiḳu 'et haẓẓadiḳ*. The *ẓaddiḳ* is the "winner" in a case at law, and the *rashaʿ* is the "loser." It is, of course, assumed that the verdict is just and that the winner is the rightful winner, and the loser guilty. The language is without cynicism; right triumphs. "To be righteous, to be in the right" means a favorable verdict, connotes success. Righteousness assures victory. So the Second Isaiah:

> Let them produce witnesses and win their case [*yiẓdaḳu*];

State your case and be judged right [*tiẓdaḳ*];

At hand is he who vindicates me [*maẓdiḳi*];

My servant vindicated [*hizdik*] many[20]

By way of victory in the law courts, i.e., vindication, the noun *ẓedeḳ* came then to mean simply: victory, triumph; at any rate that is its meaning again and again in Isa. 40–55:

Who aroused from the East
That one whose footsteps victory [*ẓedeḳ*] attends?

I strengthened you, I aided you,
Sustained you with my right hand of victory [*ẓedeḳ*].

I summoned you for victory [*beẓedeḳ*]
Holding your hand. . . .

I aroused him for victory [*beẓedeḳ*].[21]

This is the way to the one connotation of *ẓedeḳ, ẓedaḳah.* Through success in the law court, the triumph of right, it came to mean success, triumph, victory. It gathered overtones of confidence, assuredness. The first element in the expression "sure purpose" has this history.

But in the word *ẓedeḳ* as the Second Isaiah employed it and others after him, a second element was unmistakably present. *Ẓedeḳ* involved purpose. One comes to this conclusion by way of the observation that *ẓedeḳ* serves many times as the parallel, which means the synonym, of *yeshaʿ, yeshuʿah,* "salvation." God commands the skies to shower *ẓedeḳ,* the soil to produce salvation (*yeshaʿ*) and *ẓedaḳah.* He proclaims:

I have brought closer my *ẓedaḳah;* it is not far,
And my salvation will not long delay.
I shall give salvation to Zion,
My splendor to Israel . . .

Near at hand is my *ẓedeḳ,*
My salvation has gone forth . . .

And my salvation will be everlasting,

My *ẓedaḳah* will not fail.

The equation *ẓedeḳ*—salvation here in the Second Isaiah echoes clearly in Trito-Isaiah, indeed at the very start:

Near at hand is my salvation,
My *ẓedaḳah* all but evident. . . .

The exuberant author of another hymnic passage, whether speaking for himself or, as is more likely, for the community, rejoices that God has clothed him "in garments of salvation," wrapped him in "a robe of *ẓedaḳah*." And the obstinate author of chapter 62 renounces silence until the *ẓedeḳ* of Zion "appears as the dawn, her salvation as a burning torch." Everywhere in these passages *ẓedeḳ—ẓedaḳah* shares some common element with salvation, that the two can be thus frequently paired.[22]

Ẓedeḳ indeed appears, like salvation, to be a divinely set goal for creation. And, in view of the other connotations of the word, it is an end the attainment of which would mean an achievement for God—fulfillment, triumph, victory—not so much the defeat of a rival as the accomplishment of a set purpose. And in fact, God's mood appears resolute and determined in several relevant passages.

My salvation will be everlasting,
My *ẓedaḳah* will not fail.

Not in secret did I speak,
In the place of a land of darkness.
I said not to the seed of Jacob
"Seek me for naught."
I am God, speaker of *ẓedeḳ*,
Who says what is true.

Turn to me and be saved
All you ends of the earth,
For I am God and there is none else;
By myself I swear it!
There has gone from my mouth in *ẓedaḳah*
A word and it shall not return:
Every knee shall do me reverence,
Every tongue confess me.

This prophet's reference elsewhere to "the right hand of" God's *ẓedeḳ* may have the same overtones of resoluteness and determination as does the firm assurance here: "I am God, speaker of *ẓedeḳ*." [23]

This word, then, which the later Isaiahs employ practically as a synonym for *yeshaʿ*, "salvation," has for them some connotations that, if they do not go farther, at any rate add definition to the concept of salvation. The word *ẓedeḳ* brings into focus that feature of salvation which is God's purposed activity. Also, because the purpose is God's, and because it is "right," it is sure. The word may properly be rendered "God's sure purpose." *Ẓedeḳ* is the difference that God makes, the *meaning* that he gives to history.

(It is incidental to the theme of the chapter, but it would be a shame to overlook the religious optimism of the later Isaiahs who, by way of the noun *ẓedeḳ,* equated the accomplishment of God's sure purpose with righteousness triumphant.)

The Second Isaiah both announced the coming of the dawn, and proclaimed in God's name:

> Near at hand is [the realization of] my sure purpose,
> My salvation has gone forth,

but he also gave content to this abstraction:

> I, God, have summoned you for a sure purpose,
> Grasping your hand, shaping you,
> And setting you up for a covenant uniting men
> **[berit ʿam],**
> For a light to nations.
>
> Teaching [*torah*] proceeds from me.
> I arouse my truth [*mishpaṭ*] as a light for men. . . .
> My arms shall arbitrate among nations.
> The coastlands put their hope in me;
> For my arm they wait.[24]

The influence of this thought, and the implications of the Second Isaiah's whole doctrine of salvation, are nowhere more clearly expressed than in the familiar, almost identical passages in Isaiah and Micah which begin with the words: "In the end of days it shall come to pass, that the mountain of the Lord's house shall be established as the top of the mountains" and continue with the thought that nations, eager to learn the ways of God and willing to abide by his decisions, shall turn to Zion, whence proceeds his revelation, for, when they do that, their swords can be beaten into ploughshares, and each man shall sit under his vine and his fig tree, none making them afraid. According to the broadest biblical formulation of the idea of salvation, this is his light which the coastlands await.[25]

And Israel has a part in the bringing of this light and this is the mission of Israel. Israel's mission is peace. Of Israel, his servant, God said:

> In faithfulness he will publish the truth.
> He himself will neither fade nor be broken
> Until he establish truth on earth.
> The coastlands wait for his teaching.

And to his servant God said:

> I make you a light to the nations,
> That my salvation may reach
> To the ends of the earth.

And the prophet, also, said of the servant:

> God's desire shall succeed through him.[26]

How the servant Israel will implement God's sure purpose, further his work of salvation, publish the truth, make known his revelation, is also suggested: "You are my witnesses, God says, and my chosen servant." The idea of Israel as a people of prophets, as God's witnesses, is integral in the thought of the Second Isaiah. The fact to which Israel must witness is the pregnant fact that Israel's God is God.[27]

Some activity other than witnessing may be implied by the words of the servant in another of the servant songs. If the text were certain there would be no doubt. He seems to say: ". . . God gave me the tongue of disciples to know to relieve the weary." This may be such activity as is further described in the context of another song: "To open blind eyes, to release the prisoner from confinement, from the prison them that sit in darkness"—unless the darkness be only symbolic, a figure for ignorance. If the darkness is not symbolic what is meant is labor on behalf of all weary victims of cruelty and oppression, on behalf of such as suffer. Indeed, it is not impossible that such activity on the part of the servant Israel and in pursuit of his mission, may be intended. Two short statements in the description of the "suffering" servant might add to the evidence that the Second Isaiah did think in terms of such a mission. For, there God says of his servant: "My servant vindicated many" and he speaks of him "interceding for the transgressors." [28]

Though according to the Second Isaiah such activity may have been a part of Israel's mission, this prophet's emphasis was, of course, upon Israel's duty to witness. Through their witnessing this prophet-people is to produce the conviction among men that Israel's God, and he alone, directs the course of human history.

This conviction has several significant implications. The first is: one God. We are inclined to take for granted the idea of one God. Actually it is of the utmost significance. It means that one purpose moves the world. If God is unrivaled there is no divided counsel. There need be no divisiveness among men. The second is: a sure hope. The purpose of a God unrivaled must succeed. Does he not say: "My counsel stands and all that I will I do"? The third is: peace. The conviction is not merely that there is one God; it is that Israel's God is God. It matters what kind of god God is. The goal of the labor of Israel's God is peace among men, a reconciled, inhabited world.

With an enthusiasm unsullied by present realities and with spirits exuberant the immediate disciples of the Second Isaiah set out upon their mission, and this was their gospel. The inducement which they offered to prospective proselytes was a share in the salvation which their God could give, salvation at the hands of a God of proven fidelity and power, at the hands of the one unrivaled God. They set out to "be a blessing." It is against the background of their generation that God's challenging summons to Abram is best understood: "I will make you a great nation . . . and make your name great; be a blessing . . . in you shall all the families of the earth be blessed." [29]

During the fifty years or so following the appearance of the

Second Isaiah and the ensuing edict of Cyrus an active proselytizing movement appears to have achieved a considerable success. Many strangers seem then to have joined the ranks of worshipers of Israel's God and even to have made their contributions toward emerging Judaism. Then, indeed, Jews were not only aware that they possessed a redeeming truth but also conscious of a God-given urge to make this truth known among the nations for their salvation.[30]

This generous desire to share gave way in the next half century, for a while, in the days of Ezra and Nehemiah to a reactionary spirit of intolerance and exclusivism, possibly the result of a new calamity. But the exclusiveness of Ezra and Nehemiah did not, in turn, go unchallenged. The book of Ruth, for example, may best be understood as a tract in defense of the proselyte, intended as a protest against Nehemiah's dissolution of mixed marriages. The classic biblical example of a proselyte is Ruth, the Moabitess. The classic biblical formula of conversion is the words of Ruth to her Judean mother-in-law, Naomi: "Your people shall be my people and your God my God." The classic biblical words of welcome to a proselyte are the words of Boaz to Ruth: "May the Lord reward you in full; complete be your recompense from the Lord God of Israel beneath whose wings you have sought refuge." According to the beautiful imagery of the author of Ruth, to become a proselyte is "to find refuge beneath the wings of God." According to this author also, the God of Israel amply rewards all who come to him. And, apparently, according to this author, no ritual obligations are assumed by the convert; Ruth is expected only to observe the loyalty expressed in her declaration.[31]

Possibly it is because Ruth is a woman, the wife of a man of Judah on whom the obligations do devolve, that nothing more is expected of her. Another biblical passage, probably also written as a protest against the reform measures of Ezra and Nehemiah, lists the duties of the proselyte at greater length but not as concretely as one could wish: "The strangers who join themselves unto the Lord" —this is a phrase which several times describes the proselyte—"to worship him and to love the name of the Lord, to be his servants, all who observe the sabbath, not profaning it and who hold fast to my covenant, them will I give entry to my holy mountain and give cause for rejoicing in my house of prayer." Nothing is clearly specified unless it be sabbath observance, but much may be implied by the expression "to worship him" and "hold fast to my covenant." [32] These may include all such ritual and ethical conduct as the Jewish author of this passage assumed to be obligatory; and "loving the name of the Lord" and "being his servants" may include everything by way of loyalty that was incumbent on a Jew by birth.

The book of Jonah is a graphic illustration of a prophetic mission to the nations. Not to Israel but to Nineveh, a city of gentiles, the unwilling prophet Jonah goes with God's word. The message he brings is the message of doom for a wicked city. But when the king and people react as is fitting, repent and turn back from the evil and violence of their ways, then "the God of the heavens . . . who made the sea and the dry land," he who is "merciful and compassionate, long suffering and abundant in faithfulness," himself repents of the intended evil and forgives the city of "six score thousand" strangers "and also much cattle" for which he had labored, and which he had made to grow.[33]

Chronologically in the Bible the last references to the mission are in the book of Daniel. If not converted, Nebuchadnezzar, Belshazzar, and Darius were, at any rate, deeply impressed by God's wondrous aid to God's faithful servants, Daniel and his companions. These four Jews had risked all for faith, and God had saved them even from a den of lions and a fiery furnace. Their example led kings to decree that in all the dominion of their kingdom men should "tremble and fear before the God of Daniel, for he is the living God . . . his dominion shall be even unto the end." [34] This last gleaming of the missionary spirit in Bible times commends the courage which stems from faith—the courage which came, in later centuries, to be known as *ḳiddush hashem,* "the sanctification of the name."

The mission idea in the Bible displays these many facets but the glowing core of the idea is the thought of the Second Isaiah that Israel is God's chosen people of prophets, destined to serve as a light to the nations, that his salvation may reach to the ends of the earth.

CHAPTER VIII

THE SHAPES OF HOPE

Hope, when there is need, can take on many shapes; like a wild animal surrounded the mind darts here and there. Some shapes are already familiar: joined bones would be clothed with flesh, a spirit would breathe in them and a nation would live again; blow after staggering blow would flatten the ravenous foes of Zion; Jerusalem would be remade all glorious—dramatic, sensational news to spread abroad; God is one and this shall be known—his salvation shall reach to the ends of the earth; accomplished shall be God's sure purpose. These, which we have contemplated, and yet other alluring prospects made somewhat less dreary the lot of the Judean exiles in Babylonia and, in time, the life also of the weak and impoverished community that clung precariously to the slopes of Jerusalem.

Out of the multiform hope that sustained the revived Judean state in the centuries following on exile two forms found their clearest expression among the later Isaiahs, the messianic and the apocalyptic. These are here briefly described.

There is a lot of stretch in the word "messianic," and we could pack into it all of the hopes which have shone on the foregoing pages and all which shall yet dawn. But we can also conceive it more narrowly and put in it only such thoughts on a kingly messiah as we find at the beginning of chapters 9 and 11 of Isaiah.[1]

Central in the hope, indeed, is the descendant of David: "the shoot from the stock of Jesse," who shall occupy "the throne of David." [2] Actually, it would be surprising if the Jewish literature of the post-exilic period contained no expectation of this sort. Recall the history of the nation: from Saul to Zedekiah it had been a kingdom; from David to Zedekiah, for more than four centuries without interruption, a member of the family of David had sat upon the throne. What then if Judah is to be a state? A state means a king, and a king comes from the stock of Jesse. There is nothing strange about this hope which centers on a king. What is strange is the fact that all of Isaiah 40 to 66, all of the chapters known as the Second Isaiah and Trito-Isaiah, contain no reference to the prospect of a Davidic king for Judah.[3] It is to chapters 9 and 11 that we must turn for examples of messianic hopes in the book of Isaiah.

At one point early in the post-exilic period the expectation that a son of David would reign over Judah appeared realistic. The prophets Haggai and Zechariah furthered a movement to restore the monarchy with Zerubbabel as Davidic king. But apparently Persia regarded this activity as equivalent to a declaration of independence and put a stop to it. At any rate, Zerubbabel appears to have been no more than a disappointing hope, never in fact a king. The failure of the movement to make him king may be the soil on which messianism flourished. Hope deferred is hope intensified. Messianism is the sublimation of the frustrated desire for—a king. Now, enhanced and exalted, the hope is for a much more than ordinary king—a king with such virtues as a king ideally might possess, a ruler truly chosen by God and divinely gifted.

The two passages are complementary. The one in chapter 11 clarifies at least two obscurities in the preceding passage. In chapter 9 some legitimate confusion exists as concerns the tenses. At the outset that passage appears to say: "The people that were walking in darkness have seen a great light"—"have seen" as though already the dawn has come. But then, the end of the passage raises a question; it suggests that the "great light" is a future prospect, a day yet to dawn: "The ardor of the Lord of hosts will accomplish this"—not "has accomplished"—"will accomplish this," as though the light is yet to rise. If we depended upon this one passage only, from chapter 9, we would not clearly know; what appears at the beginning to be a past event seems at the end to be yet expected, and we rest in indecision. But in chapter 11 there is help. In that chapter unquestionably that blessed ruler is a prospect only, no past or present reality. Chapter 11 concerns the same matter, may be the product of the same prophetic author, and it clearly looks forward, not backward. And so doing it becomes decisive for the tense of the verbs in chapter 9. The final verb in chapter 9 is the key: "The ardor of the Lord of hosts will accomplish this," i.e., "the people that walk in darkness shall see a great light." The verbs in the perfect throughout the passage are prophetic perfect. So vividly foreseen, so inevitable because God will accomplish it, the future event can be described with forms that in less exalted style describe time past. Both messianic passages look forward to days of glorious light under a God-given king.

The passage in chapter 11 contributes also to an understanding of the name of the child-king in 9:5 (6):

> For a child will be born to us,
> A son given to us,
> And the government will be upon his shoulders;
> And this will be his name:
> Wondrous Counselor, God-like Hero,
> Father Forever, Prince of Peace.

The name is, no doubt, descriptive; as his name is, so will the person be. And the description is fairly clear. And the context of the name in this passage, and the parallel in chapter 11, make abundantly clear the characterization of the expected king. The context contemplates the breaking of the oppressor's yoke, the burning of all accoutrements of war, peace unending. It contemplates authority and stability, a reign perpetual because just and right. This context warrants at least the second half of the king's name: "Father Forever, Prince of Peace." It suggests, though somewhat less particularly, the remaining attributes: "Wondrous Counselor, God-like Hero." But whatever this immediate context lacks the second passage supplies. Upon the newly given king of David's line God's spirit will rest, a spirit of wisdom and discernment, of "counsel and strength," of knowledge of God and fear of God. This description is all to be found in 11:2. The quoted words: "counsel," "strength," are cognates of "Counselor" and "Hero" in the name. And not "God" but "God-like" is here suggested by the thought that God's spirit will be "upon" him, that he will "know" God and "fear" God. The attribute of "God-like" appears as well in the following verse, in the more than human intuition, which will permit him to see what is not on the surface and to hear the unsaid. Such was the "Wondrous Counselor, God-like Hero, Father Forever, Prince of Peace" that the messianic Isaiah dreamed. This was the form of his hope: that such a one should sit upon the throne of David in the new Jerusalem.

Three observations before we leave the vision of this Isaiah: (1) There is a sense of permanence in the picture. The king will be "Father Forever"; the peace he brings will be "unending"; his reign will be "perpetual." (2) He will exercise justice, and that will be the stability of his reign. "He will judge the poor in righteousness, and decide with equity for the lowly of the land." (3) It is not Judah alone that will enjoy the security, the peace, the stability, that his reign will bring, but nature will be regenerate and the earth will be filled with the knowledge of God as is the ocean bed with its waters.

These features tie in the messianic Isaiah with certain of his predecessors. The linking of stability with the exercise of justice and the prevalence of righteousness is strongly reminiscent of what the historical Isaiah taught. The thought that this expected scion of David enthroned in Jerusalem will introduce enduring peace the whole world over is but a variant of the Second Isaiah's dream of universal salvation, the realization of God's sure purpose. Only the person of the messianic ruler, indeed, distinguishes the passages in chapters 9 and 11 from a third passage, which is the keystone in the arch of hope. This third passage, written in the spirit of the Second Isaiah, is the one which the book of Isaiah shares with the book of Micah. It is found at the beginning of Isa. 2 and Mic. 4, and its fuller form is that in Micah. It is the passage too familiar to quote which looks to that latter day when the mountain of God's house shall be the highest of the mountains, and to it nations shall turn in search of God's word, when God's justice shall lead to reconciliation, and want and fear shall prevail no more. So much for Isaiah the messianist.

Vast as the cosmos is the hope of Isaiah the apocalyptist, and—

paradoxically—as terrifying as it is vast. The major work of this Isaiah is the extended apocalyptic vision in chapters 24 to 27. These chapters are far from clear, and in their interpretation we leave unanswered many a question.

Only, indeed, by a certain courtesy can we speak of the apocalyptic vision in terms of hope. It is hopeful if one assumes development within the vision, episodes, the last of which is blessing. Stark terror is the apocalyptic mood; but it yields in the end to peace. Worlds crash and splinter. The wobbling earth grows dizzy, overturns and spills its load of corruption. But these somehow stay; in the calm that ensues they are there—the blessed.

The thread is hard to follow through the maze of forgotten allusions and private fantasies and deliberate concealment, but there is a kind of story. It resembles Noah's flood. Primeval creation then had grown stale. God saw and resolved to flush clean his corrupted earth. He opened wide the fountains below and the sluices above, and the waters raged, fifteen cubits higher than the highest peak. So he submerged all rotting flesh. Yet God was both provident and discriminating. He closed the hatch upon one man, his wife and household. The upright Noah in his bark survived to hear God's rainbow promise: "Not again shall the waters swell to a flood to destroy all flesh." And, in other words,

> Yet all the days of the earth
> Seed and harvest, cold and heat,
> Summer and winter, day and night,
> Shall never cease.

That is the old story, the story of Noah's flood at the beginning of time, told in chapters 6 to 9 of Genesis.

That story serves as pattern for the apocalypse. The cause behind the approaching cataclysm is the same:

> The earth lies polluted under its inhabitants
> For they have transgressed the laws, violated the statutes,
> Broken the everlasting covenant . . .
> Its transgression lies heavy upon it,
> And it falls and will not rise again.

The means are still the same:

The sluices are opened on high,
The very foundations of the earth tremble.

And the closed door again preserves the few:

Go, my people; enter your chambers
And close your door behind you.
Hide for a little moment
Until the indignation is past.

Again provision for restoring the population of the earth—or, if not of the earth, at least of the land:

On that day a great trumpet shall be blown,
And those lost in the land of Assyria shall come,
And those banished to the land of Egypt,
And they shall bow down to God in the
holy mountain, in Jerusalem.

Again, finally, the eternal blessing-promise:

He will forever abolish death;
And the Lord God will wipe the tear
From every countenance
And will take away from all the earth
His people's disgrace.

The parallel is striking and the probability great that the story of Noah's flood at the beginning of days went into the shaping of this vision of the end of days. Isaiah the apocalyptist drew upon that ancient myth.[4]

But the story is only the frame and the conception is cosmic. This Isaiah foresaw a day of fierce and universal judgment:

On that day God will punish
The heavenly hosts in heaven
And the earthly kings on earth . . .
And the moon will be abashed and the sun ashamed,
For the Lord of Hosts will reign
On Mount Zion, in Jerusalem,
And before his elders will his glory be.

In the same mood another writer says:

The heavens shall be rolled up like a scroll
And all their host shall fail.[5]

The powerful accents and the crashing sounds of the Hebrew original are muted in translation but the mad dance is yet revealed:

Lo, God will empty the earth and rifle it,
He will turn it over and scatter its inhabitants.
Terror and pit and snare
Upon you, O inhabitant of the earth!
It shall be that he who flees from the noise of the terror
Shall fall into the pit,
And he who comes up out of the pit
Shall be taken in the snare . . .
Broken, utterly broken, the earth,
Shattered, utterly shattered, the earth,
Staggering, very staggering, the earth,
Reeling, the earth reels like a drunken man;
It swings to and fro like a hammock.

The apocalyptist almost disputes the word of the Second Isaiah:

Not an empty waste did he create it,
To be inhabited he formed it.

Unlike the Second Isaiah, almost he sees the world revert to the chaos before the "beginning." [6]

In the word "almost" lies the hope. Noah escaped the all-destroying deluge because his goodness had won God's favor. Similarly in the apocalyptic vision a few escape the universal catastrophe, but the author of the vision is far from explicit as to why they do. Two considerations may have entered in. The author may have excepted them from the general condemnation—silently assumed they were not among the defilers of the earth. Alternatively, or also, he may have remembered they were God's people: "Go, my people! Enter your chambers, and close your door behind you." Whatever the rationale, the hope is real. "My people" will survive though the heavens collapse—survive and see the dawn of a never-ending day. To be sure, the apocalyptist is not above paradox. He can condemn to utter destruction all the earth's inhabitants and yet go on to describe the banquet which God will prepare for them in Zion:

> And the Lord of hosts will provide on this mountain for all nations
> A feast of rich foods, a feast of wine on the lees,
> Of rich foods well fatted, of wine on the lees well refined.

Not only shall the peoples (who remain when all have perished!) partake of the fabulous banquet at which God serves as host in Jerusalem, they shall share as well in the newly granted boon of eternal life. Not from the face of his people alone will God wipe the tear, not his people's disgrace alone will he remove from this earth, but:

> In this mountain he will abolish the appearance of the wrapper wrapped about all nations and the veil woven upon all peoples: He will forever abolish death. . . .

Despite himself the apocalyptist must speak in universal terms—and not thus of the judgment alone but of the day after the last day as well.[7]

Perhaps the most strikingly original feature of this apocalypse is its suggestion of eternal life and the related idea of bodily resurrection. Actually, there is very little said about either eternal life or resurrection in the Hebrew Bible, and Isaiah the apocalyptist is responsible for the most of it. Adam, in Eden, according to one feature of that myth, failed to eat of "the tree of life" and lost the chance to live forever. Accordingly, if God does not abolish death, men will go on dying. One of the later Isaiahs thought in terms of long life in the new Jerusalem: anyone who failed to reach the age of a hundred would be thought accursed. But only the apocalyptist said: He will forever abolish death. This blessed immortality has its counterpart in the final verses of the book of Isaiah, one of the rare suggestions in the Hebrew Bible of eternal torment, a passage which shares the dark and violent mood of the longer apocalypse.

> New moon after new moon and sabbath after sabbath all flesh shall come to bow down before me, God said; and they shall go out and look upon the corpses of the men who transgressed against me, for the worm that feeds on them shall never die and the fire shall never go out that consumes them. And they shall serve as an object of horror for all flesh.

This is the grim obverse of the apocalyptic hope, the promised life eternal.[8]

The other thought, companion to the hope that men would live forever, is the thought that the dead would yet arise, "awake and sing." Isaiah the apocalyptist shares this thought with the author of Daniel—and no other biblical author. Ezekiel's vision of the bones in the valley is a parable of national rebirth and not of bodily resurrection. The fact that only Daniel and the Isaiah apocalypse contain the thought suggests that it was among the last creations of the men who made the Hebrew Bible. Only subsequent intertestamental literature shows its influence. The passage in Daniel reads:

> And many of those who sleep in . . . the dust shall awake,
> These to eternal life, and these . . . to eternal horror.

And the passage in the Isaiah apocalypse says:

> Your dead shall live . . . they shall arise,
> Those who dwell in the dust shall awake and sing,
> For your dew is the dew of lights
> And the earth shall give birth to the shades.

The language is mysterious; "dew" is a kind of vital moisture, "light," as often, is symbolic of life, "shades" are wraiths or spirits. It is mysterious, but its terms point to the hope for the return of the dead—the hope of resurrection.[9]

The passage in Daniel and the Isaiah passage are not identical. In one particular the Daniel passage is vague: "many" shall awake, where the Isaiah passage is specific: "your dead" shall live. In another particular the passage in Daniel is the more explicit. The Isaiah passage does not contemplate the destiny of the newly awakened dead. At least, it says no more than that they shall "sing," whatever that activity may signify. The Daniel passage, on the other hand, knows that some awake to bliss, others to terror. Daniel has a premonition of heaven and hell.[10]

Apocalypse is the answer when there is no answer. Desperation fathers apocalypse. Apocalypse is a defeat, a giving up, a surrender. At the end of his resources, man expects no help, no salvation short of a violent irruption of the supernatural into human history. And this irruption is apocalypse. That it takes weird forms in the frantic mind is not surprising. What awakens our wonder is this: that the apocalyptist is capable of retaining a balanced sense of right: not any whim, demonic or divine, is responsible for the cataclysm, but the unbounded transgression of the earth's inhabitants. And also this: that, with a sublime faith which looks beyond the visible, he can say of God:

> You keep in perfect peace the spirit
>   of him who trusts
> If in you he trusts.
> Trust in God forever
> For God is a rock of ages.[11]

These two new forms: the messianic and the apocalyptic, took their place enduringly among the shapes of hope—contributions of prophets who confidently awaited the kingly messiah and of others who in terror invited the thunder crash of judgment. With expectations such as these they advanced the process by which the book of Isaiah became a song of consolation. These prophets are to be identified neither with the historical Isaiah nor with his legendary counterpart, not either with the Second Isaiah. They had their separate qualities and they joined their varied voices to the swelling sound.

But the eleven chapters which conclude the book resoundingly echo the hopes of the Second Isaiah, hopes spurned by his own generation.

CHAPTER IX

HOPE IS A DUTY

Two quite different causes may result in lethargy. As well as the lethargy which stems from opulence and characterizes the smugly arrogant, there is the awful lethargy of despair. Even though their message be sanguine prophets must expect disappointment.

Ezekiel's public were an apathetic lot; they were bogged down in despair. He heard what they said: "Our transgressions and sins have overtaken us; in them we waste away. How can we live?" This was soon after 586 and the fall of Jerusalem. The captive Judeans with Ezekiel in Babylonia, defeated in spirit as in battle, lay down to die. "Our bones are dry," they wailed, "our hope is lost, we perish all." In words like these they gave voice to their hopelessness. Ezekiel heard them, adopted their figure, granted they were "dead" (if so they wished) and sought to counter their despair with promise of new hope. He said that the nation would rise from its grave.[1] But there is nothing in Ezekiel to suggest that even when he spoke of life abundant he faced a responsive congregation. The repetition "We perish all!" of the desperate question "How can we live?" indeed, suggests the contrary, although it is not now possible to say how much of the prophet's spent effort separated the people's two cries. At least once his grudging tone betrays feelings of frustration:

> Not for your sake am I doing it, says the Lord God; let it be known to you. Be ashamed and abashed at your ways, O house of Israel.[2]

Though the evidence is meager it appears wholly probable that the exiles damped Ezekiel's ardor with indulgent smiles.

At any rate it was so in the next generation in exile; the Second Isaiah offered his good tidings to a strangely unresponsive public. The first Isaiah had evil things to say that made men uneasy and uncomfortable, and it is small wonder that a prophet with his message went unheard—small wonder, too, that he gave vent to his frustration in terms of bitter irony. But it was otherwise with the Second Isaiah; he had a different story to tell. And it is strange and, at first thought, unnatural that he, too, seemed to fail. But so he did. He was all eagerness and anticipation, his cup ran over. But it seemed to him, as it had seemed to Ezekiel, as it seemed to the most of the prophets, that he failed. Though his was an evangel of redemption it was to him as though he spoke to stout and stubborn minds which persistently and effectively shut him out. Impatient then, he called them "numbskulls, far from salvation." Though he summoned them to hear that God's sure purpose was soon to be realized, he saw no results. For God he had said:

> I have brought closer my sure purpose, it is not far;
> And my salvation will not long delay.
> I shall give salvation to Zion,
> My splendor to Israel,

but the people scorned all hope and the prophet's language, as he spoke for God, must remain bitter. He heard God say to them: I announced it all beforehand

> [Only] because I knew your inertness,
> That your neck is iron stiff and your forehead brass.

He summoned them:

> Hear and see, you people deaf and blind!

and then went on to lament their insensible state:

> Who but my servant is blind!
> Or deaf as my commissioned messenger!

Prophets must expect disappointment.[3]

Now, despite their own obvious misgivings, these Exilic prophets, Ezekiel, the Second Isaiah, appear from our perspective in fact to have enjoyed some measure of success. If not their rhapsodic and persuasive words, then certain events of the latter half of the sixth century were quite well calculated to produce the conviction that perhaps the prophetic promises were not mere vaporings after all. Jehoiachin's release, Babylon's fall, the edict of Cyrus, Sheshbazzar's return, the excitement about Zerubbabel, the temple rebuilt—there were some high moments that might suggest the plausibility of hope. And the partial realization of promises feeds the desire and strengthens the appetite for their total fulfillment. And the words of the Second Isaiah, in particular, together with the auspicious events that did indeed follow upon them may be the source of the air of expectancy which we find in Trito-Isaiah.

Trito-Isaiah is, of course, only a convenient way of referring to chapters 56 to 66 of Isaiah. Probably no single prophet composed them, and if one man did his name was certainly not Trito-Isaiah. The name is an invention and the implication of single authorship misleading. And yet the compositions which make up these eleven chapters do to some extent justify the designation. They have some things in common and share a certain mood. And one thing that they have in common is that they clearly show the influence of the Second Isaiah. Another thing is that, for the most part, they seem to be the product of the fifth pre-Christian century. And the mood that they share is an air of expectancy.

Though in his own mind a failure the Second Isaiah was probably responsible for this air of expectancy in the next generation. One says "probably" because surely a mere fragment of the literature of early post-Exilic times survived, and writings and authors unknown to us may quite as well be responsible, or may be also responsible along with the Second Isaiah, for this feeling that now something is about to happen, this air of anticipation, this presentiment of destiny. But, because such exuberance as his must be infectious, the probability remains.

It is with a faithful echo of the Second Isaiah that the chapters of Trito-Isaiah begin, making use, as they do, of the very terms: *yeshu'ah,* "salvation," *zedakah,* "God's sure purpose." Through the Second Isaiah God had announced:

Near at hand is my sure purpose,
My salvation has gone forth,

and through the later Isaiah now again he says:

Near at hand is my salvation,
My sure purpose all but evident.

It would surely have pleased the Second Isaiah to know that his words had really lived. Seemingly lost in outer space they had yet lodged somewhere nearer home, and for a subsequent generation they held reality. The rejected promise of the one century became the dogma of the next.[4]

This last-cited passage does not have the tone of a polemic. It seems to anticipate agreement. The author of this utterance was not alone in believing that salvation was thus near at hand. Unlike the Second Isaiah, this Isaiah was speaking to a people who also believed. He urged them, only to make the little extra human effort which might alone be needed to convert the emergent promise into splendid fact. This is the meaning of the plea:

Preserve justice and do the right,

which accompanies the repeated promise:

For near at hand is my salvation. . . .

Trito-Isaiah assumed that the people expected what he expected and that they asked only: When? and: Why the delay? and: What can we do?

That he was not alone in his expectation the following verses also suggest. In them two types of persons among the Jewish population, the castrates and the proselytes, express their concern lest they be excluded from salvation. They did not doubt, they expected the fulfillment of God's sure purpose; they were worried only that they might be left out. The prophet reassured them. Just do God's will, he said. Isa. 56:1–8 is a comprehensive invitation: Partake!

The comprehensive character of the invitation is, incidentally, another sign of the influence of the Second Isaiah. If the dimension of God's purpose was world-wide for the author of Isa. 56 it had also been so for the Second Isaiah, according to whom God was resolved:

> Every knee shall do me reverence,
> Every tongue confess me,

and generously offered:

> Turn to me and be saved
> All you ends of the earth.

Through Trito-Isaiah God only confirmed his earlier resolve, when, as the climax of this utterance in chapter 56, he said

> For my house shall be called
> A house of prayer for all peoples

and repeated the invitation: Partake!

> Preserve justice and do the right,
> For, near at hand is my salvation,
> My sure purpose all but evident.

The first of the utterances known as Trito-Isaiah clearly reveals the source of the expectation that salvation is at hand: directly or indirectly the Second Isaiah was responsible for the terms as well as for the spirit of the passage. And this same utterance is clear evidence of the widespread air of expectancy at the time of Trito-Isaiah. The new day was dawning in all its splendor before the eyes of men.[5]

Not to be overlooked is the demand with which the passage opens: "Preserve justice, and do the right," and its implication that men can nudge history, so to speak, and by acceptable conduct hasten, or, at any rate, not hinder, the dawning of the desired day. The implication of a second passage in Trito-Isaiah is the same and it is very specific. The passage is Isa. 58:1 to 12. There the answer to the question: What can we do? is as follows:

> Is not this the fast which I prefer:
> To loose the fetters of wickedness,
> To cut the bonds of the yoke,
> To free the enslaved,

And that you break every yoke?
Is it not to divide your bread with the hungry,
And that you open your home to the homeless poor,
And cover the naked when you see him
And do not hide from your own flesh? . . .

If you remove from your midst the yoke,
The pointing of the finger and speaking evil,
And give of yourself for the hungry
And satisfy the want of the afflicted. . . .[6]

This in chapter 58 is the equivalent of the formula "Preserve justice and do the right" in chapter 56. And both statements appear to be the answer to the questions: Why does the dawn delay? What can we do? That this is so in chapter 58 is suggested by the immediate continuation of the foregoing passages: If you do these things, then

Light shall break forth for you like the dawn
And healing for you shall spring forth speedily,
And your triumph shall go before
And the glory of God after you. . . .
Light shall rise for you in the darkness,
As the noonday shall be your deep darkness.[7]

These and like symbols in chapter 58 stand for "salvation" and "sure purpose" of God in chapter 56. Again the expectation, here as there. It is merely a matter of: Why not yet?

This is what they ask, aggrieved, earlier in this 58th chapter:

Why do we fast and you not see?
Why do you not heed when we afflict ourselves? [8]

People and prophet in this situation were differently oriented. What, unlike the prophet, the people thought should be effective is ritual in nature: fasting and self-mortification. But only their prescription differed—that is all; like his, it had the purpose of inviting salvation.

The words of Trito-Isaiah in this chapter and his formula in chapter 56, his broad statement: "justice," "the right," as well as his particulars: "set free the enslaved . . . divide your bread with the hungry . . . open your home to the homeless poor . . . cover the naked . . . satisfy the want of the afflicted," both agree notably with the staccato imperatives of the first Isaiah:

> Wash, be clean.
> Remove from my sight
> The evil of your deeds.
> Cease doing wrong.
> Learn to do good.
> Seek justice.
> Correct oppression.
> Secure the orphan's right.
> Take up the widow's cause.[9]

The demand was the same, but the motivation was different; and this difference is an essential difference between the first Isaiah and Trito-Isaiah. The one expected disaster, the other expected salvation. The one spoke of national calamity, the fruit of man's corruption, the other of triumph, the gift of a resolute God. The first Isaiah prescribed the works of righteousness as a means to *avert catastrophe;* Trito-Isaiah prescribed the works of righteousness as a means to earn salvation, to *invite redemption.* And of course the difference is understandable. Between the time of the one Isaiah and of the other catastrophe had fallen, an Ezekiel and a Second Isaiah had appeared with God's promise of glory, partial fulfillment had pricked the appetite, and all were expectant. Expectancy is the new note, the mood of the times of Trito-Isaiah.

To be sure, the mood of the eleven chapters is not uniform. All too frequently it seems to be one of bitter disappointment. But even the presence of disappointment testifies to the mood of expectancy. For, disappointment is inconceivable without an antecedent hope. Much of what appears in Trito-Isaiah can be understood only as the prophetic reaction to popular dismay over the nonfulfillment of cherished expectations.

Why the vision faded we cannot certainly know, but something surely happened to dash all hopes. Perhaps that fifth century about which too little is clearly known, was in fact the dreary converse of all earlier promises. At a distance we telescope history. The moments of triumph, from Jehoiachin's release to the restoration of Jerusalem's walls, span at least a century—no single lifetime; and for most men, for the most part no doubt, the triumphs were rare and life was drab and unprofitable. There were without doubt serious depressions and reverses. The edict of Cyrus and the return of some exiles would have been forgotten amid such hard times as Haggai described: "sowing much, harvesting little. . . ." The sack of Jerusalem some decades later, if the evidence is correctly interpreted, was a staggering blow.

There is more history than is on record. No available source tells of a devastating attack upon Judah between 516, when the temple was rededicated, and the middle of the fifth century, when Nehemiah heard with dismay of the desolate state of the capital city, but it can only be because the records are fragmentary. An abundance of indirect evidence converges upon the conclusion that Jerusalem suffered a grim experience then.[10] The temptation was doubtless great to abandon all hope and it became the prophet's new responsibility to cup his hand about his own still dimly burning hope and to keep alight as well what little faith yet burned in others, threatened as it was by the wind of harsh realities.

If the devastation which the following passage describes was not the result of the assumed assault upon Jerusalem early in the fifth century, it was the result of a similar calamity unrecorded and unguessed. The vividness of the language points in this context to an event much more recent than the destruction of the first Temple in 586:

Your holy cities are a wilderness,
Zion is a wilderness,
Jerusalem a desolation.
Our sanctuary, our pride,
Where our fathers praised you,
Is burned.
All our pleasant place is a ruin.[11]

This is not conventional language reminiscent of battles long ago. It is, in its context, a witness' awed description of a major catastrophe within the fifth or a later century, one which dashed hope to the ground and raised all manner of doubts in the minds of the survivors as to God's benign purposes and his power to effect them. The author of Isa. 63:7 to 64:11 (if it is one piece) was swept along in the flood of despair which followed in the wake of the catastrophe. He was sharp and impatient with his God, but he had nothing to say to restore the spirits of his fellow sufferers.[12]

We do not know how many such major calamities and minor reverses conspired to produce the mood of disappointment, but the mood is unquestionably present and, if not the author of this lamentation, others in other chapters of Trito-Isaiah did have words to say to counter a newborn despair.

First there is the author of 57:14 to 19. In v. 14 God speaks not to his people but about them. Those whom he addresses appear to be God's spokesmen, his prophets. He gives them a charge concerning his people:

> Cast up, cast up, prepare the way.
> Remove the obstacle from the way of my people.

Here it is the task and mission of a prophet to clear a way, to remove an obstacle. And what is this obstacle? In the figurative language of this passage, "obstacle" appears to symbolize bewilderment and despair. At any rate, it is to the task of removing such an obstacle in the way of his people that the author of the passage as if in obedience to the divine charge immediately turns. As against the people's bewilderment he denies that God is either remote or indifferent to their misery.

> I dwell [God says] on high in holiness,
> But [also] with the crushed and lowly
> To revive the spirit of the lowly,
> To revive the courage of the crushed.

And as antidote to their despair the prophet brings God's assurance:

> I will not contend forever . . . ;
> I will heal him . . . ,

and again:

> I will heal him.

He knows himself called to keep the failing hope alive.

The thought of a large part of chapter 59 is related to the thought of these verses in chapter 57. Like them it is directed against the growing despair. And there is in it, as in so much of Trito-Isaiah, an echo of the Second Isaiah. The Second Isaiah had phrased God's challenging query:

> Why do I come and find no one?
> Why does no one respond to my call?
> Am I too utterly weak to redeem,
> Powerless to deliver? [13]

The last, of course, was a rhetorical question. It constituted an indignant denial: of course God is not too weak. And this is the phrase which the author of Isaiah 59 picked up and employed for his own double denial:

> God is not too weak to save,
> And he is not deaf to entreaties.[14]

Such a denial could only be the answer to a contrary claim. Speaking thus the prophet could only be defending God against calumny —against the accusation: God cannot help, and the frightening surmise: God is remote and indifferent. With a knowing glance over his shoulder at the Second Isaiah, the prophetic author of chapter 59 emphatically rejected any such accusation or surmise:

> God is not too weak to save;
> And he is not deaf to entreaties.

Speaking thus he was not only defending God but also salvaging a failing hope.

The author of chapter 62, in his way, also tended the dimly burning wick. His way is notable, but his goal was the same: to keep the vision fresh, constantly to rehearse the promise. He was impatient for the consummation, and he was determined.

> For Zion's sake I will not keep quiet,
> For Jerusalem's sake I will not hold my peace,
> Until her triumph appears as the dawn,
> Her salvation as a burning torch.
> And nations shall behold your triumph

And all kings your glory;
And you shall be given a new name
Which God's own mouth will designate . . .
You will no more be termed "Forsaken,"
Nor your land termed "Desolate"
But you will be called "God's Delight"
And your land "Espoused,"
For God will take delight in you
And your land will be espoused. . . .[15]

The words translated "triumph" and "salvation" are *ẓedeḳ* and *yeshu'ah,* words already familiar in this context. Long ago and repeatedly God had promised all of what the prophet here recalled and the prophet was resolved only that it should not be overlooked. How far this resolution went appears in the following verses. But a brief note on v. 4 should come first. The name "God's Delight" is not a translation of the received text; it is based on a necessary correction of that text. The correction involves the omission of one Hebrew consonant, reading *ḥefeẓ-yah* in place of *ḥefẓi-bah.* The change is necessary because the received text (from which we get the name Hephzibah) means "My delight is in her," "my" being God's, and this would be the only place in the first half of the chapter where God speaks. Until v. 8, where he is introduced as speaker, he is consistently spoken of as "he" or "the Lord" or "your God." The recognition that "my delight" is an error and that "God's delight" is the original text removes all possibility of confusion here. Down to v. 8, then, the prophet alone is speaking, and vv. 8 and 9 are God's reaffirmation of his former oath, the basis of the prophet's hope.[16]

Until God is introduced as speaker in these last two verses the prophet has the word, and it is he who with set jaw vows: "I will not keep quiet . . . will not hold my peace" and who still is speaking in the spirited verses which follow:

Upon your walls, O Jerusalem,
I have stationed watchmen.
Neither by day nor by night,
Never shall they hold their peace.
You remembrancers of God

Allow yourselves no rest;
Yea, and give him no rest
Until he establish it,
Until he make Jerusalem
An object of praise in the earth.[17]

This man, impatient, calls God to account; he incites his fellows to do likewise, to importune God unceasingly, denying him peace, so long as his promise lies neglected. The prophet and the followers whom he exhorts are clinging desperately to the receding vision, believing against all evidence in the long dormant promise. Still they hope—they are resolved to hope—for the dawn of God's sure purpose with Zion, the coming of the radiant salvation. Hopeful, expectant, they are yet not passive; they do not lie down and wait supine. They invite the future. They undertake with clamorous prayer to bring on the "time to come." Their spirit and their behavior are somewhat unusual, though not unique. To the author of Isa. 62 hope is a contest.[18]

The Second Isaiah never doubted God's ability to fulfill his word and accomplish his purpose. His classic expression of the thought was the word of God:

My counsel stands,
And what I will I do.

In concise nonfigurative terms the Second Isaiah thus phrased his confidence in the imminent consummation of God's sure purpose.[19]

In a later century and a later chapter, the last in the book of Isaiah, a prophet rephrased the thought in deep and elemental symbolism. The author derived his fantasy from the process of birth. He spoke of his times as pregnant with the future and of his God as the life-giver. His creator God stills all dark doubts. No panic! The womb will yield its fruit and the issue will be sound.

Does such a one as I bring to delivery and
withhold the fruit? . . .
Do I, the life-giver, bind up the womb? . . .[20]

With feelings that probe deeper than artistry the writer of this passage drew upon fantasies which attend the biological source of human anxiety, the perilous moment of birth itself, for the symbol he had to find to allay all human anxiety and to overcome despair. His symbol was profound but a symbol it was and what he meant by the expected birth was the salvation long promised, the fulfillment of God's sure purpose.

It was probably not long after Trito-Isaiah found this symbol that "Isaiah the apocalyptist" borrowed the figure without changing the meaning. To the complaint of the people:

> We were pregnant, in labor—as though we bore wind!
> We have not wrought salvation on earth,
> The world's inhabitants have not dropped from
> the womb—

to their complaint God replied through the apocalyptist:

> Your dead shall live. . . .[21]

There as before, God rejected the implication that the times will remain eternally pregnant. Because of God's unrivaled power, the expectant earth beyond all doubt shall experience the birth of salvation. The apocalyptic passage in chapter 26, one of the few in the Bible which suggest resurrection, appears to have derived its powerful symbolism from the passage in the last of the chapters known as Trito-Isaiah.

In those chapters, then, and in nearly every one of them, we meet the characteristic mood, the air of expectancy.

Now there is something special about this air of expectancy in these Trito-Isaianic chapters. The discovery of its special essence was the goal of the survey in the foregoing paragraphs and the discovery now rewards the search. An expecting, a hoping, may be just that and nothing more—a mere passivity, a waiting, openmouthed, an infantile expectancy. But such is not the spirit of Trito-Isaiah. He and all who are infected with his spirit cherish a hope that is active, a creative expectancy. That is the something special: a hope that is active, a creative expectancy, pervades the chapters.

Hope is a duty. With imperatives God addresses the leaders of a despondent community:

> Cast up, cast up, prepare the way.
> Remove the obstacles from the way of my people.

To the author of this passage it is the people's hopelessness which looms as an obstacle in their way, and through him God commands its removal. God demands hope.[22]

And the prophetic authors of Isa. 56 to 66 in splendid succession devote themselves to the fulfillment of this divine command. On God's behalf they call for hope. We have seen it. The author of Isa. 59 insists:

> God is not too weak to save;
> And he is not deaf to entreaties.

And, appealing to the deepest recesses of man's consciousness, another author speaks up for God:

> Does such a one as I bring to delivery
> and withhold the fruit?
> Do I, the life-giver, bind up the womb?

With bold affirmation they thought to keep expectation alive and by such means to invest it with substance.[23]

A creative hope is yet more. It expresses itself in conduct. And the Trito-Isaianic chapters contain several attempts at defining the conduct which implements hope. There are three such attempts in chapter 58. There is the definition which concludes the chapter; reverting to an earlier emphasis, its author invokes Sabbath observance as man's part in the task ahead. According to him, refraining from one's own pursuits on God's holy day and calling the Sabbath a delight will insure the fulfillment of all hope. A second prescription is that of the populace whom the writer quotes. According to their words they propose by fasting and self-mortification to invite the dawn. When they ask:

> Why do we fast and you not see?
> Why do you not heed when we afflict ourselves?

they describe what, according to their lights, they, the prophet's public, have been doing to implement their hope. The third prescription, of course, is that of the author of the chapter. Opposing the people's ritually oriented answer (as well as the answer which now appears at the end of his chapter) he prescribes conduct strikingly similar to that which God demanded by the hand of the first Isaiah: morality, ethical conduct conforming to the standard of social justice. It was this which man could do to implement his hope as his part in God's work of salvation.[24]

Three times in these chapters the thought occurs that moral conduct is the key which will unlock the gates of hope: here in chapter 58, in the next chapter, and at the very beginning of Trito-Isaiah. The author of chapter 59 advocates justice and integrity; he believes it is the lack thereof that has postponed the day. God is not too weak to save (he says),

> But your iniquities have kept
> You apart from your God,
> And your sins have turned him
> Away from you, that he hears not.
> For your hands are gory with blood,
> Your fingers with guilt;
> Your mouth has spoken falsehood,
> Your tongue uttered wickedness.

And he continues in this vein. His words, too, are strongly reminiscent of the first Isaiah. The third passage is phrased as a commandment:

> So God has said:
> Preserve justice and do the right,
> For, near at hand is my salvation . . .[25]

Again the ancient moral demand—this time in broad terms: "Preserve justice . . . do the right," *mishpaṭ, ẓedaḳah*. Again in the concluding chapters of the book, among the latest, resounding tones also from the first, the earliest Isaiah.

Now, if hope is a duty, if faith is moral activity, if confidence is not a sitting still but a doing, if expectancy is a creating, then prophetic challenge and prophetic consolation are not at odds; they have achieved a synthesis. The two prophetic emphases flow on together. So strong, indeed, was the sense of obligation aroused by the earlier prophets, the first Isaiah among them, that this development was inevitable: it had to be recognized and acknowledged that hope, too, is a duty. To the writers collectively known as Trito-Isaiah it was obvious. Hope was not so much a heavenly gift as a divine requirement. God commanded these prophets to clear the way, and they, faithful to their charge, decried despair, demanded hope. And their hope was half determination. They and their people were frontiersmen of the spirit looking to the future with a creative expectancy.

CHAPTER X

"AND ALL OUR VIRTUES"

But hope is hard. It may be a setting of the jaw and a gritting of the teeth. It may be a squaring of the shoulders and a stubborn determination, not indeed unlike rebellion. In the midst of a lament among the chapters known as Trito-Isaiah there is a brief passage which hints at the presence of just such a defiant mood, and this note concerns that passage.

The text of the passage in part is very difficult. If one reads it in an English translation one has no idea that a mood of defiance lurks behind the words. As a matter of fact, if one reads it in an English translation one has hardly an idea even as to what the passage means. The half verse Isa. 64:4b is so obviously meaningless even in the Hebrew that the text can only be at fault. And the first task of the interpreter must be to speculate upon the original form of the text.

That the text of this half verse is not satisfactory becomes evident when one looks at the translations. The King James version has:

> Behold thou art wroth for we have sinned.
> In those is continuance and we shall be saved.

The later Revised version is no better:

> Behold thou wast wroth, and we sinned.
> In them have we been of long time, and shall we be saved?

These translations do not agree with each other and neither makes any reasonable sense. But it is the Hebrew text, not the translator, that is at fault—as the Revised version indeed admits on the margin: "The text is probably corrupt."

The ancient translations are no help in restoring the text. The Targum, Peshitta, and Vulgate all appear to be translations of the same confused text that has come down to us in the Hebrew; and the Greek translation went its own way. After the equivalent of "Behold you were angry and we have sinned" the Greek translation continues "therefore we have gone astray." This cannot be a translation of the received Hebrew text or of anything nearly resembling it. It sounds as if the translator abandoned the text as untranslatable and invented a substitute. His was a good invention because it closely approximates the spirit of what seems to have been the original text. Somewhat boldly he let the prophetic author suggest: because God was angry the people went astray. He may have come to this thought by way of the even more challenging query which occurs in 63:17, a few verses earlier in the same composition: "Why, O God, do you make us stray from your ways?" The Septuagint translator impressed by the tone of that earlier question apparently sensed the same spirit in the untranslatable words of 64:4b, and his "translation" is merely his surmise of what should have stood there. The translator's instinct was good but his guess so little resembles the received text that it is of no use for the restoration of the original.

The best current attempt to restore that text is that of Paul Volz. In place of *bahem ʿolam vannivvasheaʿ*, "In them have we been of long time and shall we be saved?" Volz has suggested reading *beheʿalemeka vannirshaʿ*, which he takes to mean: because you hid yourself we became guilty. In transliteration this suggestion may appear radical but actually the difference between the received consonant text and the proposed reading is slight, as a matching of the Hebrew letters of the two readings will show. The proposed *beheʿalemeka* is a *niphʿal* form of *ʿalam*, "to hide." The verb is very much in place here and, with a minor modification only, the proposal is to be accepted. It is the proposed passive form of the verb which is not entirely suitable. That form is less suitable than the reflexive would be. The proposed form means "because you were hidden." "When you hide yourself" would be better. With this modification, reading *behitʿallemeka,* Volz's suggestion is good and it is to be adopted. Of the original reading the received text has lost the one letter pronominal suffix *-ka,* and misread or miscopied two letters, a *mem* for a *tav* in the first word and a *vav* for a *resh* in the last.[1]

The proposed reading is not only very nearly the same, consonant for consonant, as the preserved text but it also yields a most suitable sense. It is a completely synonymous parallel to the preceding line. This becomes apparent on closer inspection.

The *hithpaʿel* of the verb *ʿalam* means: to hide oneself, turning away, not wanting to help. It is used of men hiding, in the humane legislation in Deut. 22: "You shall not see the ass or the ox of your brother fallen on the way and hide yourself from them. Help him to get them up." It is used of men also in a neighboring chapter in Trito-Isaiah:

> That you cover the naked when you see him
> And do not hide from your own flesh.

And it is also used of God in a psalm:

> Hear my prayer, O God;
> Do not hide yourself from my petition.

This is the sense in which the verb is used in the proposed reading: "When you hide yourself." [2]

"When you hide yourself" is really only another way of saying "when you are angry," and as such it forms a perfect parallel to that very expression in the preceding line. By hiding himself God expresses and implements his anger. The more common expression is "hiding his face." Only two verses later, in this same composition, the author complains to God: "You hid your face from us." And in another Trito-Isaiah chapter God's anger and the hiding of his face are similarly paired: "I was angry and smote him, hiding in anger." [3]

When, in the Bible, God "hides his face" he may (a) just be (humanly) forgetful or (b) unmindful. It is worse if (c) he is consciously casting one off, abandoning or rejecting his people or servant, (d) leaving him at the mercy of his enemies. Worst of all

(e) when he hides his face in angry opposition. This may (f) cause terror and (g) even death.[4]

The proposed reading: "when you hide yourself," parallel as it here is to the thought: "you were angry," stands near the pole of greatest intensity in this scale of dreadful connotations.

The other expression in the proposed reading, *vannirsha'*, needs also to be understood. What this word means here depends upon the meaning of the preceding line, because the two lines are parallel. The preceding line is commonly translated: Behold you were angry and we sinned. But this translation is not quite right. The trouble with it is that it suggests no relationship between the two ideas: God's anger and our sinning. The other familiar translation is also inaccurate: You are angry for we have sinned. This latter translation does suggest a relationship between the two ideas but it suggests a wrong one. It makes good sense and it is quite in line with the teaching of post-Exilic orthodoxy. The thought is expressed, for example, in Josh. 22:18: "If you rebel against God to-day, to-morrow he will be angry with the whole congregation of Israel." Even in the Trito-Isaianic composition here considered, a part of which reflects the prevailing orthodoxy, the causal nexus between man's disobedience and God's anger finds expression:

> Be not exceedingly angry, O God.
> Do not remember transgression forever.[5]

There is certainly nothing wrong with the idea—it is only that the text of 64:4b cannot be translated: You are angry for we have sinned. It does not say: You (now) are angry (because, first) we sinned. What it seems to say is actually just the reverse: Behold you were angry and (then, or and so) we sinned. The usual translations fail to take into account the fact that the second verb in the Hebrew text follows upon the first as a consecutive imperfect.

The consecutive imperfect, following naturally the preceding perfect, expresses the conditions which represent the logical consequence of what preceded. With this same force, the consecutive imperfect is used, for example, in Gen. 39:2: "And the Lord was with Joseph and he was [i.e. and so he was] a prosperous man," and in Gen. 1:3: "And God said 'Let there be light' and there was [and, as a consequence of his saying it, there was] light." So also here: Behold you were angry and (as a consequence) we sinned. The construction requires this causal nexus rather than the reverse.[6]

Nevertheless it must be admitted that the resulting sense is somewhat strange. The idea that men may be brought to sin as a consequence of God's anger is not, in itself, impossible. As a matter of fact, another verse in this same composition might seem to support such an interpretation. In 63:17, in their agony the people ask:

> O Lord, why do you make us stray from your ways
> And harden our heart that we fear you not?

quite as though they must hold God responsible for their apostasy. David might have made the same plea, that angry with Israel God misled him and made him guilty of the offense of counting the people.[7]

The idea is not in itself impossible, but another thought in close proximity to the questionable line makes it improbable that it really means: As a consequence of your anger we sinned. That other thought occurs in the very next half verse:

> And we have all become as an unclean thing
> And all our virtues as a filthy rag.

These words are not an admission of guilt. They refer to the appearance only of guilt, for note, it is their "virtues" which are "as a filthy rag." Though, indeed, they are compared to a filthy rag it is "virtues" not sins that are thus compared. In a confession or admission of guilt the words "and all our virtues" would be quite out of context.

The line is most vivid and its meaning beyond question. "We have all become as an unclean thing" is a proper translation—not "as one that is unclean." The parallel to "an unclean thing" here is not a person but an object, "a filthy rag." Traditionally this latter expression refers to a garment soiled with menses, a symbol of ritual impurity. For the word translated "virtues" most translations have "righteousnesses," despite its barbarous sound. The rendering "and all our virtues" is taken from C. C. Torrey. Virtues are not otherwise so compared but sins are—in Isa. 1:18: "If your sins be as scarlet. . . ." The sense of the line in 64:5 is quite clear—and it is not an admission of guilt.[8]

For this reason it is at least improbable that the foregoing line contains such an admission and means: as a consequence of your anger we sinned. There is ambiguity here and it lies in the word translated "we sinned." Actually the verb so translated occurs in this line in one of its less common meanings—less common but well attested. The verb *ḥaṭa'* has this special meaning twice in the Joseph story in Genesis. There, Judah, guaranteeing the safe return to his father of the young Benjamin, says: "If I do not bring him back to you I will forever stand condemned." The verb in question has the meaning "to stand condemned," "to assume the blame," "be convicted by the circumstances." It does not have the usual meaning: "to sin." [9]

Using this less common meaning of the verb *hata'* in the verse in Trito-Isaiah we may then render it so:

> Behold, because you were angry we are presumed guilty.

And if we understand this part of the line in this way then we are ready for the remainder of the line:

> You hide yourself and . . . [what?]

After all that has been said the conclusion of this thought must be ". . . we stand convicted":

> Behold, because you were angry we are presumed guilty;
> You hide yourself and we stand convicted.

The last words are a legitimate translation of the restored Hebrew word *vannirsha'*. This meaning for the verb *rasha'* is not uncommon. The *hiph'il* often means "to convict." Moreover, it frequently refers to the unjust conviction of the innocent. Job, for example, complains:

> Even though I am righteous my own mouth must condemn me.

And in a passage in Exodus the two verbs *ḥaṭa'* and *rasha'* occur together in a meaning similar to that required in the Trito-Isaiah passage. After hail has destroyed all the vegetation of Egypt what

Pharaoh says to Moses and Aaron can not be taken as an admission of guilt. Pharaoh can be saying no more than this: (By the desolation which the hail has wrought) this time I am presumed guilty; Yahveh wins his case, and I and my people stand convicted. And the manner in which Job and Pharaoh use the words in the two passages here cited confirms the reading and interpretation proposed for the passage in Trito-Isaiah. The stricken community, not conscious of any wrongdoing commensurate with its sufferings, neither confesses nor laments, but in the striking words of the two half verses bitterly complains:

> Behold, because you were angry we are presumed guilty;
> You hide yourself and we stand convicted.
> Yea, we are all become as an unclean thing
> And all our virtues as a filthy rag.[10]

Now, if this interpretation is right, a rare spirit breathes through this composition—one akin to the spirit of the author of Job. Trito-Isaiah here, spokesman of a people who are crawling in the dust, dares to point an accusing finger at God. Because of a calamity which in his unprovoked wrath God has let befall his people, this people has become wrongly suspect. Judea, here Job's national counterpart, is, like Job, presumed guilty, convicted by the incredible circumstances that foes have laid low its capital city and sanctuary. The undated occasion for the prophet's complaint has been considered already. Some overwhelming catastrophe, more recent than the deportations of 597 and 586 and the destruction of Jerusalem, evoked the word picture in 64:9:

> Your holy cities are a wilderness,
> Zion is a wilderness,
> Jerusalem a desolation.
> Our sanctuary, our pride,
> Where our fathers praised you,
> Is burned.
> All our pleasant place is a ruin.

Probably, as we have noted, Jerusalem was besieged and taken, plundered and burned, not only by the Babylonians in 586 but again early in the fifth century, and it is to this event that Trito-

Isaiah refers. Though the occasion may be uncertain, its nature is wholly apparent, and the magnificent composition Isa. 63:17 to 64:11 was written while the survivors were yet reeling from the suddenness and force of the blow.[11]

There is bewilderment in the piteous cry in 63:19.

> We have been as those for long not ruled by you,
> Even as those not bearing your name.

The people reveal no awareness that they have been unfaithful—on the contrary, inexplicably God has cast them off. It is as if he had led them astray, lured them to a fateful error, as indeed they have suggested just a few lines earlier:

> Why do you make us stray from your ways
> And harden our heart that we fear you not?

And this bewilderment is certainly responsible in part for the unorthodox spirit which breathes in the utterance.

To be sure, the author of this composition cannot elude wholly the conventions of his medium. He is writing in the shadow of the tragedy, and he casts his thoughts in the mold of a "Klagelied," a psalm of public lamentation. He is writing a lament; and in the pattern of a lament, an admission of guilt is a usual if not essential element. It is not at all surprising, then, to find in his composition some reference to sin and guilt, and even in the verses which follow immediately upon the bold words of 64:4b-5a:

> You have delivered us up to our sin.
>
> Our sin like the wind is bearing us away.
>
> Remember not sin forever.[12]

The presence of allusions to sin is not surprising. What is surprising is this: that the author is able sufficiently to escape the bonds of the form to air thus openly his grievances against God—even to say in the words of our passage:

> Behold, because you were angry we are presumed guilty;
> You hide yourself and we stand convicted.
> Yea, we are all become as an unclean thing
> And all our virtues as a filthy rag.

Most startling of all is the last of these phrases: "and all our virtues as a filthy rag." "All our virtues," those acts even which we count meritorious, even they find no acceptance; nothing we can do is good enough. Nothing is good enough.

Two or three centuries earlier, in the eighth pre-Christian century, the first Isaiah would have called this spirit stubborn pride, stiff-neckedness, or worse. And even in its own historical context, in the fifth century, the attitude is, to say the least, heretical. Yet this spirit does exist, and not in isolation. The author of this passage is only one of a company of stout hearts who, like Job, hold fast to their righteousness.[13]

CHAPTER XI

"GIVE HIM NO REST": THE PROMETHEAN ELEMENT IN BIBLICAL PRAYER

The Prometheus among the prophets was the author of Isa. 62. He undertook to force God's hand. His weapon was prayer.

Men who pray figure prominently in Hebrew Scriptures and Jewish tradition. But these men do not all pray alike. Some of them pray in a mood of submissive penitence—this is the commoner, the approved way. Others, strange though it sounds, stand up to God in prayer and demand their due. In distress and danger, they defend their rights, the rights of men, against the encroachments of an arbitrary and tyrannical God. We may call them Promethean. In the modern romanticized sense of the term, these men and the spirit of their prayer are Promethean. It is no dominant theme but there is a considerable amount of biblical material which may be called Promethean.

The sources are of two kinds. First, there are the narratives—the tales of colorful personalities who figure in the Bible story and play the Promethean role. And secondly, there are the Promethean prayers; our interest is in the motifs of these prayers. The persons in bold color illumine the manuscript on which the words of prayer are written.

Not all of the biblical personages, real or mythical, who challenge divine authority, illustrate our theme. "The infernal serpent" and "all his host of rebel angels" (the Lucifers of the Bible) who rivaled or sought to supplant God or to share his prerogative—these ... separate category.

The Promethean personalities do not, for example, include that mythical figure "Helal, son of the morning" nor his fellow who "walked up and down in the midst of the stones of fire" in the "mountain of God" nor yet those "sons of God" whose forbidden commerce with "daughters of men" failed to lift the veil of man's mortality, instead of which they themselves were doomed to "die like men." [1]

Nor do they include those paler shadows of the stars, the men who questioned God's primacy and sought to frustrate his decrees, not "our grand parents" who, had they only eaten of the right tree, might have compelled God to share his immortality, not the ill-fated builders of the "tower," not, in later generations, that boastful axe the stouthearted king of Assyria and his successor the king of Babylon, who made the earth tremble and kingdoms quake, nor yet the "virgin daughter of Babylon" who said in her heart "I am unrivaled," and not the prince of Tyre, proud because of his beauty, who said "I am a god." Fascinating though they are themselves, these are not the Promethean figures associated with biblical prayer.[2]

It is not, indeed, among the rebels that we find them, but among the faithful. They hold fast to God even while they question his decrees. Though they defy, they do not deny him.

It is seldom, too, that we find them in physical contest with God. Isolated are the obscure narratives of Jacob who struggled through a dark night with God and prevailed, and Moses the "bridegroom of blood," whom also God proved at Massah, with whom God strove at the waters of Meribah.[3]

But we do find them among the numerous accounts of men wrestling with God in prayer; it is these which illustrate our theme.

Two biblical passages list persons apparently credited with more than ordinary influence, persons whose prayers God cannot lightly ignore. In the one, speaking to Jeremiah, God denies that either Moses or Samuel, much less the prophet himself, could sway him toward the faithless nation and, in the other, similarly, God reveals to Ezekiel his intransigence: In a time of retributive calamity, Noah, Daniel, and Job would intercede with him in vain; though for their own righteousness the three might themselves escape, they could not rescue any others. But both passages imply that if the prayers of any mortals could avail, it would be the prayers of these named heroes of virtue: Moses, Samuel, Jeremiah, Noah, Daniel, and Job.[4]

Properly the name of Moses leads all the rest; for he more often than others and more successfully takes issue with God. When, after they had made the golden calf, God decided to destroy the stiff-necked people, Moses produced two reasons why he should not do so. And, whether because of the cogency of his argument or because it was Moses who presented it, God acceded to his request. And when the people, alarmed at the majority opinion of the spies, determined to return to Egypt and God lost patience, again it was Moses who intervened and again "the Lord said: 'I have pardoned according to your word.' "[5]

Probably it was the record of these incidents which, in later centuries, created the Rabbinic legends of a Promethean Moses. Two such legends refer, in fact, to the scene at Sinai:

An authority in the Babylonian Talmud comments on the somewhat remarkable words spoken by God to Moses in Exod. 32: "Now therefore let me alone." This teacher exclaims: "Were it not written in the Bible, it could not have been said. Moses held on to God as a man his friend by the garment and said, 'Lord of the world, I will not let you go until you forgive and pardon them.' "[6]

An aggada in the Palestinian Talmud, less restrained than the Bible, permits Moses on this occasion in fact to prevail over God in physical contest. When God was about to hand the two tablets of stone to Moses, God still grasping them above and Moses below, the people sinned with the golden calf and God resolved to withhold the gift. Indeed the precious ten commandments would never have come into man's possession had not Moses then, at the last moment, with sheer physical strength, actually wrested the tablets from the reluctant fingers of God.[7]

The reference to Samuel as an intercessor comparable to Moses may be related to the passage in the first book of Samuel where his persuasiveness is concisely noted: "And Samuel cried out unto the Lord for Israel and the Lord answered him." In its present form, this narrative makes him responsible for a military victory; but originally Samuel may have prayed successfully for rain—here as in chapter 12 where there can be no doubt of it. There Samuel calls for rain and it falls on that very day.[8] At the time of the drought to which Jeremiah's list pertains, however, so great was the offense that neither a Moses nor a Samuel would have done any good. Nor yet a Jeremiah. The prophet Jeremiah, too, deserves his place among these bolder spirits; repeatedly in times of trouble he prayed for the people and repeatedly God denied him the high privilege of prayer.[9]

If we ask why—why was Jeremiah forbidden to pray? Could God not merely turn a deaf ear to his prayers?—we may be left with the surmise that God did indeed find it hard to wave aside his prayers and the prayers of men like him. And if we ask further why God cannot simply refuse their petitions, we are reminded of Abraham of whom it is said: "he believed in the Lord and he accounted it to him for righteousness," even as it is said of Moses that he found favor in God's eyes—and of Noah.[10]

Noah heads Ezekiel's list of potential mediators. If, at such a time, any mortal could persuade God to spare his fellows, Ezekiel implies, it would be such a one as Noah. Of him it is said: "Noah had found favor in the eyes of the Lord," and it is also said: "Noah in his generations was a righteous man and blameless." [11]

Along with Noah, Ezekiel names Daniel and Job. But, since the biblical books which celebrate these two heroes of the spirit are most certainly later than Ezekiel's reference and are, therefore, no sure guide to his meaning, all we may confidently say about Daniel and Job is that already in Ezekiel's day (if not before), they enjoyed a reputation like that of Noah, whose virtue had set a limit to God's freedom and prevented the extinction of mankind.[12]

Noah became the pattern for other later heroes, too—those who on the "last day" will survive the cosmic catastrophe, those in the Isaiah apocalypse instructed, like Noah, to enter their chambers, to close the door behind them, and to hide "until the indignation is past." [13]

Abraham ranks with Moses and with Noah among the biblical personages whose persuasive powers God had to acknowledge.

Abraham would surely have snatched Sodom from destruction if only those few—ten, even—had been worthy of his prayer.[14] But that was while he lived. In the Hebrew Bible it is living men who lift the people's prayer to God, not angelic intermediaries nor departed saints. The author of Isa. 63 toys with the idea that still the patriarchs of old may serve as intercessors only to reject it and direct his eyes to God, himself the redeemer: ". . . Abraham knows us not," he lets the people say,

> And Israel does not acknowledge us;
> You, O Lord, are our Father,
> Our Redeemer from everlasting is your name.[15]

Now our sources afford glimpses not only of persons who strove with God in prayer but also of the strife itself. And for news of the strife, we can turn to other persons than those who are mentioned by name—others in addition to Abraham, Moses, Samuel, and Jeremiah. The Promethean figures include many an unnamed psalmist and advocate, not least among them one or more of the later Isaiahs, whose personalities are preserved only in the daring words they spoke. The words of these named and unnamed heroes reveal a number of recurrent themes, propositions with which a man armed himself when he approached God in unequal contest. These propositions are not the more common expressions of submissive piety and humble petition. Like the figures in the narratives, these are the compelling reasons, the cogent postulates, the barbed weapons in the arsenal of prayer.

Prominent among these arguments is the appeal to God's self-interest. If unwilling to act on behalf of the individual or the nation in distress, God is advised then to act for his own sake, for his name's sake. This is the first of the two arguments with which Moses persuades God not to destroy the nation worshiping the calf. "What will people say?" Moses asks. "Egypt, for example. That you delivered the Israelites from bondage only to slay them in the wilderness." In the incident of the spies, he repeats this argument more pointedly still: "What will they say? That it was for want of ability to fulfill your promise that you slew them in the desert." [16]

In a spirit of independence, the one who uses the argument "for his name's sake" renounces any claim for special treatment. "I am not," he seems to be saying, "asking any favors. I merely call your attention to the fact that in your own interest you must act in such and such a manner."

> Arise, O God, plead your own cause;
> Remember your reproach all the day at the
> hand of base men. . . .[17]

As a matter of fact, the argument "for his name's sake" is theologically respectable. It is not, as it may sound, an appeal to God's vanity. It is an aspect of the larger concept of universal salvation, which has to wait until God's sovereignty is universally accepted. In this context God is expected to be jealous for his good name with an altruistic jealousy.[18]

But the theme of God's own interest is given a special twist, somewhat less respectable, in Psalms 6, 30, and 88. Assuming as they do that human adulation is pleasing to God, the authors of these psalms remind him, with what amounts to blackmail, that none but the living render him praise—and it is therefore not to his interest to surrender his worshipers to death.

> For in death there is no remembrance of you;
> In the nether-world who will give you thanks?
>
> What profit is there in my blood when I go down to the pit?
> Will the dust praise you? Will it declare your truth?
>
> . . . Do the shades arise and give you thanks?
> Is your mercy declared in the grave?
> . . . Are your wonders known in the dark?
> Your righteous deeds in the land of forgetfulness? [19]

The second decisive argument with which Moses confronts God in the molten calf affair is the reminder that God himself has, so to speak, restricted his own freedom. Once in the past, when he chose Abraham and the seed of Abraham forever, God exercised his freedom—and in doing so limited that same freedom henceforth. His choice then became a commitment for the future. "Remember," Moses says, "remember Abraham, Isaac, and Israel, your servants to whom you swore by your own self and said to them: I will multiply your seed as the stars of heaven, and all this land that I have spoken of I will give unto your seed, and they shall inherit it forever." Again and again, as in this argument of Moses, men refer to God's commitment not only to Israel in general but also specifically to the house of the kings of Judah by way of their founder, David.[20]

They had what amounts to a technical term for the divine commitment; they called it a *ḥesed*. To designate God's alleged commitment to the patriarchs, they used this term along with the word *berit* ("covenant") and *shebuʿah* ("promise"), but to designate his commitment to the line of David, they definitely preferred the term *ḥesed*. Having the tradition of these divine commitments, it is perhaps understandable if the presumed beneficiaries sought the presumed benefits. They could, by the way (and this is a significant aside)—they could have respect only for a God whose word was sure.[21]

At times this second argument appears disguised as a hymn. Do not be misled. The recital of God's former mercies is not a mere mentioning for gratitude. Since to the faithful it is axiomatic that God is consistent, his past conduct is also a warranty for the future. Having not only pledged his word (*ḥesed*) but also embarked upon a matching course of action, God is not now at liberty to depart from that course, for in him caprice would be intolerable. Therefore, if God acted as, in a lament, his worshipers claim, the mention of past favors, so different from his recent inexplicable conduct, is not praise but a reproach and the hymn not wholly innocent. Hear just one of a number of such hymns:

> I mention the faithful deeds of God,
> The praiseworthy acts of God,
> . . . What he did for them, in accordance with his love,
> In accordance with his great faithfulness.
> He said: "They are my people,
> Children not prone to falsehood."
> And he was their savior
> In all their trouble.
> Not a deputy or messenger—
> His own presence saved them;

Because of his love and compassion
He himself redeemed them,
And he took them up and carried them,
Always in times past . . .
. . . Where is he who brought them up from the sea
With the shepherds of his flock?
Where is he who placed in their midst
His holy spirit?
Sending along to the right of Moses
His glorious arm,
Dividing waters before them,
To his everlasting fame.

The hymn leads back to one of the later Isaiahs, to the author of the lament in Isa. 63:7 to 64:11. It is with this piously phrased hymnic passage that the lament begins, though it goes on to the less piously phrased, reproachful, if not, indeed, indignant expression in 64:4 f. ". . . And all our virtues." [22] The Isaiah who wrote this hymn, capable as he is of defending himself and his people, recalls the past: "I mention the faithful deeds of God. . . . What he did for them. . . . Always in times past" and bemoans the present: "Where [now] is he who brought them up from the sea . . . ? Where [now] is he who placed in their midst his holy spirit?" and the question is both groan and accusation.

"I remember" is the common introduction, and the recollection is clamorous rather than nostalgic. Remembered for the most part is the deliverance from Egypt with the attendant wonders and subsequent care, or—evidence not only of God's good will but of his unlimited power as well—the epic of the world's creation.[23]

How, indeed, can a friendly and powerful Lord betray his servants whom he has, so to speak, trained to put their trust in him?

The soil upon which this argument thrives is the confidence that a permanent bond unites this people and its God. The doctrine of the covenant has wholly recovered from the challenge of the first Isaiah, and Amos, and Micah, and their sort. That "God is with us" is beyond all question—nevertheless: Why? and Where? and Oh that!

The third argument is one which Abraham proposes, which God

accepts as valid, and which all but saves Sodom. It is the demand that God remain true to his moral nature. "Will you indeed sweep away the righteous with the wicked? . . . Shall not the Judge of all the earth do justice?" All biblical writers bear witness to this basic concept, notably among them Jeremiah and the author of Job. The "confessions" of Jeremiah are one persistent demand that, by repudiating Jeremiah's detractors and upholding the prophet himself, God should give evidence of his just nature. And what does Job require of God except that he be just? [24]

There are two courses open to the afflicted: they may confess, repent and seek atonement—that is the usual course; or they may regard themselves as victims of injustice and adopt the attitude of aggrieved innocence, disclaiming guilt and insisting upon a rectification of the wrongs they have suffered. It is the bolder spirits who take this latter course, the Jobs and Jeremiahs who claim that the fault is God's, not theirs.

Their disclaiming of guilt takes a variety of forms. They say: though our fathers sinned, *we* are innocent and with manifest injustice we suffer for *their* sins. These are the authors of the "sour grapes" proverb repudiated by Jeremiah and Ezekiel. In the sense that the youth is father to the man, one psalmist expresses a variant of this same thought when he pleads: "Remember not the sins of my youth." Sometimes the denial of guilt takes the form: if we have sinned, we are indeed not aware of it; and what kind of a God would exact a penalty for an unrecognized offense? And now and then it is said: God's standards are simply too high. Men cannot be expected to attain perfection. "There *is* no man that does not sin." [25]

The author of Ps. 143 betrays ambivalence: he both wants and does not want God to judge him. Although he appeals to the righteousness of God: "Answer me in your righteousness," without transition he continues: "Enter *not* into judgment with your servant; for in your sight shall no man living be justified." Perhaps it is untempered justice which in the latter verse he fears, whereas the divine righteousness, which in the former he invokes, recognizes and discounts the common frailty of mortals. Let God judge, he seems to say; let him judge indeed, but let him not be petty, let him not be unreasonable.[26]

Similar is the denial—not of all guilt, but of guilt commensurate with the penalty. The thought is that a proportionate relationship must prevail between them. According to the Second Isaiah, even God accepts this principle. This is the prophet's meaning when he says of Jerusalem: "She has received of the Lord's hand double for all her sins." The penalty has been excessive and Zion may now claim reparations. Zechariah agrees: the agents of God's anger, turned loose against Israel, exacted a disproportionate penalty—"for I was only a little angry and they wrought excessive evil." The seventy shepherds in Enoch are guilty of the same excess and, according to that apocalyptic parable, they are treated accordingly on the Judgment Day.[27]

Finally, the denial of guilt may be only that and nothing more. The author of Ps. 44 does not mince words. He bluntly declares:

> All this has come upon us although we did not forget you—
> Although we were not false to your covenant.
> Our heart did not turn back
> Neither did our steps decline from your path . . .
> If we had forgotten the name of our God
> Or spread forth our hands to a strange god
> Would not God search this out?
> For he knows the secrets of the heart.

And boldly the author of the great lament interpreted in the foregoing chapter calls the people's guilt an illusion. No fault of theirs invited this disaster; quite the contrary! the disaster produced the guilt—no, it produced only the appearance of guilt.

> Behold, because you were angry we are presumed guilty;
> You hide yourself and we stand convicted.
> Yes, we are all become as an unclean thing
> And all our virtues as a filthy rag.[28]

So much, then, for the compelling arguments. Not these alone but also the manner of the praying was counted on to insure the prayer's effectiveness. The psalmist applied to his own situation the mocking words which Elijah addressed to the prophets of Baal: "He is musing, or he is gone aside, or he is on a journey, or peradventure he sleeps and must be awakened," and, thinking thus, the psalmist also called him "louder" and louder, and louder still, until, in spirit, his prayer resembled the tempestuous clamor of the Baal prophets in the oratorio.[29]

The psalmist is sometimes overwhelmed by the thought, not that God is being unusually severe with him or his people, but that God is doing something much, much worse, that he is looking the other way, indifferent to their fate, that, in biblical terminology, he is "hiding his face." This phrase denotes various degrees of estrangement, from a passive forgetting or not heeding to an active rejecting and leaving unprotected. When the terrifying thought arises that God is indeed hiding his face, at such a time unimpassioned, temperate speech gives way to an insistent, importunate demand bordering on panic.[30]

The arguments are the same, but there is an added urgency. This urgency is expressed in three different ways. It is expressed as an accusation—an accusation addressed to God bluntly and directly: "You have enticed me," "You have been to me like a deceitful stream." [31]

Or it has the form of an impatient demand, a variant of the imperative: "Look at me!" or its companion: "Awake! Why do you sleep, O Lord?" [32]

This demand, "Awake! Why do you sleep, O Lord?" is cited in the *Talmud*. In a list of the reforms of the High Priest John Hyrcanus, the *Mishnah* says: "He abolished the awakeners." And in the *Babylonian Talmud* someone asks: "Who were these awakeners?" They were the levites, he learns, who were assigned the special duty, day by day to ascend a platform and to cry aloud: "Awake! Why do you sleep, O Lord? Awake! Why do you sleep, O Lord?" [33]

And last among the forms which give expression to this unbridled urgency is the desperate question. The question is a variant of: "How long, O Lord?" or "My God, my God, why have you forsaken me?" The question: "How much longer?" occurs apparently as a conventional formula in Babylonian ritual laments and its use in our psalm literature seems at times to be similarly conventional. Indeed a liturgy adopts and repeats bold phrases which were no mere phrases when a crisis begot them. And, certainly, not every occurrence in this literature of the accusation, the question and the demand, is equally earnest. The psalms will contain the borrowed conventional phrase as well as the fresh hot demand.[34]

Isaiah 62, described at some length a few pages back, is one of the finest compositions in the minor anthology that goes by the name of Trito-Isaiah; it is also the best biblical expression of this fresh urgency. The opening words of its author reveal his spirit:

For Zion's sake I will not keep quiet,
For Jerusalem's sake I will not hold my peace,
Until her triumph appears as the dawn,
Her salvation as a burning torch.

We miss the whole point of the chapter if we fail to recognize the speaker of these lines. As we have seen, it is the psalmist who vows he will not hold his peace or rest. And it is still the psalmist who is speaking in vv. 6 and 7:

Upon your walls, O Jerusalem,
I have stationed watchmen.
Neither by day nor by night,
Never shall they hold their peace.
You remembrancers of God
Allow yourselves no rest;
Yea, and *give him no rest*
Until he establish it,
Until he make Jerusalem
An object of praise in the earth.[35]

As the speaker, in v. 1, denies himself peace until he sees salvation dawn for Jerusalem, so precisely, in v. 6, he denies his watchmen peace until that day. And these appointed watchmen are men like him—men who pray, who pray urgently and ceaselessly ever the same prayer for the salvation of Jerusalem.[36] It is their business, his business and theirs, to remind God of his commitment to Jerusalem. Their function as "remembrancers" is very like what God requires of Israel in Isa. 43:26:

Put me in remembrance; let us argue together;
State your case that you may be justified.

As in that passage, so here the remembrancers are "stating their case" and stating it with all the power they can muster and with unwearying persistence. So sure of himself and the right of his cause is the author of Isa. 62 that he leads a protesting chorus in uninterrupted prayer designed to force the hand of God.

MAN TAKES THE FIRST STEP

If it is possible at all to speak of *the* religion of the Isaiahs, if there is any ground at all which the many prophets whom we call Isaiah together occupy, it is the area of hopeful faith.

With just such variety as a succession of earnest seekers would offer—men dedicated to the same quest but living in different times and other circumstances, not committed in advance to one only orientation, though all in search of a guide through dark places—with just such variety as these would offer, the Isaiahs all urge a hopeful faith.

Particularly noticeable is the divergence of opinion among the Isaiahs as concerns the basis for hope and its source: whether hope springs solely from the anticipation of divine intervention in human affairs or is founded also upon purposeful human activity and effort. In the single biblical book we find the ultimate of both positions on the whence of human confidence.

Isaiah the apocalyptist saw no escape from the encircling terror save in flight to the sheltering chambers, there to wait out God's violent irruption into history, but

the historical Isaiah, who prized contentment no less than others did, and himself believed it attainable, that Isaiah said to his people: This is the way: *Give the weary rest;* this is security for you.

And the Isaiahs move between these poles: surrender and effort, receiving and giving, supine expectancy and earned repose.

Near the one pole is the Isaiah of legend who "believes." He is the Isaiah to reassure an Ahaz or a Hezekiah: Jerusalem is safe beneath the sheltering wings, and trusting God is virtue.

Near, too, stands Isaiah the messianist, whose savior king is divinely given and endowed.

In Trito-Isaiah, in passages where Israel plays a passive role in the unfolding of God's purpose, that role, too, involves only a sitting, a resting, a waiting.

But Israel's active role, noble ideal of the Second Isaiah; the service done by God's servant Israel, witness to God's divinity; the mission undertaken by a prophet-people—that is human effort; that is purposeful activity along with God; that is the bolstering of hope with doing.

And finally, among the chapters of Trito-Isaiah, the mustering of man's spiritual resources which occurs in prayer; the affirmation of hope, which is prayer; the watchfulness, the fruit of faith, which is creative prayer—these make of hope a contest, a program.

With them, with the idea of mission and the concept of creative prayer we arrive at the other pole, the pole of human effort—"human effort," of course, as an aspect of faith. The extremes, the two poles, are extremes in the meanings of faith as these meanings emerge in the book of Isaiah.

Arrived at the pole of human effort we find ourselves again in the company of the first, the historical Isaiah. And it is he, in fact, who sums the matter up. He does so in a meaningful verse, the 15th of chapter 30. Although he lays great store by "quietness and confidence," in first place he puts a man's "return":

> By returning and rest you can be saved,
> In quietness and confidence lies your strength.

Man takes the first step.

NOTES

CHAPTER I. ISAIAH: THE PROPHET AND THE BOOK

1 Isa. 1:2; 5:1 f.
2 Isa. 1:11–15.
3 Isa. 9:11b (cf. Deut. 5:15); 28:21 (cf. II Sam. 5:20; Josh. 10:10–14); 29:1 (cf. II Sam. 5:6–8); 29:14.
4 Isa. 32:9; 28:14 f.; 30:2; 31:1.
5 Isa. 5:5 f.; 1:2–5; 31:6; 1:21–24.
6 Isa. 1:11–15; 29:13.
7 Isa. 9:7–20 (esp. vv. 12, 11, 16, 20); 28:19, 21; 29:14; 2:12, 11, 17 (cf. Amos 5:20).
8 Mic. 3:12; Jer. 26:6, 11, 18; Isa. 29:1 f.; 31:9; 31:4.
9 Isa. 28:12; 30:9, 15; 6:10.
10 Isa. 5:2; 1:19.
11 Isa. 1:3; 28:12; 1:21; 1:4 f.; 31:6; 30:15; 9:12.
12 Isa. 1:21; 28:16 f.; 5:7.
13 Isa. 28:12; 1:17; 5:8, 22 f.; 10:1 f.
14 Isa. 22:16; 3:15, 14; 30:10.
15 Isa. 30:13; 17:5 f.; 10:33 f.; 28:4; 10:5 f.; 7:20; 5:26–29; 8:7 f.
16 *Babylonian Talmud Baba Batra* 14b.
17 Isa. 6:1.
18 Isa. 31:1–4.

CHAPTER II. THE ISAIAH OF LEGEND AND THE SEVENTH CHAPTER

1 Isa. 29:3, cf. 30:3 and 16. In the last verse of the first cited passage (31:1–4) the expression "lay siege to" is a proper translation; the idiom does not mean "to fight for" (AV) or "upon" (RV), but "to fight against" (RV margin), as it does also in 29:7: "the multitude of all the nations that fight against Ariel" (RV). Cf. also Num. 31:7 and Zech. 14:12 where the same idiom occurs. The comparison with the lion is clear though cruel. The lion stalks his prey in silence, roars and growls when he has taken a victim (cf. Amos 3:4). God is the lion in the simile, Jerusalem his prey, and Egypt's hosts the futile

shepherds. God (represented here by the besieging army of Assyria) has caught his prey and none can take it from him (cf. Isa. 5:29) not even Egypt. Assyria, the staff of God's indignation (Isa. 10:5) is poised for the blow. Describing his campaign the Assyrian king congratulated himself and said of Hezekiah: I made him a prisoner in Jerusalem "like a bird in a cage." Like Sennacherib Isaiah believed that Jerusalem was caught and nothing could prevent the kill. The Sennacherib inscription is available in James Pritchard, *Ancient Near Eastern Texts Relating to the Old Testament* (Princeton: 1950), pp. 287 f.

2 Isa. 22:14.

3 Isa. 8:18, 16, 1–3; 30:8.

4 Isa. 37:6 f.; 37:22a, 29b; 37:33–35; 38:5 f.

5 I Kings 13:1–6; 18:38; II Kings 2:8; 6:6 and Isa. 38:7 f.—Also in 37:30 Isaiah promises a sign to authenticate his words—a different kind of sign; see below, pp. 27–29.

6 II Sam. 12:13; I Kings 21:27–29; II Kings 22:19 f. and Isa. 38:1–5; II Kings 4:40 f.; 5:14 and Isa 38:21.

7 II Kings 8:7–15 and Isa. 37:7, 38.

8 Isa. 37:36, 37 f. and I Kings 13:2; cf. II Kings 23:15–18.

9 Isa. 29:8, and cf. 8:9 f.

10 Cf. II Kings 15:37; 16:5, 7–10; II Chron. 28:5–8.

11 In his *Lehrbuch der Einleitung in das Alte Testament* (Tübingen: 1912), p. 483.

12 In somewhat greater detail the suggestion concerning v. 9b is that both verbs originally had the form *ta'aminu,* both in the *hiph'il* (the second is now *niph'al*); also that the two particles *ki* and *'im* with which, respectively, the first and the second clauses begin, are merely alternatives, since both can mean "if"; and the text leaves the choice to the reader. In other words, there were two textual traditions (as with an instance of *ḳeri* and *kethib*) and the text is conflate: "If (*ki*), or if (*'im*), you do not believe. . . ."

13 In v. 4 "Ephraim" has been added from v. 5 for the sake of symmetry. In v. 10 the translation has: "And again Isaiah spoke"—where the text has: "God spoke." This may be the same thing since God spoke through his prophet. But the narrative in this part of chapter 7 appears to be biographical in form; it is a story about Isaiah, as already v. 3 has suggested: "And God said to Isaiah." Probably this third-person narrative had Isaiah speaking here again in v. 10, and again in v. 13. Perhaps at some stage in the transmission of the text Isaiah's name was written by initial only and then, later, this single letter *yod* was mistaken for an abbreviation of the name of God. For references to other errors resulting from the use of abbreviations, see p. 118, n. 1, below.

14 So in 1:24; 5:13, 14, 24; 10:16; (28:14;) 29:14; 30:13. The parallel between Isa. 7:13 and 17 and Amos 7:16 and 17 is striking.

15 6:1, 5, 6, 7, 8 and 11; 8:1, 2, 3, 5, 11, 17 and 18. The Immanuel prophecy, to the contrary, is biographical; cf. n. 13, above.

16 Isa. 5:8, 20, 23; 10:1 f.; 3:15; 1:16 f., and see above, pp. 5 f.

17 Isa. 5:5 f., reading *ve'ashbitehu* for the first two words of v. 6; Isa. 8:6a, 7a. For the equation "River"—Euphrates—Assyria see the comment on 7:20, above, p. 21.

18 Judg. 6:39; Num. 14:21–23.

19 Ps. 106:13 f.; Ps. 78:19; Ps. 78:17, 40 f., 56; Ps. 78:22, 42; Ps. 106:15; Num. 14:22 f.
20 Exod. 17:7.
21 Isa. 38:1 ff. discussed above, p. 13.
22 "The Elohist Narrative in Exodus 3:1–15," *American Journal of Semitic Languages,* XXXVII (1921), 252 f.
23 Cf. 38:7 f. with 7:11; 37:30 with 7:14 and 16.
24 Cf. Isa. 7:1 and II Kings 16:5.
25 "A Suggestion Regarding Isaiah's Immanuel," *Journal of Biblical Literature,* XIV, 26.
26 The interpretation of the name and explanation of 8:4 agree in large part with those of R. H. Kennett, *The Composition of the Book of Isaiah, The Schweich Lectures, 1909* (London: 1910), pp. 14 f. Kennett also refers to 10:6 for the original significance of the name and connects 8:4 with 7:16. He thinks of the 8:4 as a "variant" of 7:16.
27 I have presented it recently in an essay entitled "Traces of Prophetic Agony in Isaiah," *Hebrew Union College Annual,* XXVII (1956), 81 ff.
28 It is only a step from the legend to the messianic interpretation of the name in Isa. 10:21.

CHAPTER III. THE MEANINGS OF FAITH

1 Jer. 7:4 (cf. vv. 9 f., 14; also 48:13); Mic. 3:11 (cf. Amos 5:14); Amos 5:20; Jer. 6:14; Ezek. 13:10 (cf. Jer. 14:13 f.; 28:15; 29:31).
2 Jer. 7:8; Amos 6:1; Isa. 32:9–11.
3 Hos. 2:21 f.; Jer. 5:1 (cf. v. 3); 9:2; Isa. 11:4 f.; 26:2; 59:4.
4 Isa. 8:2; 22:23, cf. v. 25; Jer. 15:18; Isa. 33:16; 55:3 (cf. II Sam. 7:15 f.).
5 Isa. 49:7 (cf. Isa. 25:1); Jer. 42:5.
6 Cf. Isa. 1:21 and 26.
7 The translation assumes a commonly accepted change in the vowels of one word, omits a dittograph of another, and adopts a meaning for *yaḥish,* "be agitated, in a panic," proposed by G. R. Driver in *Journal of Theological Studies,* XXXII (1931), 253 f.
8 Jer. 40:14; Jer. 12:6 (so Mic. 7:5); Hab. 1:5; Isa. 53:1.
9 Isa. 47:8–11 and Zeph. 2:15; Jer. 48:13, 7; Jer. 49:3 f. (cf. Jer. 49:31 and Ezek. 39:6); Isa. 42:17 (cf. Hab. 2:18).
10 Isa. 31:1 (cf. 30:2 f., 7a and possibly 28:15, 17b, 18 f.); Jer. 37:7b; 2:36 f. (echoed in Ezek. 29:16).
11 Hos. 10:13 (cf. Jer. 17:5); Isa. 22:8–11; Jer. 5:17; Ezek. 16:15; 33:13; Isa. 30:12; 59:4; Jer. 13:25–27.
12 Isa. 2:8, 11.
13 Jer. 17:5–8 (cf. Ps. 1).
14 See the analysis of Isa. 7 above, especially pp. 25–27.
15 Isa. 31:1; 22:8–11 (cf. 9:12).
16 Isa. 30:15 f.
17 Cf. Isa. 1:19 f.; 28:12; 30:9, 15.
18 Isa. 6:10; 9:12; 31:6 and 8 (v. 7 is out of context); Jer. 7:3.
19 Jer. 17:17; 39:18.

20 Zeph. 3:2; Isa. 50:10; 40:31; 49:23.
21 **Isa. 7:9 and 11, see above, p. 18 f.; II Chron. 20:20.**
22 Cf. A. Cronbach, *Religion and Its Social Setting* (Cincinnati: 1933), pp. 185 ff.
23 Isa. 57:13 (cf. Jer. 14:8); Isa. 25:4 (cf. Zeph. 3:12; Jer. 49:11); Isa. 26:3 f. (omitting a dittograph in v. 4).

CHAPTER IV. ISRAEL'S GOD IS GOD

1 Rashi's comment is to Amos 1:5. "Rashi" (Rabbi Solomon bar Isaac) was a French Jewish exegete of the eleventh century.
2 Isa. 44:28; 45:1–4; 41:2–4, 25; 43:14; chap. 47.
3 Isa. 46:1 f., reading "their," *-hem* for "your," *-kem,* in v. 1.
4 Isa. 40:1, 9; 41:9.
5 Isa. 40:19 f. with 41:6 f.; 44:9–20; 45:20b; 46:1 f.
6 Isa. 44:12; 41:6 f. and 40:19; Gen. 1:31; Milton, *Paradise Lost,* Canto VII, line 568.
7 This challenge is contained in Isa. 41:21–29, with v. 27 omitted—a verse which does not appear to be a part of the argument. A few words and phrases in the above translation assume a slightly different Hebrew text: The word translated "your strongest arguments" is ambiguous but the synonymous parallel "your case" determines its meaning here.—The order of the clauses "announce for us the coming events" and "that we may know their conclusion" has been reversed.—The received text preserves two traditions as to the reading of the word translated "fear." The marginal reading is "see," but "fear" is better. The neighboring v. 10 contains the same combination of "look amazed" and "fear." —The reading "misguided is he that prefers you" assumes a slightly different text: *toʿeh habboḥer bakem.* This reading is proposed by C. C. Torrey, *The Second Isaiah* (Edinburgh: 1928), p. 319.—The word "tread," the needed synonym for "trample," also assumes the change of one letter and reads *veyabos.*—The text has an extra conjunction before the clause "no adviser among these" and lacks a necessary conjunction before "their works are naught."—The translation "nothing" involves a minor change.
8 Isa. 43:9a and b. The singular verb "foretell" in the a part of the verse suggests that also the verb "announce" should be read as a singular, contrary to the received text.
9 Isa. 42:8 f. (cf. 41:21 ff.); 43:12a.
10 Isa. 44:8.
11 Isa. 45:21.
12 Isa. 46:9 f.
13 Isa. 48:3.
14 Amos 7:17; Mic. 3:12; Isa. 30:3; Jer. 37:8; Ezek. 5:12.
15 Isa. 22:14 (see above, pp. 10 f.).
16 See above, pp. 11 f.
17 See S. Blank, *"Of a Truth the Lord Hath Sent Me": An Inquiry into the Source of the Prophets' Authority, the Goldenson Lecture for 1955* (Cincinnati: 1955).
18 Jer. 29; Ezek. 13; Jer. 29:8; Ezek. 13:4.
19 Deut. 13:2a, 3b–4a, 6, later amplified by vv. 2b–3a and 4b.

20 Deut. 18:20–22.
21 Jer. 17:15; Ezek. 12:27; Jer. 32:6–8; 1:11 f.; 37:19 (cf. *Goldenson Lecture,* pp. 6 f.); Ezek. 12:28; 12:25; 33:33.
22 Isa. 55:11; 40:8.
23 Isa. 8:1 f., see above, pp. 31 f.
24 Isa. 44:8; see above, p. 57.
25 Isa. 44:8 f.; 43:9 f.
26 Isa. 43:9 f. and 49:3–5; see below, p. 85.
27 Cf. Isa. 8:16 and 30:8.
28 Isa. 6:9; 42:19 (cf. the entire passage 42:18–25, also 40:27; 43:8; 48:4 f. *et al.*).
29 Cf. Jer. 5:21; 6:10; 11:21; 18:18; Ezek. 12:2.
30 Josh. 24:22; Job 16:19–21; Isa. 43:10.
31 Isa. 45:6 and 14. The last line of the first cited passage: "No God but me" now appears in v. 5. It seems originally to have been the end of v. 6. Accidentally omitted, it was written in the margin along with the immediately preceding phrase, "I am God and there is none else," which now appears in v. 5 as well as in v. 6.
32 Isa. 55:4 f., reading "you" for Hebrew "him" in the first line, with the Peshitta.
33 Isa. 44:9, 18; 45:20b; 45:4 and 5 (but the repetition here may be an accident).
34 Isa. 41:23; 40:28; 43:10 (see above, pp. 62 f.); 41:20. Related to the thought, though less clearly so, are 45:3b; 49:23, 26; 52:6.
35 Isa. 40:27 f.; 43:10; 45:4 f.; 44:9, 18 f.; 45:20; 45:6 (see above, p. 65).
36 I Kings 11:33; Isa. 46:1, *et al.* The peoples probably pronounced the names otherwise.
37 Isa. 45:22 and 46:9, compared with 45:6 and 45:18b.
38 To the thoughts presented in this section Julian Morgenstern has added some very interesting and highly significant observations; cf. "Deutero-Isaiah's Terminology for 'Universal God,'" *Journal of Biblical Literature,* LXII (1943), 269–80.
39 Isa. 45:21 and 46:9b. See above, p. 57.
40 Isa. 43:11 f.; 44:6.
41 Isa. 44:24; 45:18.
42 Isa. 41:13. Similarly 41:17: "I, Yahveh, will answer them; I, Israel's God, will not forsake them"; 43:3: "For I am Yahveh, your God, the Holy One of Israel, your savior"; 43:15; 45:3; 48:17. Cf. also 49:26 and 51:15.
43 Isa. 42:8; Exod. 6:2 f. (cf. Ezek. 20:5).

CHAPTER V. AND ISRAEL IS HIS PROPHET

1 Isa. 42:22; 41:14 (reading *rimmat* for *mete*); 47:6; 49:6; 44:26 and cf. 49:7; 50:6; 51:23 and chap. 53.
2 Isa. 48:5.
3 *Der Prophet Jesaia,* III (Leipzig: 1821), pp. 10 f.; cf. p. 168.
4 *Der Gottesknecht bei Deuterojesaja* (Halle: 1933), p. 17.
5 The data are to be found, together with a very useful chart, in H. A.

Fischel, "Die Deuterojesajanischen Gottesknechtlieder in der Juedischen Auslegung," *Hebrew Union College Annual,* XVIII (1944), 53–76.

6 The address, the vocative, appears to extend through the words "you are my servant," and the statement only begins with "I favor you."

7 42:18 f.—The symmetry of the verses requires "deaf" in the last phrase instead of "blind," which stands in the Hebrew text.—The word *meshullam* seems to be a name for Israel, those addressed in the preceding verse. Its meaning and relevance are not clear. One could alter the last letter, divide the words differently, and read *meshullaḥo,* were it not that such a reading fits the hypothesis so well that it might seem to be made for the purpose. That reading would yield the meaning:

> Who so blind as the one sent by him,
> Deaf as God's servant!

The word for "the one sent by him" is a form of that verb which the first Isaiah used when he responded "Here am I. Send me" (6:8).

8 43:10a. See above, pp. 62–65.

9 44:1 f. Jeshurun, like Meshullam (42:19), seems to be a name for Israel; cf. v. 1b.

10 44:21. With 44:8 plus 21 cf. 43:10.

11 44:26. "He," of course, is God—see v. 24b. What he does for his "messengers" is the opposite of his behavior toward the (Babylonian) diviners, according to v. 25. On "messenger" as prophet, see above, note 7.

12 50:10. Except in the songs the Second Isaiah refers to God's servant in these eight passages only. In two other passages he speaks of servants but in neither is the reference relevant. He refers to Israel in 49:7 as the servant not of God but of kings, and he only approaches the concept in 54:17 where he uses the plural: "This is the lot of the servants of God."

13 Isa. 47:1 f., 8 f.; 40:9.

14 In v. 4 "nor be broken" assumes a change in the vowels of the Hebrew word. The received reading means "nor run." The proposed reading is a form of the verb translated "break" in the preceding verse. "Faithfulness" is a justified translation of the word *'emet* in v. 3; cf. above, p. 36.

15 Isa. 1:10–17; 5:24; 8:16; 30:8 f. (cf. 28:9).

16 Paul Volz, *Kommentar zum Alten Testament, Jesaia II* (Leipzig: 1932), p. 153, has suggested this meaning for the term *mishpaṭ* in this context.

17 The translation departs from the order of the Hebrew text at one point. It reads the c part of v. 5: "and I am honored in God's sight, and my God has been my strength," at the beginning of the verse, where it forms the proper continuation of v. 4. When this part of v. 5 is removed from its present disturbing position, the rest of the verse suitably introduces v. 6. "He said" in v. 6 resumes "And now God has said," in v. 5. "Adopted me" is a legitimate rendering of the idiom in v. 1 which is literally "mentioned my name." The servant says of himself here what God says of him when, in 42:1, he calls him "my chosen one."

18 If the translation of v. 4 and the beginning of v. 5 seems confusing it is because the original is confusing. The translation "to relieve" is a guess at the meaning of an obscure word. The combination of two infinitives "to know to relieve" is awkward. The repetition of "he stirs up" with a different object is

unexpected, as is the repetition of "my ear." How the whole is to be phrased is questionable. The translation is tentative and, barring conjectural changes, as good as any. The expressions "he who vindicates me" and "Who can prove me in the wrong?" are taken from the language of the law court. For a description of this setting—see Blank, "The Confessions of Jeremiah and the Meaning of Prayer" in *Hebrew Union College Annual* XXI (1948), 334 f.

19 Isa. 49:3.

20 Isa. 8:16.

21 "To relieve the weary" may be related to the middle phrase of Isa. 1:17: "Correct oppression" and to the admonition "Give the weary rest" in Isa. 28:12, cf. above, p. 24.

22 The continuation: "his looks," "his appearance," "at him," certainly shows the need for reading "at him" at the beginning of the verse. The Targum and Peshitta also have the pronoun of the third person.

23 *Yirgezu* is pure conjecture but makes excellent sense and uses most of the consonants of the two words it replaces. The suggestion is found in a number of commentaries. The word occurs with this same meaning in Exod. 15:14 and Ps. 99:1, and the thought of this line occurs again in Isa. 49:7.

24 The kings are speaking in the whole passage vv. 1–9 and seem here to be saying what they said in v. 5: "He was wounded because of our transgressions"; therefore "our transgressions" here again, and not the unrelated "transgression of my people."

25 The reading "stricken unto death" is a conjecture suggested by the parallel ("cut off from the land of the living"), with some help from the Septuagint.

26 The reading "doers of evil," proposed by others and suggested by the parallelism, does not greatly depart from the consonants of the received text.

27 "His simple grave" is wholly guesswork. The proposed reading uses the noun occurring in Neh. 3:34 and there means "mound of earth or rubbish"; cf. Volz, *op. cit.*, p. 171.

28 The word "light" appears here in the Dead Sea Isaiah Scroll and it may have stood in the text used by the translators of the Septuagint. Both consonants of the Hebrew word appear in the word "see," and this chance may have occasioned its loss. At any rate the verb "to see" requires an object.

29 "Knowledge" is literally "his knowledge." Assuming a usual abbreviation of the name of God, Volz (*op. cit.*, p. 172) obtains the meaning: "He shall be sated with knowledge of God." His suggestion is so attractive that one is both tempted to adopt it and urged to caution.

30 On the reading "vindicated" see the discussion below, p. 92.

31 The reference to a guilt offering may be significant, but if so its significance is lost in the present confusion. The subject of the verb "would give" is either second person masculine or third person feminine. Either would be strange. No one is directly addressed in the context and the only feminine noun that could serve as subject is "his life." The Philistines, afflicted with a plague by the God of the ark, "put a guilt offering" (the same words as here) of golden objects into the chest on the cart which returned the ark to Israelite territory (I Sam. 6:3, 8). For the sake of their lives they did this, to halt the plague; it was not their lives that did it. The only translation grammatically possible here "if his life would give a guilt offering" is not the same, and its meaning is, to say the least, obscure.

32 The stative verb in v. 10 can be either participle or perfect, but in view of v. 6 it is probably the latter: "God wanted."

33 53:4, 5, 6, 12.

34 Isa. 53:4a, 5 f., 8 (see the note on the translation of v. 8, above, p. 89).

35 Isa. 53:11 (see the note on the tense above, p. 92), 12b, 9b.

36 Isa. 53:4b, 10a.

37 The idea of *musar* is discussed below, pp. 96 f.

38 Isa. 53:5 f., 8, 11b, 12b, 4a.

39 Isa. 53:10.

40 Isa. 53:5b.

41 Jer. 18:20; 15:11; 7:16. The translation of 15:11 is based on an altered text. For the suggested reading, for the interpretation of the passage, and for the suggestion that the confessions are the prophet's defense before the divine judge, see S. Blank, *op. cit.* (n. 18, above), pp. 331 ff. and n. 24 there. With 7:16 cf. 14:11; cf. also 21:2 and 42:2 in one of which passages the king and in the other the people, urge the prophet to pray for them; and for a discussion of this theme see Blank, *The Goldenson Lecture for 1955* (Cincinnati: 1955), pp. 12 f.

42 Isa. 53:11b, 12b.

43 Isa. 53:5.

44 Amos 4:6–12; Jer. 31:18; Isa. 9:7–20, esp. vv. 12, 11, 16, 20.

45 Jer. 2:30.

46 Deut. 13:12; Jer. 3:6–11 (though he does not himself call it *musar* Jeremiah here clearly suggests the possibly salutary vicarious experience of another person's grief) .

47 Exod. 14:30 f. For an exhaustive treatment of the theme cf. Jim A. Sanders, "Suffering as Divine Discipline in the Old Testament and Post-Biblical Judaism," *Colgate-Rochester Divinity School Bulletin,* Special Issue 1955. I had the pleasure of working with the author in his preparation of this study, originally a Ph.D. dissertation at Hebrew Union College, and we are in close agreement. Sanders considers this "vicarious" aspect of *musar* on pp. 97–100 of his study. He lists five other examples of what he calls "The Lesson Learned by Observing Others Suffer": Ps. 64:8–10; Prov. 24:30–34; Deut. 11:2; Ezek. 5:15; and our passage, Isa. 53:5.

48 Dan. 12:2; Isa. 26:19 (see below, pp. 168 f.).

49 Ezek. 37:11; 33:10; 37:12, 14.

50 Isa. 53:8.

51 Cited from *The Fifty-Third Chapter of Isaiah according to the Jewish Interpreters,* by S. R. Driver and Adolf Neubauer, *I Texts* (Oxford, London and Leipzig: 1876), p. 43.

52 *Ibid., II Translations* (1877), p. 19.

53 On pp. 16 ff. of the monograph referred to above, p. 77 and n. 4, Otto Eissfeldt has listed some of the contacts between the servant and Jeremiah.

54 I.e., Jeremiah 11:18 to 12:6; 15:10 f. plus 15 to 20; 17:14 to 18; 18:18 to 23; 20:7 to 11 and 14 to 18; 1:4 to 10 plus 17 to 19. There are contacts also with 16:1 to 9.

55 Jer. 1:4 f. and Isa. 49:1, (5).

56 Jer. 11:19 and Isa. 53:7. We may not exclude the possible alternative to borrowing, that both writers used proverbial phrases.

57 Jeremiah: ". . . I am called by your name, Lord, God of Hosts" (Jer. 15:16).
The servant: "He said to me: You are my servant" (Isa. 49:3).

58 Jeremiah: "God put forth his hand and touched my mouth and said to me: Lo, I have put my words in your mouth" (Jer. 1:9).
The servant: "My Lord God gave me the tongue of disciples" (Isa. 50:4). "He made my mouth a sharp sword" (Isa. 49:2).

59 Jeremiah: "Lo, I turn my word in your mouth to fire, and this people it will consume as fuel" (Jer. 5:14). "Is my word not so: as fire? . . . and as a hammer that crushes rock?" (Jer. 23:29). "If I say: I will not remember him or speak any more in his name, then there is in me, as it were, a raging fire pent in my bones. I weary myself to contain it—but in vain" (Jer. 20:9).
The servant (as in n. 58): "He made my mouth a sharp sword."

60 Jeremiah: "When your words presented themselves I devoured them, and your word was a pleasure to me . . ." (Jer. 15:16). "I have not sought to escape serving you. . . . You know what comes from my lips; it is ever before you" (Jer. 17:16). "If you repent [God is speaking] I will take you back—you may minister to me [again]. . . . You may [again] serve as my spokesman" (Jer. 15:19) and cf. 1:7, 17.
The servant: "To know to relieve the weary he stirs up a word in the morning. In the morning he stirs up my ear to hear as disciples. My Lord God opened my ear, and I was not stubborn, did not turn away" (Isa. 50:4b–5).

61 Jeremiah: "God says, I will put my teaching [*torah*] within them, I will write it on their hearts . . . and they shall no more teach each other: Know God, for all of them shall know me . . ." (Jer. 31:33 f.).
The servant: "The coastlands wait for his teaching [*torah*]" (Isa. 42:4).

62 Isa. 51:7, *'am torati belibbam.*

63 Jeremiah: "And Pashhur flogged Jeremiah the prophet" (Jer. 20:2). "And the nobles were angered at Jeremiah and flogged him" (Jer. 37:15).
The servant: "I gave my back to them that smote me" (Isa. 50:6).

64 Jeremiah: "My sickness" (Jer. 10:19b), "my pain . . . my wound" (Jer. 15:18).
The servant: "A man of pains, familiar with sickness" (Isa. 53:3).

65 Jeremiah: "Know that for your sake I have borne disgrace" (Jer. 15:15). "Daily I have been an object of ridicule, everyone taunts me. . . . The word of the Lord has become for me a constant source of disgrace and insult" (Jer. 20:7 f.). Cf. also Jer. 12:6; 17:15; 18:18.
The servant: "[I gave] my cheek to those that plucked it. I hid not my face from insult and spittle" (Isa. 50:6).

66 Jeremiah: "You know, O Lord, that they plotted my death" (Jer. 18:23). "This man deserves death, for he prophesied of this city as you yourselves have heard" (Jer. 26:11). "You shall not prophesy in God's name lest you die by our hands" (Jer. 11:21). "Let us destroy the tree in its sap. Let us cut him off from the land of the living that his name be remembered no more" (Jer. 11:19). Cf. Jer. 20:10; 26:16, 24; 38:7–13; 37:20.
The servant: "He was cut off from the land of the living . . . was stricken

unto death. They placed his tomb with the wicked, with the doers of evil his simple grave" (Isa. 53:8 f.).

67 Jer. 26:14 and Isa. 53:12.

68 Jeremiah: "I have been neither a lender nor a borrower, yet everyone curses me" (Jer. 15:10). "Is good to be rewarded with evil? Remember how I have stood before you to speak good on their behalf" (Jer. 18:20). "Give heed to me, O Lord, and hearken to the voice of them that contend with me" (Jer. 18:19).

The servant: "He was wounded because of our transgressions, crushed because of our iniquities" (Isa. 53:5). "He had done no deeds of violence and no deceit was in his mouth" (Isa. 53:9).

69 Isa. 50:8. On the nature of Jeremiah's confessions see S. Blank, *op. cit.* (n. 18, above).

70 Jeremiah: "God is with me. . . . Therefore my persecutors will stumble and fail, will suffer great shame in their defeat . . ." (Jer. 20:11, cf. 11:21 f.). "Though they contend with you they will not prevail, for I will be with you to save and deliver you . . ." (Jer. 15:20, cf. 1:18 f.).

The servant: "God hid me in the shadow of his hand . . . concealed me in his quiver" (Isa. 49:2). "I am honored in God's sight and my God has been my strength" (Isa. 49:5). "My Lord God helps me; so am I not abashed. I set my jaw as stone and know that I will not be disgraced" (Isa. 50:7). ". . . My cause is with God; my God has a reward for me" (Isa. 49:4).

71 "If you return, O Israel . . . if you remove your abominations . . . and swear: As God lives, in truth, in justice and righteousness, then nations shall find blessing in you, and get themselves praise through you" (Jer. 4:1 f., assuming a reading *beka,* "through you," instead of *bo,* "through him," twice in v. 2). Cf. Jer. 1:5 and 10: "prophet to the nations."

72 Jeremiah probably died as an old man in Egypt before the Second Isaiah was born. Jeremiah's disciple Baruch also appears to have spent his last years in Egypt (Jer. 43:5–7). We have no knowledge of how the Second Isaiah came into possession of the words of Jeremiah. Did he belong to some "circle" in Babylonia which possessed, cherished, and studied the prophetic books? And did the book of Jeremiah somehow reach them from Egypt? Or a pre-Egyptian recension of the book, from Judea?

73 Amos 3:8; Jer. 1:9; Isa. 6:5–8; Ezek. 2:7–3:4 (cf. 3:17).

74 Exod. 4:10–12 and 14–16; Exod. 7:1 f.; Num. 12:8; Deut. 18:18; Num. 22:38 (cf. 23:5 and the whole Balaam narrative); I Kings 22:14, 23, 24; Jer. 18:18.

75 See above, p. 82.

76 Isa. 40:8; 55:10 f.; 40:5; 48:13.

77 Isa. 42:9; 46:10 f. (cf. 52:6); 45:23 (on "sure purpose" as a rendering of *ẓedeḳ* and *ẓedaḳah* in these chapters see below, pp. 152–156); 45:19; 51:4; 42:4; 42:21.

78 Isa. 42:19; 44:26.

79 Jer. 7:25; 25:4; 26:5; 29:19; 35:15; 44:4; II Kings 17:13; 21:10; 17:23; 24:2; 9:7; Ezek. 38:17.

80 Zech. 1:5 f.

81 Amos 3:7.
82 Num. 12:2, 7 f.; Deut. 34:10 (cf. 18:18); Num. 16 (cf. vv. 3 and 5); see S. Blank, The Dissident Laity in Early Judaism," *Hebrew Union College Annual,* XIX (1945–46) 27 ff.
83 Isa. 20:3 f. No certain conclusion is possible. As a matter of fact the word "my servant" may be a gloss added under the influence of the familiar formula. In some Septuagint manuscripts it precedes, in others it follows the name Isaiah. On the Isaiah legends see chap. II, above.
84 Amos 3:8; Jer. 20:9; 20:7.
85 Isa. 42:1–4; 49:3 and 6; 50:4; 53:10 f.
86 Isa. 40:15, 22, 18, 25, 13, 26 (cf. 46:5).
87 Isa. 42:5 (cf. 44:24); 48:13; 45:7.
88 Isa. 41:4; 43:10; 48:12.
89 Isa. 44:28 to 45:6; 53:10; 46:10; 45:18; 45:22 f.
90 See above, p. 109.

CHAPTER VI. "FOR THE SAKE OF HIS NAME"

1 In a study entitled "Isaiah 52:5 and the Profanation of the Name" which appeared in *Hebrew Union College Annual* XXV (1954), 1–8, I discussed the text of this verse in detail and proposed this translation. The translation assumes that *ne'um yahveh,* "God says," came into this line by mistake; the fact that the same two words occur in the previous line made it easy for a reader to mistake the first person singular pronominal suffix *-ni* for the initial letters of *ne'um yahveh* and so to repeat the phrase here. It assumes, further, that this suffix originally was attached to a form of the verb *ḥalal,* thus reading *yeḥalleluni.* Finally, it assumes that the conjunction "and" before "constantly" is a dittograph of the preceding *yod.* The study cites examples of errors occasioned by abbreviations or supposed abbreviations, and refers to literature touching on this phenomenon, and likewise to certain commentaries in which Isa. 52:5 is considered.

2 Cf. also Ps. 74:22 f. As a matter of fact, the pairing of the two terms as parallels is of frequent occurrence. But the tautologous expression "constantly, daily" also occurs; cf. Isa. 21:8 and 51:13. Both arrangements suit the biblical idiom.

3 In v. 16 of the same chapter in Ezekiel, "And you shall be profaned through you in the sight of nations" is probably an error for "And I will be profaned through you . . ."

4 Cf. the critical apparatus to *Biblia Hebraica,* 3d. ed. Also A. Geiger, *Urschrift u. Uebersetzungen der Bibel* (Frankfurt: 1928), pp. 312–14. This tradition is not included in the usual lists of *tiḳḳune sopherim* (cf. Frensdorff, *Ochlah W'ochlah* [Hannover: 1864], p. 113).

5 The unquestionable cases are Ezek. 13:19 and 22:26, to which add Mal. 1:12 according to rabbinic tradition and Isa. 52:5 here proposed. For examples of the reticence which probably reduced an originally larger number to these four, cf. S. Blank, "The Curse, Blasphemy, the Spell and the Oath," *Hebrew Union College Annual,* XXIII, Part One (1950–51), especially there the section on blasphemy, 83 ff.

6 Rom. 2:22–24 quoted from RSV. As to whether Paul misunderstood the ambiguous text or consciously interpreted it loosely to suit his purpose, cf. Wm. Sanday in the *International Critical Commentary* to Romans, p. 67.
7 *Babylonian Talmud, Sukkah* 52b.
8 Amos 2:7; Jer. 34:16; Ezek. 20:39; Mal. 1:12 (but see above, p. 119); Lev. 18:21; 19:12; 20:3; 21:6; 22:2, 32 (cf. also Ezek. 13:19; 22:26).
9 Jer. 34:16; 34:22 plus 37:7b–10.
10 Isa. 48:11 and 52:5.
11 Ezek. 36:16 ff.
12 Isa. 52:5 and 48:11.
13 Ezek. 20:8–10, 14, 22.
14 Ezek. 20:41; 36:23. The thought is echoed in Ezek. 28:25 and 39:25–27.
15 As here quoted, in 5:15, 17; 21:22; 30:12; 34:24; "For I have spoken, says my Lord Yahveh" in 23:34; 26:5; 28:10; 39:5; "For I, Yahveh, have spoken, says my Lord Yahveh," in 26:14.
16 Ezek. 17:24; 22:14; 36:36 and 24:14 (here reading *dabar* for *ba'ah*).
17 Ezek. 12:21–28.
18 Cf. Deut. 18:22 and the discussion above, p. 60.
19 Cf. Jer. 26:12 and 15.
20 Ezek. 12:23–25, reading *dabber ve'asoh* in v. 25a with A. B. Ehrlich, *Randglossen zur Hebräischen Bibel* (Leipzig: 1912), *ad loc.* For the translation "I, Yahveh, I will speak . . ." cf. 14:4 and 9 where the same construction occurs. The thought of this paragraph is echoed in Isa. 46:12 f. with an ironic twist; see below, p. 172.
21 Ezek. 2:4 f. and 33:33.
22 By restoring a dead child to life Elijah earned the recognition which Ezekiel coveted. What the child's mother afterward said to him approximates the formula in Ezekiel: "Now," she said, "I know that you are a man of God and that the word of God in your mouth is true" (I Kings 17:24).
23 Ezek. 13:6 f.
24 I am now inclined to favor this alternative, thus modifying the conclusion I had reached when I wrote "Studies in Deutero-Isaiah," Appendix II (*Hebrew Union College Annual,* XV [1940], 34–41) on which these present paragraphs are based.
25 (a) Ezek. 7:4; (b) Ezek. 34:27; (c) Ezek. 25:11; (d) Ezek. 36:23.
26 For the Second Isaiah's position see above, pp. 63–65.
27 See above, pp. 82–86.
28 Ezek. 33:33 and Isa. 48:3.
29 **Isa. 45:6 and see the section "That all may know," above, pp. 65 ff.**
30 Exod. 12:12.
31 Exod. 7:8–13, 19–20a*a*, 21b–22; 8:1–3, 11b, 12–15; 9:8–12.
32 Isa. 47:6; 48:20 f.; 52:12; cf. 11:16 *et al.*
33 Isa. 47:13 f. and 44:25 f., omitting the preposition "from" as a dittograph in 47:13.
34 Isa. 52:4 f. (cf. Gen. 17:1 ff. and 35:11 f.).
35 Isa. 45:2; Ezek. 20:35.
36 Exod. 18:8–11; 1 Kings 18:24, 39; II Kings 5:15.

CHAPTER VII. THE MISSION OF ISRAEL: BIBLICAL ORIGINS

1 Isa. 55:8 f.

2 Joel 2:17. An addition to Jer. 22, vv. 8 f., explains the calamity to the passers-by: It was deserved.

3 Zech. 8:23; Jer. 16:19; Isa. 45:23; Isa. 56:7; I Kings 8:41–43; Ezek. 47:1–12; Zech. 14:9.

4 Isa. 45:22; 49:6.

5 Mal. 1:5; 1:1–4; 1:11; 1:14.

6 Isa. 45:1–6. Cf. also Isa. 47; 41:2; 11:13; Zech. 2:12–15; 14:17–19.

7 Isa. 18:7; Mal. 3:12; Jer. 33:9. In the last of these passages the name "Jerusalem," the required feminine subject of the verb, appears now to be concealed in the three Hebrew words which follow the opening verb.

8 Isa. 60:17; 54:11–13 (reading "builders" instead of "sons," with the change of one vowel); 60:11; 60:6; 66:19; 61:9; Zech. 8:13.

9 Zech. 6:15; Isa. 60:10; 61:5 f.; 66:21; 66:23; Zech. 14:16.

10 Isa. 52:13; 54:11–14.

11 Isa. 53:10.

12 Cf. Deut. 20:10–14; Mic. 4:11–13; 5:7 f.; Amos 9:12; Joel 4:9–20; Isa. 41:15 f. For a discussion of this and related material see S. Blank, "Studies in Post-Exilic Universalism," *Hebrew Union College Annual,* XI (1936), 159 ff.

13 Isa. 51:7; 51:16; 51:4.

14 Isa. 59:21.

15 Isa. 45:22.

16 Isa. 55:2.

17 Isa. 45:18.

18 Isa. 42:6; 54:8–10.

19 Isa. 48:1; 56:1; 58:2; so, too, in 59:4; 59:14; 60:17.

20 Isa. 43:9; 43:26; 50:8; 53:11 (see above, p. 92).

21 Isa. 41:2; 41:10; 42:6; 45:13 (cf. v. 25). The related idea, *ẓedaḳah,* as national triumph for Judah, appears in 58:8; 61:11; and 62:2.

22 Isa. 45:8; 46:13; 51:5 f.; 56:1; 61:10 f.; 62:1.

23 Isa. 51:6; 45:19; 45:22 f.; 41:10.

24 Isa. 51:5; 42:6; 51:4 f. On the meaning of the expressions *torah* and *mishpaṭ* here, see above, pp. 82 and 82 f.

25 Isa. 2:2–4; Mic. 4:1–4.

26 Isa. 42:3 f.; 49:6; 53:10.

27 Isa. 43:10.

28 Isa. 50:4; 42:7; 53:11 f.

29 Gen. 12:2 f.

30 Cf. Isa. 56:1–8; Ezek. 44:9; Neh. 13:1–3.

31 Ruth 1:16; 2:12.

32 Isa. 56:6 f.; cf. also, 56:3; 14:1; Zech. 2:15, and Lev. 16:29; 17:8–16; 18:26; 22:18; 24:16, 22; Num. 9:14; 15:14–16, 26a, 29; 19:10.

33 Jonah 1:9; 4:2; 4:10 f.

34 Dan. 6:27 f. (cf. 3:31–33; 4:31–34).

CHAPTER VIII. THE SHAPES OF HOPE

1 The two passages are 9:1–6 and 11:1–9. The former begins: "The people that walked in darkness . . ." which in some English translations is the second verse of the chapter.

2 Isa. 11:1; 9:6 (7).

3 This statement would be wrong were the "servant" in the Second Isaiah a messianic figure, but he is not. The expression "sure mercies of David" in 55:3 is not messianic; it is merely another way of saying "dependable" (like the promises God made to David, cf. II Sam. 7:15 f.).

4 Isa. 24:5 and 20 (RSV); 24:18; 26:20; 27:13; 25:8. Cf. especially Gen. 6:5, 11–13; 7:11; 7:13, 16; 9:1; 8:22; and 9:12–17.

5 Isa. 24:21, 23; 34:4 (perhaps not "fail" but "fall" is intended here; there is as little difference between the two words in Hebrew as in English).

6 Isa. 24:1, 17–20; 45:18 (above, pp. 151 f.). The translations in this paragraph lean heavily on George Adam Smith, whose style is still hard to match. Isa. 24:17–20, he suggests, "is like one of Dante's visions," cf. *The Expositor's Bible, The Book of Isaiah, I* (London: 1889), p. 417.

7 Isa. 25:6, 7 f.

8 Gen. 3:22; Isa. 65:20; 66:23 f. (cf. 33:14).

9 Dan. 12:2 (omitting two words); Isa. 26:19 (omitting a word and reading the verbs "awake and sing" as future forms, as the context requires).

10 As a matter of fact, in 24:21 f., Isaiah the apocalyptist contemplates a kind of purgatory, a dungeon where "after many days" fallen angels and earthly kings will be punished.

11 Isa. 26:3 f., see above, p. 48.

CHAPTER IX. HOPE IS A DUTY

1 Ezek. 33:10; 37:11 (reading *kullanu* in place of *lanu*); 37:12–14. Ezekiel's message of hope is largely confined to his chapters 18, 33–34, 36–37, which, for the most part, come from his latter period following on the fall of Jerusalem.

2 Ezek. 36:32 (cf. the whole passage, 36:16–32).

3 Isa. 6:9 f. (and see above, p. 4); 46:12 f.; 48:4; 42:18 f. (cf. v. 20 and 43:8).

4 Isa. 51:5; 56:1.

5 Isa. 45:23, 22; 56:7b, 1.

6 Isa. 58:6 f. and 9b–10a.

7 Isa. 58:8 and 10b.

8 Isa. 58:3a.

9 Isa. 1:16 f.

10 Cf. Neh. 1:1–4. Julian Morgenstern has assembled the evidence for an attack on Jerusalem early in the fifth century and presented a part of it in an article entitled "Jerusalem—485 B.C." which has recently appeared in the *Hebrew Union College Annual,* XXVII (1956), 101–79. He concludes that the neighbors of Judah, notably Ammon and Moab, under Edom's leadership, laid siege to the city, took it, wrought great havoc, razed the Temple and plundered the inhabitants and sold many into captivity in the slave markets of the world.

There is much to commend this theory, and in its larger outlines it is unquestionably correct.

11 Isa. 64:9 f. An awkward text at the end of chapter 63, probably a part of the same composition, seems to refer to the same matters. The second part of 63:18 is clear enough: "Our foes trampled your sanctuary . . ." but the parallel first half of the verse yields no suitable sense as it stands. In view of the parallel, and with 64:9 as a model, we may modify the first half of 63:18 to read *lammidbar samu ʿir ḳodsheka*. The Hebrew consonants in the received text are almost identical with those of the suggested text, and the verse as modified yields the excellent meaning:

> They made your holy city a wilderness,
> Our foes trampled your sanctuary.

So read, the verse 63:18 adds to the vivid (and indignant) description in 64:9 f., of Zion's recent fate. Morgenstern deals with this composition on pp. 147–50 and 175 f. of the article mentioned in the preceding note; he includes it among the evidence for the hypothetical sack of Jerusalem in the fifth century, but his interpretations differ from ours in some details.

12 On 64:4 f. see below, Chap. X.

13 Isa. 50:2a.

14 Isa. 59:1.

15 Isa. 62:1, 2, 4.

16 As the words "my sanctuary" at the end of 9b suggest, we require "praise me" (*'oti*) and not "praise the Lord" (*'et yahveh*) at the end of v. 9a—a case of abbreviation wrongly assumed; see above on Isa. 52:5, p. 118, n. 1.

17 Isa. 62:6 f.

18 Related biblical material is surveyed in chap. XI, below.

19 Isa. 46:10.

20 Isa. 66:7–9.

21 Isa. 26:17–19.

22 Isa. 57:14.

23 Isa. 59:1; 66:9.

24 Isa. 58:13 f. (which verses are probably an appendix to the chapter)—cf. 56:2 and 6; 58:3 and 8; 58:6 f. and 9b–10a. On the idea of self-mortification see S. Blank, "The Nearness of God and Psalm 73," *To Do and To Teach* (Lexington, The College of the Bible: 1953), p. 12.

25 Isa. 59:2 f., 4–8, 12–14; 56:1.

CHAPTER X. "AND ALL OUR VIRTUES"

1 Volz's proposal is to be found in his *Kommentar zum Alten Testament, Jesaia II* (Leipzig: 1932), p. 267. The *niphʿal* of the verb *ʿalam* occurs also in Lev. 4:13; 5:2–4; Num. 5:13; I Kings 10:3 (II Chron. 9:2); Job 28:21; Eccles. 12:14; and questionably in Ps. 26:4. The passage in Kings is typical: Solomon could answer all the questions of the queen of Sheba; "there was nothing too recondite [*neʿelam*] for the king."

2 Deut. 22:4; Isa. 58:7; Ps. 55:2. See S. Blank "'And All Our Virtues'—

An Interpretation of Isaiah 64:4b–5a" in *Journal of Biblical Literature,* Vol. LXXI (1952), 149–54.

3 Isa. 57:17.

4 (a) Ps. 10:11; 13:2; 44:25; (b) Ps. 22:25; 69:18; 102:3; Isa. 59:2; Mic. 3:4; (c) Ps. 27:9; 88:15; Deut. 31:17 f.; 32:19 f., and questionably, Isa. 8:17; (d) Isa. 64:6; Jer. 33:5; Ezek. 39:23 f., 29, the symbolism also of the iron plate in Ezek. 4:3; (e) Ps. 89:47; Isa. 54:8; 57:17; Job 13:24; (f) Ps. 30:8; (g) Ps. 104:29; 143:7.

5 Isa. 64:8a; the thought occurs also in 64:6b and 63:10, and cf. Num. 16:22.

6 Cf. *Gesenius' Hebrew Grammar* edited by Kautzsch, English edition by Cowley, (Oxford: 1910), paragraph 111 *l*. Other examples are Gen. 24:35 and Ps. 33:9.

7 II Sam. 24:1 ff.

8 For the tradition concerning the meaning "filthy rag," cf. the *Aruch Completum,* VI, p. 168b, under *'ad,* and the Vulgate: *pannus menstruatae.* The Targum employs the same Aramaic term to translate the word here rendered "filthy" and the word meaning "impurity" in Lev. 20:21. The reference to Torrey is to C. C. Torrey, *The Second Isaiah* (Edinburgh: 1928), p. 271.

9 Gen. 43:9 and 44:32. For the verb in this context, the Buhl edition of Gesenius' Hebrew dictionary recognizes the meaning "to stand condemned as a sinner" and for the *hiph'il* of *ḥaṭa'* in Isa. 29:21 the corresponding meaning "to hold guilty."

10 Cf. Job 9:20 and Exod. 9:27. Cf. also, Job 9:29; 10:2; 15:6; and Prov. 17:15. In Ps. 109:7 nouns related to the two verbs *hata'* and *rasha'* are paired as in the two lines in Trito-Isaiah, and there as here it appears that a conviction is not in itself a proof of guilt. On these two verbs see also above, p. 153.

11 On the possible occasion for the composition, cf. above, p. 178.

12 Isa. 64:6, reading a form of the verb *magan;* 64:5b, reading the verb as a singular form; 64:8.

13 Job 27:6.

CHAPTER XI. "GIVE HIM NO REST"

1 Isa. 14:12 ff.; Ezek. 28:11–19; Gen. 6:2 f. (cf. Isa. 25:7 f.; Ps. 82:7).

2 Isa. 10:12, 15 (cf. 37:23–25); Isa. 14:4, 16; Isa. 47:1, 7, 10; Ezek. 28:2, 17.

3 Deut. 33:8.

4 Jer. 15:1 (cf. 14:11); Ezek. 14:12 ff.

5 Exod. 32:9–14 (cf. Deut. 9:25–29; Ps. 106:23); Num. 14:11–20 (cf. also Exod. 5:22 f. and Num. 11:11–15, where Moses is quite out of patience with God).

6 *Babylonian Talmud Berakot* 32a. Here and often rabbinic fantasy sharpens the point of the biblical phrase.

7 *Palestinian Talmud Ta'anit* IV. 8, 68c.

8 I Sam. 7:5–10; 12:16–18.

9 Jer. 42:4; 18:20; 15:11 (cf. 32:16); 7:16; 11:14; 14:11.

10 Gen. 15:6 (cf. Neh. 9:7 f.; Ps. 105:42; 106:30 f.); Exod. 33:17.

11 Gen. 6:8 and 9.

[12] Cf. the Daniel who figures in the Ugaritic "Tale of Aqhat" V 4–8, etc., to be found in translation in Pritchard, *Ancient Near Eastern Texts* (Princeton: 1950), pp. 149 ff. Before he became the hero of the biblical book, Job, too, may have been celebrated as one who possessed intercessory powers (cf. Job 42:8 ff.). Job and Prometheus are frequently compared; see E. Bussler, *Hiob und Prometheus, zwei Vorkämpfer der göttlichen Gerechtigkeit* (Hamburg: 1897); W. A. Irwin, "Job and Prometheus," *Journal of Religion*, XXX (1950), 90–108; H. G. May, "Prometheus and Job," *Anglican Theological Review*, XXXIV (1952).

[13] Isa. 26:20 (cf. Gen. 6:18; 7:16), and cf. above, pp. 165–167.

[14] Gen. 18:22 ff. (cf. 20:7, 17).

[15] Isa. 63:16 (cf. 51:1 f.; Jer. 31:15).

[16] Jer. 14:7; Ps. 25:11; 79:9 f.; Exod. 32:12; Num. 14:15 f. (cf. Isa. 59:1 f.), and often. See chap. VI, above.

[17] Ps. 74:22 (cf. 74:10, 18).

[18] I Kings 8:41–43; Isa. 45:6; Ps. 98, and see above, p. 140 f.

[19] Ps. 6:6; 30:10; 88:11–13.

[20] Exod. 32:13; Deut. 9:5; II Kings 13:23; Jer. 32:22; Mic. 7:20; Neh. 9:8; II Sam. 7:13b, 15 f.; I Chron. 17:12b–14; Ps. 89:29 f., 34–38; Jer. 33:17, 20–21a; II Chron. 6:42; Isa. 55:3. Cf. S. Blank, "The Dissident Laity in Early Judaism," *Hebrew Union College Annual*, XIX (1945–46), 11 f., 33 ff.

[21] Cf. the references in n. 20; also Deut. 7:8 f., 12; Dan. 9:4; Isa. 54:10; II Chron. 1:8; Ps. 18:51; Isa. 16:5.

[22] Which was the subject of the foregoing chapter and will be recalled a few paragraphs later. The more pertinent parts of the hymn are quoted above (63:7ab, 8, 9, 11bc, 12). The translation assumes a different reading of the vowels in the Hebrew words for "deputy" and "messenger," a different division between vv. 8 and 9, and the reading: "in their midst" for "in his midst" in v. 11c, and it admits the obscurity of the phrase "with the shepherds of his flock" in v. 11b. It supposes that "children not prone to falsehood" in v. 9 suggests good faith on the part of the people. Hymns like this in 63:7–14 appear also as Ps. 22:4–7; Ps. 44:1–10; Ps. 80:9–13. In each of these examples one observes the reproachful tone of its final verse. For a recent discussion of this hymn cf. Julian Morgenstern, "Isaiah 63:7–14," *Hebrew Union College Annual*, XXIII, Part One (1950–51), 185–203.

[23] Ps. 77:12 ff.; 143:5; 44:2–4; 80:9; Isa. 51:9 f.; Dan. 9:15; Ps. 74:12–17; 102:26.

[24] Gen. 18:25; Jer. 11:20; 12:1; 18:19 f. discussed in S. Blank, "The Confessions of Jeremiah and the Meaning of Prayer," *Hebrew Union College Annual* XXI (1948); Job 13:15, 18; 23:3 f.; 27:2.

[25] Jer. 31:28; Ezek. 18:2; Ps. 25:7; Job 13:23; I Kings 8:46; cf. Job 4:17; Ps. 130:3.

[26] Ps. 143:1, 2; cf. 130:3.

[27] Isa. 40:2; Zech. 1:15 (where, though the last phrase is awkward Hebrew, the meaning seems to be as above); Isa. 10:5–7; 47:6; 61:7 and Enoch 89 f., especially 89:62, 69; 90:22, 25.

[28] Ps. 44:18–22; Isa. 64:4b–5a.

[29] I Kings 18:27.

30 See above, p. 190.
31 Jer. 20:7; cf. Blank, "The Confessions of Jeremiah" etc., p. 344; Jer. 15:18.
32 Ps. 13:4 (cf. Isa. 64:8; Ps. 25:16, 18 f.; 59:5; 80:15; Lam. 1:9, 11; 5:1); Ps. 44:24 (cf. Ps. 35:22 f.; 59:2–6; 80:2–4; Isa. 51:9).
33 *Mishnah Sota* IX.10; *Babylonian Talmud Sota* 48a.
34 Ps. 13:2 f. (cf. Ps. 74:10; 79:5; 89:47; 90:13; 85:6; Hab. 1:2); Ps. 22:2 (cf. Ps. 10:1; 42:10; 43:2; 74:1; 88:15; Lam. 5:20; Jer. 14:8, 19); H. Zimmern, *Babylonische Hymnen u. Gebete,* in *Der Alte Orient* VII (Leipzig: 1905), p. 8; M. Jastrow, *Die Religion Babyloniens u. Assyriens,* II, 1 (Giessen: 1912), pp. 16, 43, 109.
35 Isa. 62:1, 6 f.
36 Cf. the Sumerian "Lamentation over the Destruction of Ur" translated and annotated by S. N. Kramer in Pritchard, *op. cit.,* pp. 455 ff., especially line 80 ff. and n. 25. Cf. also I Kings 8:59 and Ps. 55:18.

INDEX OF BIBLICAL PASSAGES

The reference will be found on the page listed or in a footnote pertaining to the page.

Where corrections in the Hebrew text are adopted or proposed the page number is printed in italics.

JEREMIAH

GENERAL INDEX

The item will be found on the page listed or in a footnote pertaining to the page.

HEBREW TERMS CONSIDERED